Denn was ging uns Preussen an?
Es war die Persönlichkeit des grossen Königs,
die auf alle Gemüter wirkte.   (Goethe)

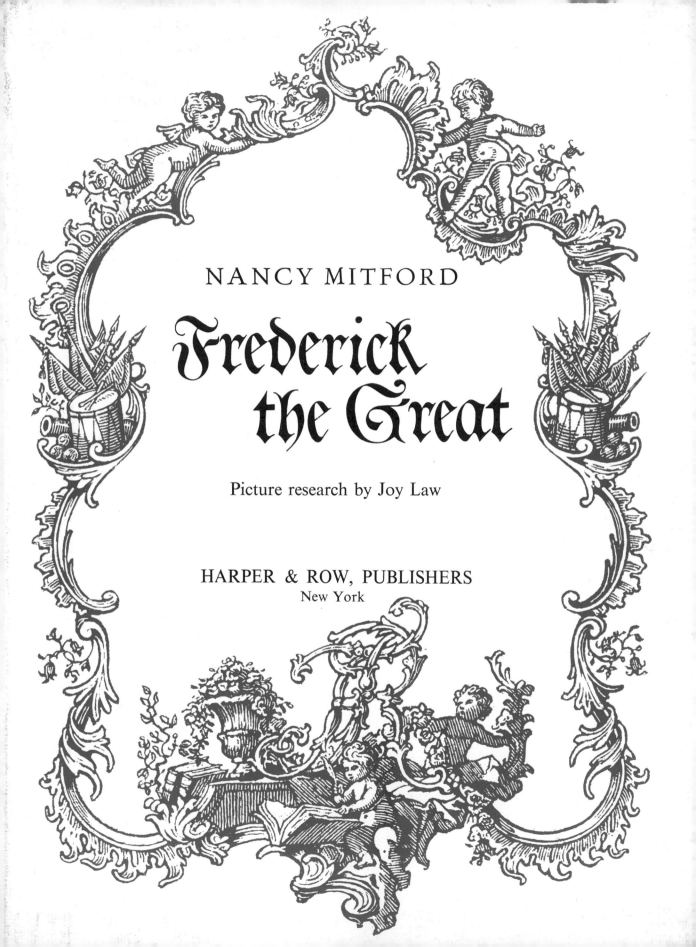

NANCY MITFORD

Frederick the Great

Picture research by Joy Law

HARPER & ROW, PUBLISHERS
New York

Designed and produced by George Rainbird Ltd
Marble Arch House 44 Edgware Road London w.2

House Editor: Gabrielle Wilson
Designer: Michael Mendelsohn
Maps: John Flower
Index: Irene Clephane

Text set in Monophoto Poliphilus
Printed and bound by Jarrold & Sons Ltd Norwich
Color plates and jacket originated and printed by
Westerham Press Ltd Kent

Library of Congress Catalog Card Number 73-116435
ISBN 06-012986-7

PRINTED IN ENGLAND

Dedicated to my sister Diana

ACKNOWLEDGMENTS: My principal helpers have been Prince Clary and Mr Nicholas Lawford, both learned in matters concerning the Empire. Prince Clary has saved me from making many a gaffe and has read my manuscript. Mr Raymond Mortimer has once again put his taste and learning at my disposal. Professor Francis Carsten has kindly read the book and made some useful suggestions. Miss Madeau Stewart provided me with facts about Frederick and his flute. Madame Gaudin has helped in many ways and has typed the book. Miss Irene Clephane has done a splendid cleaning-up and the index. The Librarian of the London Library has been indispensable. I am also indebted to Mr Peter Fleetwood-Hesketh, Monsieur Michel Catargi and Herr Martin von Katte.

I stayed in Prague with His Excellency the French Ambassador, Monsieur Roger Lalouette, who arranged for me to see what was relevant to the book. I was taken round the town by Monsieur Ousovsky and given many facts by Professor Polisensky. Mademoiselle de Passavent made everything easy.

In East Germany Mrs Law and I had the greatest kindness. Dr Joachim Menzhausen of the Grünes Gewölbe at Dresden, Herr H.-J. Giersberg at Potsdam and Frau A. Kondeyne at Rheinsberg showed us many wonderful things, while Professor Mittenzwei at Berlin gave me an invaluable history lesson. Herr Ernst Friedlander organized our visit and was unfailingly thoughtful. Miss Elizabeth Matthews arranged everything from London. My sister Pamela kindly came to Germany and was a great help.

Owing to illness I was unable to go to Silesia, but Prince Donnersmark and Dr Grossman have provided much information.

Finally, Mrs Law has been the king-pin of the book and I can hardly believe that without her it would have seen the light of day.

Contents

Color Plates

ABOVE: *An Austrian soldier.*
BELOW: *A French soldier.*

North Sea

DENMARK

HOLSTEIN

MECKLE

WEST
POMERANIA

HANOVER

UNITED

Hanover

Brunswick

PROVINCES

The Hague   Utrecht

Wesel
CLEVES

MARK

SAXE-
WEISSENF

Nieuport

BERG
Cologne

HESSE

Brussels

AUSTRIAN

Aix-la-
Chapelle

JÜLICH
Bonn

SAXE-
GOTHA

Rhine

Frankfurt-on-Main

BAYREU

NETHERLANDS

Darmstadt

Main

Mannheim

PALATINATE

Erlangen

ANSBACH

Metz

LORRAINE

Lunéville

Strasbourg

WÜRTTEMBERG

BAV

ALSACE

Munich

F R A N C E

Neuchâtel

SWITZERLAND

VENETIA

MILAN

PIEDMONT

PARMA

GENOA

MODENA

Mediterranean Sea

LUCCA

TUSCANY

SWEDEN

Baltic Sea

Memel

Konigsberg

EAST PRUSSIA

Danzig

SWEDISH
POMERANIA

P R U S S I A

Kolberg

WEST PRUSSIA

ANDENBURG

Stettin

URG

RANDENBURG

Oder

Vistula

Warsaw

Berlin
Fürstenwalde
Frankfurt-on-Oder
andenburg

P O L A N D

S I L E S I A

WOHLAU

LIEGNITZ

SAXONY

eipzig
ubertusburg
Meissen
Dresden

Breslau

BRIEG

GALICIA

Prague

JÄGERNDORF

IA

BOHEMIA

MORAVIA

Vienna
Pressburg
Danube

AUSTRIA

H U N G A R Y

REPUBLIC

Adriatic Sea

ABOVE: *An English soldier.*
BELOW: *A Prussian soldier.*

Boundary of the
Holy Roman Empire

0 ———————— 100 Miles
0 ———————— 100 Kilometres

CHAPTER ONE

The Father

Frederick the Great was born on 24 January 1712, the year of Denain, Louis XIV's final and victorious battle in the War of the Spanish Succession; when he died, seventy-four years later, people were discussing Marie Antoinette's diamond necklace. Few would deny that, for a member of the European ruling classes, this was an enviable span of life, since it encompassed the essence of the eighteenth century. Frederick used to say that he was happy to have spent his first three years in the reign of the Great King and to have been the con-temporary of Voltaire. He was the third son of his parents: two little Fredericks had died, one from having a crown forced upon his head at the time of the christening and the other when the guns greeting his birth were fired too near his cradle; the third Frederick, allergic to neither crowns nor guns, survived, and so, luckily for him, did his elder sister, Wilhelmine.

The preponderant power in Europe was France, richer and more powerful than the Empire, and the centre of art, literature and learning. Many of the German states were politically dominated by the French, although the evident aim of French statesmen was to keep Germany weak and divided. When the princes began to desire a better way of life than that of the robber baron it was to Paris rather than Vienna that they turned. Those who could read did not care for German writers (the Prussian Queen Sophia Charlotte's patronage of Leibniz was an exception); they sent to Paris for their books. Anybody with pretensions to gentility, and rulers everywhere, spoke French. The German princes, according to how much money they could squeeze out of their subjects, built palaces, pavilions, orangeries, follies, theatres and opera-houses modelled upon Versailles and often designed—in a more florid taste to suit less civilized people—by French architects. The admirable German craftsmen, the best of whom went to work in Paris, made furniture and panelling for these buildings in the French style but with a charmingly rustic air and more than a touch of peasant art. The French influence was strengthened in the Protestant states, especially in Prussia, by the thousands of Huguenots who had settled there during the persecutions of Louis XIV; a high proportion of the Prussian bourgeoisie in the early eighteenth century had been born in France. Frederick the Great's great-grandmother was a French refugee, Eleanor d'Olbreuse who was married for her charm and beauty by the Duke of Celle—he was also descended from Admiral de Coligny.

A tabagie held by King Frederick William; painting by an unknown artist.

The head of the House of Hohenzollern, Elector of Brandenburg since the fifteenth century, became King in Prussia in 1701. After 1714, when the Elector of Hanover became King of England, there were three German Electors with kingdoms outside the Empire, since the Elector of Saxony was King of Poland. All preferred their electorates to their kingdoms. Prussia had belonged to the Hohenzollerns since 1618; geographically it was part of Poland, most inconveniently divided from Brandenburg by the Polish province of West Prussia. By degrees the Hohenzollern properties which were scattered over the Empire became known collectively as Prussia. They were difficult to defend—it was said of them that their frontier was the army—and difficult to administer. The most important of them, Brandenburg, though not directly engaged in the Thirty Years' War, had been ruined by the opposing armies which fought all over its territory, the Elector George William having been too weak to keep them out. His son Frederick William, known as the Great Elector, was the founder of modern Prussia; single-handed and at a very early age he put his country on its feet again; he reformed and strengthened the army; with French help, he countered Imperial diplomacy at the Peace of Westphalia and acquired six hundred square miles of new territory. He taught his people to put the State before the individual and regarded himself as its first servant. During his reign Prussia became the most powerful of the minor German states and leader of the Protestants in the Empire. The Habsburgs began to realize that the Hohenzollerns were uncomfortable neighbours.

The son of the Great Elector was King Frederick I of Prussia. He was a civilized man with a love of art, but there was something absurd about him. Though the newest and the least important of European kings, he modelled himself upon the most important, the Sun King. He copied him slavishly, even to the extent of taking a mistress, though vastly preferring his wife. His time-table was that of Louis XIV until the hour of the evening party at Versailles, when he reverted to German ways and held a *tabagie*, shutting himself up to drink beer in a small smoky room with a few pipe-puffing friends. His wife, Sophia Charlotte, the friend of Leibniz, was the sister of George I of England, a charming, clever, musical princess. She saw her husband as he was and used to say that he was taken up with the infinitely little. His finances were always in a disastrous state—he overspent on such unproductive things as silver, pictures and fine furniture; he loved all forms of pomp and the outward display of riches. He left some beautiful buildings, having fallen upon a talented architect, Andreas Schlüter. The houses of Frederick I and his Queen were those in which Frederick the Great lived until he began building for himself. They were the royal palace at Berlin, Charlottenburg, a garden residence for Queen Sophia Charlotte, at that time outside the city, and the palace at Potsdam.

After losing his first two grandsons in infancy Frederick I, by then a widower, married again, thinking to secure the succession. It was an unfortunate venture, and unnecessary, as his daughter-in-law soon had a third son, Frederick the Great, and thereafter eleven more

King Frederick William receiving homage from his troops; engraving by Pieter Schenk.

children. At fifty, Frederick I was incapable of making love; his second wife was a perfect nuisance, and proved the death of him. She went mad and surged into his room in her underclothes. Frederick, not expecting the apparition, thought she was a certain White Lady who appears to Hohenzollerns presaging death. '*Weisse Frau*', he cried, fell unconscious, and died a few days later. The Queen had to be kept, an expensive lunatic, for another twenty years. Frederick's son, Frederick William, buried him as he would have wished, with expensive, long-drawn-out ceremonies and as much pomp as if he had been an emperor. Then he settled down to reign in his own, different way. He was twenty-five.

The first twenty-eight years of Frederick the Great's life were overshadowed by his curious, furious but in some ways touching father. When all passion between the two men was spent, and old Frederick, now the Great, was writing his memoirs, he said of Frederick William: 'His spirit was transcendent; he penetrated and understood great objectives and knew the best interests of his country better than any minister or general.' These interests were a sound economy and a valid system of defence. In his own father's time, Frederick William had seen the Swedes and the Russians dictating the policy of a weak, bankrupt Prussia; he was determined to be independent; for this a full exchequer was necessary. After his accession to the throne he began to practise a frugality considered by his fellow princes as a comical miserliness; unlike them he did not treat public funds as his own pocket-money. He dismissed the Council of State and reduced the power of the ministers or took over their departments himself. He had no facility for communicating with his fellow men; he never read and could hardly write, but he had a talent for finance and administration, and understood the foreign affairs of his day. He said a king must not lead an easy, woman's life: 'I am the King of Prussia's Finance Minister and his Field Marshal.' He established a vast building programme to attract people to the towns, depopulated during the Thirty Years' War, reorganized the police, created arsenals and factories and built hospitals 'for those unlucky objects of our disgust and our compassion'. In ten years Frederick William had a sound exchequer and a full treasury and was the only German ruler who could say as much.

Frederick William hated everything that his father had liked; above all he abominated the French, their ways, their civilization and even their food. When criminals were to be hanged he dressed them up in French clothes in order to give people a horror of such fashions. He practised German, Protestant virtues, was faithful to his wife, honourable, brave and hard-working. When he came to the throne he sold most of his father's horses, the best of his furniture and all his jewels, dismissed nearly all the courtiers and settled down to the life of a country gentleman, giving himself no royal airs. He said, 'I', 'my wife', 'Fritz', instead of 'we', 'the Queen', 'the heir to this great country', as his father would have; and he dined every night with his wife and his children of whom he saw much more than most upper-class people did in those days. He had married, for love, his first cousin Sophia Dorothea, the sister of George II, and he always loved her.

Frederick William had few intimates. His only advisers were his cousin and greatest friend, the Prince of Anhalt-Dessau, and General Count von Grumbkow. These two men, and especially Grumbkow, had a good deal of influence over the events of the young Frederick's early life. Anhalt-Dessau, known as the 'Old Dessauer', was the ruler of a tiny principality marching with Brandenburg. He was ten years older than Frederick William, and a Field Marshal in the Prussian army. Although, like the King, he was rather inarticulate, the advice he gave was always to the point. A remarkable soldier and strategist, he had spent his life in camps—his very face was the colour of gunpowder. He invented modern drill, marching in step, most of the words of command that are used to this day, and he increased the fire power of the infantry by the invention of iron ramrods. Prince Eugene thought that he and his Prussians had been indispensable to the Allied victory at Blenheim. He helped Frederick William to turn the Prussian army into a first-class fighting machine, the most up-to-date in Europe. The Old Dessauer was a violent and wilful man. When very young he had fallen in love with a bourgeoise, the daughter of an apothecary, murdered her fiancé, and committed the unheard-of eccentricity of marrying her. He was perfectly happy with her for more than fifty years. The Emperor legalized the marriage, a most unusual step in such a case, and the children were Princes of Anhalt-Dessau.

Grumbkow was a very different sort of person, an able minister, civilized and witty. Frederick William knew that he was sold to the court of Austria; he was not at all disturbed

LEFT: *Prince Leopold I of Anhalt-Dessau, 'The Old Dessauer'; engraving by Adam Manyoki.*
CENTRE: *General Count von Grumbkow; engraving.*
RIGHT: *General Count von Seckendorf; engraving.*

—he said it brought in foreign currency and made no difference to his policy. But he underestimated the devilish cleverness of Grumbkow, and he may not have known quite to what extent all his servants were bought for the Emperor. The concierge of the palace at Berlin was an Austrian agent, and so was Frederick William's minister in London. General Count von Seckendorf, the Austrian minister to Prussia, was one of those accomplished bribers or blackmailers who know exactly how to succeed with each individual. He also had a high military reputation — Prince Eugene told the Emperor that if anything happened to him he must send for Seckendorf; probably for this reason Frederick William liked him and admitted him to his own little coterie. His colleagues did not enjoy such favour — Frederick William loathed foreigners so much that Berlin was said to be the purgatory of ambassadors.

Unfortunately King Frederick William, in whom there were excellent qualities and who did much for his country, was ill. Like George III he had an hereditary disease, prevalent among descendants of Mary Queen of Scots, which drives its victim mad with prolonged and terrible sufferings. It is now known as porphyria, a derangement of the metabolism; its symptoms are some of the most horrible miseries with which mankind is afflicted — gout, piles, migraine, abscesses and boils, as well as appalling, unexplained pains in the stomach. Frederick William was strange at the best of times and, under the influence of the agonies he endured, his eccentricities became past a joke. He was the terror of those who had to do with him; uncontrollable rages were triggered off by apparently harmless

17

remarks or even looks. One key-word which never failed in its effect was 'France'. In the streets of Berlin and in the intimacy of his home he would make play with his dreaded cane, hitting people in the face, breaking their teeth and noses. There was no redress; anybody who tried to defend himself would have been killed. The King had a pathetic desire to be popular: 'Love me', he roared at a passer-by who, he thought, had given him an unfriendly look—whack, whack, whack. Once, in a rage with Augustus the Strong, he smashed up a whole dinner service because it was made at Meissen. While still very young he was enormously fat, with bulging eyes and an unhealthy-looking marbled complexion; with the years his disease became more agonizing.

In his misery he took to drink. Every evening he held a *tabagie* where the smoking and

A caricature of Baron Gundling; engraving.

drinking released some sort of communication with his fellow men. The company, which always included the Old Dessauer and Grumbkow, and often Seckendorf, consisted mainly of soldiers. All got drunk, and the grossest scenes would occur, most of them connected with the baiting of Gundling. Half-way between a fool and a professor, Gundling came into Frederick William's household to read the newspapers to the family at dinner. He could explain any points of history or geography that might crop up—his mind was crammed with odd, unrelated, perfectly accurate facts on which he would gladly dissert at boring length. He was made to be teased. But at the *tabagie*, when they were all drunk and Gundling more drunk than any, they began by teasing and ended by physically torturing him. When they exaggerated, by setting him on fire for example, he would ask to leave the court but Frederick William always got him back by some sort of bribe; he made him a baron or raised his wages or simply hugged him. In fact Gundling

18

King Frederick William; painting by Antoine Pesne.

could not have borne to leave—he was a masochist and the *tabagie* was the joy of his life.

Frederick William's oddest whimsy was the collection of giants for his Potsdam Grena-diers. They were an obsession; he would spend any money, even risk going to war with his neighbours, to have tall men (often nearer seven than six feet in height, and generally idiotic) kidnapped, smuggled out of their native lands and brought to him. Finally, he acquired over two thousand of them. His agents were everywhere. Kirkman, an Irish giant, was kidnapped in the streets of London, an operation which cost £1,000. A tall Austrian diplomat was seized when getting into a cab in Hanover; he soon extricated himself from the situation, which remained a dinner-table topic for the rest of his life. The biggest of the giants was a Prussian—no ordinary man could reach the top of his head. When the Grenadiers marched beside the King's carriage they held hands over it. The kidnapping became so expensive that Frederick William tried breeding giants. Every tall man in his dominions was forced to marry a giantess. But that method proved slow and unreliable—too often the children of such marriages were a normal size. So he went on with the kidnapping while letting his fellow rulers know that the most acceptable present to him would be a giant. The Russians and the Austrians were particularly obliging in this respect. The Grenadiers were his greatest joy; when he was ill or depressed he would have two or three hundred of them marched through his room to cheer him up. The philosopher Wolf, thought by the civilized world to be the brightest jewel in Frederick William's crown, was banished on pain of hanging because somebody saw fit to tell the King that one of Wolf's propositions, if reduced to its fundamental meaning, would allow the Grenadiers to desert without committing a sin against God.

Frederick the Great's childhood and youth have been described by his sister Wilhelmine in her memoirs. She is fundamentally truthful and her account is borne out by the foreign diplomats in dispatches to their governments. She and Frederick were more like twins than an ordinary brother and sister—exactly alike to look at. They were not always on the best of terms, but there was an affinity. At an incredibly early age Wilhelmine encouraged her brother to read and study, and it was she who spurred him on to fame. From her book one would think that these two were the only children, but in fact a large family was arriving: Sophia Dorothea had a new baby nearly every year; fourteen in all were born, and ten lived to be grown up. But Wilhelmine and Frederick were the most interesting of them and they clung together through the storms of their early days.

In spite of Frederick William's loathing and contempt for the subjects of His Most Christian Majesty, he put his little son in the charge of two French Protestants. Mme de Roucoulle was appointed governess to the royal children and Jacques Duhan de Jandun tutor to Frederick. Mme de Roucoulle had brought up Frederick William; she must have been like her name, a cooing, laughing, agreeable, rather silly person – deeply religious. She had been a great friend of Queen Sophia Charlotte and was always talking about her; little Princess Wilhelmine decided to model herself on this grandmother.

A painting by Frederick William of himself (in the centre), some of his Grenadiers and servants at Middachten Castle where he went to recuperate from an illness with its owner, who had been Dutch Minister to Berlin.

King Frederick William and Queen Sophia Dorothea with their family; pen and ink sketch by Georg Wenzeslaus von Knobelsdorff.

Jacques Duhan had an enormous influence over Frederick's intellectual formation. He was born in 1685; his father, who had been the secretary of Turenne, Louis XIV's general, had emigrated to Brandenburg in 1687. As far as possible the Protestant *émigrés* were given the same jobs as they had held at home, and the nobles became officers. So the elder Duhan went into the army. He educated his son himself and when he was old enough Jacques Duhan also became a soldier. He was noticed by Frederick William for his extraordinary courage at a siege; the King had no idea that he was a scholar. He had a horror of intellectuals and would never willingly have delivered his son into the hands of one.

As well as a tutor, Frederick, at the age of seven, had a governor, the sixty-year-old General Count Finck von Finckenstein, a well-known European warrior. In those days a soldier could join any army as long as he was not asked to fight against his own king—it was considered a good military education to go campaigning with different leaders. Finck had fought with the Prince of Orange against the French in 1676; then in the French army under Luxembourg against the Spaniards; then he joined the Great Elector, Frederick's great-grandfather, and thereafter always fought against the French. The Emperor ennobled him, at the request of Prince Eugene, after Blenheim. Frederick's household was completed by Lieutenant-Colonel von Kalkstein, and Rentzel, another Prussian, who was a drill master and a flautist. It was he who started Frederick on music and taught him to play the flute, an accomplishment which was to mean so much to him. He loved these men: they were to be lifelong friends, and all the elements of his future can be found in them: French civilization, warfare and music.

LEFT: *Mme de Roucoulle; painting by the school of Pesne.*
RIGHT: *General Count Finck von Finckenstein; painting by the school of Pesne.*

Frederick William laid down rules for the education of his son. He was to learn no history before the sixteenth century and then only that which had some bearing on the House of Hohenzollern. Latin was forbidden. Frederick William had the deepest contempt for the Classical civilizations which the Germanic race had brought low; he tolerated only those political, social, religious and artistic schools of thought which sprang from a German source. The French were written off as derivative and effeminate. Frederick, said his father, is destined to rule over Prussia in this century; a lot of knowledge which might be useful to the Emperor or the King of France will clutter up his brain to no purpose. (Frederick William seemed to think that a brain is like a box and can hold only a certain amount.) Fusty old rules of etiquette are also to be avoided: the King of Prussia can get up in the morning without assistance and go to bed when he feels sleepy, after smoking his pipe. The child must know about his father's lands, scattered all over central Europe, and about those to which his family lay claim: Western Pomerania[1], Silesia, Mecklenburg, Jülich and Berg. He must learn mathematics, essential to the art of warfare, must study political economy and human rights and be able to express himself clearly and elegantly in French and German. (Frederick William himself always spoke French with his wife.) The Prince should have attractive manners and the greatest horror of laziness and Catholicism. The horror of laziness remained; as for Catholicism, Frederick grew up with contempt for

[1] Frederick William had already taken a good part of Western Pomerania from the Swedes—the rest was to become Prussian only in the general European settlement of 1815.

all religions, but he always thought the Roman Catholic the most mischievous. He must learn theology and hope, as his father does, that Calvinists and Lutherans will soon make up their differences (which partly hinged on the interpretation of Christ's words at the Last Supper: 'is', said Luther, 'represents', said Calvin). He must never be left alone night or day. He should rise at 6 a.m., kneel, thank the Almighty for having allowed him to live through the night and ask that he should be prevented from doing anything which would separate him from God. Then, at the double, he must wash his hands and face without soap, have his hair combed, but not powdered, while he drinks his tea or coffee. At 6.30 a.m. Duhan comes in with all Frederick's servants and reads prayers, a chapter of the Bible and a psalm. From 7 a.m. to 11 a.m. lessons. Then he washes with soap, is powdered and goes to the King, staying until 2 p.m. Lessons until 5 p.m. when he can do as he likes until bedtime at 10.30 p.m. 'He must try to be clean and tidy and not so dirty. That is my last word', said Frederick William who, himself, had such a mania for cleanliness that he allowed no upholstered furniture or curtains in his rooms. But Frederick was dirty, all his life.

All went well until Frederick was eight when he began to implore Duhan to teach him Latin and Classical history. Duhan, who was longing to do so, was unable to resist; but one day the King came in and found them reading the Golden Bull which, since it was the charter of the German Electors, was thought by Duhan to come within the King's curriculum. Unfortunately, the Golden Bull is in Latin. The cane, from which Frederick William was never separated, flailed in all directions. '*Ich will dich Schurke, be-auream bullam!*' (I'll Golden Bull you). Duhan was not dismissed, but that was the end of Latin lessons for Frederick, to his lifelong regret. More divinity was prescribed: 'Anybody would have thought my father wanted me to be a theologian!' Duhan was a born teacher; the boy soon knew how to learn by himself from books; he acquired a good style in French prose, an abiding passion for French literature and a grounding in history and geography. In spite of much reading of Luther's Bible, which was the model for the German language, Frederick's German was always idiosyncratic, incorrect, colourful and amusing; he very seldom spoke it and was hardly capable of writing it.

At first Frederick William loved his little Fritz and was proud of him. He hoped that they could be more like two brothers than father and son. He took the child to army manœuvres and gave him a toy in the shape of a regiment of 131 small children, the Crown Prince Cadets, to do as he liked with. It was reviewed by both Peter the Great and Grandfather George I and got a barrel of beer for good marksmanship. But the bright morning soon clouded over. Frederick William's disease began to take a terrible hold; he suffered tortures. To distract himself he learnt to paint—the strange results are signed *F.W. in tormentis pinxit*. In 1719 he was thought to be dying of 'nephritic colics'; eight years later he had a nervous breakdown and talked of abdicating. As his illness grew worse so did his temper.

Unfortunately, Queen Sophia Dorothea was no help to him. He loved her, she knew, always treated her with respect and never hit her (or an officer—nobody else was spared).

But she pretended to be frightened of him. She bore him a grudge for the simple life she led; she thought she was cut out to be a real queen with a court and much gallant coming and going, balls for visiting sovereigns and so on—she would have preferred her silly father-in-law as a husband, a thousand times. She was a gossip, a bore and a snob, attaching importance to trivial things and looking down on the Hohenzollern family. Her father became King of England in 1714 and this inflated her ideas. Her influence on Frederick and Wilhelmine was not good. Always grumbling about their father, she turned them against him and encouraged them to displease him. She was a luxurious woman—her trousseau had been bought in Paris, chosen by Madame, the sister-in-law of Louis XIV—and her rooms in the palace, decorated in her own way with curtains and upholstered furniture, seemed a haven of civilization to the children, who loved to be with her. They took her at her own value when they were little; when they first grew up they saw through her, but in her old age they loved her again. She had charm, but she was a shallow, idle person full of pretence—by way of liking the arts without bothering to learn about them, and fond of political intrigue though without knowledge of politics.

Her aim in life was to marry Wilhelmine and Frederick to their English cousins, Frederick Prince of Wales and Princess Amelia; this 'affair of the English marriages' bore no fruit except tons of archives. Carlyle devotes to it one of the eight volumes of his *History of Friedrich II of Prussia*; and it is a curious and amusing example of the diplomacy in those days. The children set their hearts on marrying their grand relations and though they had never seen them imagined themselves in love. Their father was unfavourable to the English connection and the Queen told them that he was standing in the way of their happiness, as usual. George I might have liked the marriages but George II was always lukewarm. He loathed his cousin and brother-in-law who had bullied him ferociously when they were small—indeed their grandmother had to stop Frederick William's visits to Hanover for fear he should kill little George—and the loathing was reciprocated. The two men called each other 'my brother the drill-sergeant' and 'my brother the play-actor'. As for Sophia Dorothea, Lord Hervey says George II had for her the contempt she deserved and a hatred she did not deserve. It must be said that she was good to her unfortunate mother, shut up for life by George I, and did all she could to get her out of prison. She seemed to be succeeding when Dorothea of Celle died the year before her husband's death would have released her.

By the time Frederick was twelve it had become obvious that he and his father were on the worst of terms. Frederick was a polite, delicate little boy who hated rough ways. He was always in trouble: was beaten for wearing gloves in cold weather, for eating with a silver fork, for throwing himself off a bolting horse. If his father's rages terrified him they also fascinated him, and as he grew older he and Wilhelmine leagued together to tease the King, going as far as they dared and then skipping out of his way when they had worked him up to a frenzy. In this game their mother's room was 'home', the sanctuary; she had an arrangement of screens behind which they could dodge, making their escape through a second door or crawling under her bed, giggling audibly, sometimes knocking down a screen on purpose to make sure their poor, distracted father knew exactly what was going on. Sophia Dorothea never took her husband's part. She must have known how ill he was but never showed him any sympathy; she told all and sundry that he was mad and that she went in fear for her life. Nor did Frederick try to please his father; he treated him like an enemy and did everything in his power to annoy. He paraded scepticism in matters that he knew would hurt, mocked the Scriptures, scoffed at ghosts and yet was annoyingly clever in flooring Frederick William with theological arguments. When he really agreed with his father which, in the bottom of his heart, he often did, he would have died sooner than admit it. They seemed to have no tastes in common. Frederick William's favourite pastime was hunting, which Frederick disliked all his life. He loved riding—a day never went by without several gallops—but thought that hunting was cruel and dull. He was forced to ride to hounds by his father, but infuriated him by disappearing, to be found talking to his mother in her carriage or playing the flute in a forest glade. Worse still, he hated or pretended to hate anything to do with the army. His father knew that he called his uniform his shroud. If he was beaten, starved, humiliated and generally ill-treated it was to a large extent his own fault and his mother's.

Frederick William was not only profoundly irritated by him but also puzzled. 'What goes on in this little head?' Frederick never gave himself away; the only person with whom he talked secrets was Wilhelmine and even she hardly understood his nature. He had icy self-control, never flew into rages, and received his father's blows and insults with an air of maddening indifference. There is no doubt that he was treated with intolerable cruelty. Terror reigned in the house; the Queen, generally pregnant, cried every day. Luckily the King was by no means always there: he travelled incessantly seeing to the administration of his lands.

When Frederick was fourteen he was appointed Major of the Potsdam Grenadiers, in other words the giants, and spent part of his time at Potsdam. A very small major he must have seemed; as a grown-up man he measured five feet seven; he was a particularly thin and peaky boy whose face seemed to contain only two enormous blue eyes—dazzling, like the sun. He began to go out in society, to Mme de Roucoulle's Wednesdays, sometimes to Finck and sometimes to his father's *tabagie*. Here he had to pretend to smoke and drink, both of which habits he loathed to the end of his days, while his father watched him with bloodshot eyes: 'What goes on in this little head?'

Other people who saw him were struck by his great and growing intelligence. Duhan was with him at Potsdam and together they laid the foundation of Frederick's library. The catalogue still exists, written in Frederick's own hand. There were books on mathematics and science, history books of every sort, books on art, music and politics, and translations from the classics—practically all, even German histories, were in French. He also had every great French writer since Rabelais, everything so far published by Voltaire, the works of Mme Guyon and a French rhyming dictionary. He already longed to become a

French poet and his eyes were turned with rapture towards Paris. Like many Francophils he adored the French for reasons which would bring cynical chuckles from a Frenchman; indeed Lavisse says that if he was sometimes disappointed by the French *émigrés* in Berlin he put it down to the years they had spent being contaminated by Germans. He made no attempt to hide these feelings from his father: on the contrary he flaunted them in order to tease. He made French jokes—*esprit à la française*—and pathetic attempts at elegance, growing his hair and combing it in the French style. When Frederick William saw this he took him off to a barber and said the disgusting locks were to be sheared there and then. Frederick cried. The kind barber snipped and snipped, hardly cutting anything at all; wetted the hair; flattened it and left quite enough to be fluffed up again when the King was not about.

Frederick, aged twelve; painting by F. W. Weidemann.

Frederick William now greatly preferred his second son, Augustus William, aged four. 'I wouldn't put much money on any of my children but I think this one will be a gentleman' (*honnête homme*). Excessive in everything, he sometimes kissed the poor child for a quarter of an hour at a time. He was thought to be casting about for ways of disinheriting Frederick in favour of Augustus William. Frederick, for his part, began to plot against his father, trying to form a faction which would be attached to himself in the event of the King being shut up. He set about it with a brilliant deceitfulness far beyond his fourteen years. He made friends with Rothenburg, the French minister to Berlin, to whom he confided sentiments and activities so dangerous that Rothenburg dared not write a report of them to his government. There was plenty of inflammable material in Brandenburg; people were getting tired of being governed by an autocrat whose sage administration was less apparent than his mad behaviour. Fortunately, Rothenburg was a sensible fellow: he talked to Frederick like an uncle and told him to do nothing rash, that his only hope was to wait and make himself loved. Meanwhile, Frederick William, who always knew more of what was going on than he seemed to, began to have his suspicions. He made Frederick drunk and interrogated him but the child gave nothing away.

The crux of the whole matter was the English marriages, which were an obsession with the Queen and her children. Wilhelmine was now of marriageable age and Frederick quite old enough to be betrothed. The King's only adviser on such matters, Grumbkow, was taking his orders from Vienna, and the Emperor was violently against the marriages— France and England were enjoying one of their rare and fleeting moments of friendship and this was giving him much anxiety; he had no wish to see English influence spreading in Germany. On the whole Frederick William was loyal to the Emperor as a matter of German policy. He despised Charles VI and said he was as poor as a painter, but he considered that Germany must have an emperor and might as well stick to the House of Austria. He would have thought it very low to fight the head of that house with France as an ally. At the same time, the weaker the Emperor was the better, and the less likely to interfere with the internal policies of the princes. Charles VI used to hold out hopes that he would arrange for Frederick William to succeed the childless ruler of Jülich and Berg, two duchies which he greatly coveted: he had no real intention of doing so; it was a dishonest way of keeping the King on his side.

Frederick William's policy over the marriages never really changed, though sometimes, probably to stop his wife's nagging, he seemed more or less agreeable to them. He was always ready to send Wilhelmine to London, but never wanted an English wife for Frederick. Grumbkow had put it into his head that a rich English princess at Berlin, where everybody was so venal, would have too much power. If Frederick William really believed this, he had little understanding of his son's nature. George II, on the other hand, always said (and stuck to it): 'Both marriages or neither.' While George I was alive there seemed to be some hope for Wilhelmine, but in 1727 he died. Frederick William's lifelong *bête noire*, George II, infuriated him by making away with his father's will. There had almost certainly been a legacy to Sophia Dorothea, but she never got a penny. The cause of the English marriages was not helped by this.

The various ambassadors at Berlin reported all these things to their sovereigns; they also mentioned the fact that Frederick looked wretched, pale, worried and old; the poor little persecuted boy was an object of interest all over Europe.

Wilhelmine, aged four, and Frederick, aged two. This is the first recorded painting of Frederick by Antoine Pesne, and it hung in Sophia Dorothea's bedroom. She wrote to Frederick William on 17 April 1714: 'I have had the children painted and I think their portraits will be good.'

28

OVERLEAF: *Dresden from the right bank of the Elbe; painting by Bernardo Bellotto.*

CHAPTER TWO

The Unhappy Family

In 1728 it was announced that Frederick William would pay a State visit to Dresden. The Elector of Saxony was also King—Augustus II—of Poland, having been elected by the Polish aristocrats in 1697. It was necessary for the King of Prussia to be on good terms with his neighbour because he was obliged to cross Polish territory when he wanted to visit his duchy of East Prussia, but lately the two Kings had had differences which had flared up over the kidnapping of a Saxon giant. However, this state of affairs suited neither of them and Augustus sent Field Marshal Flemming to Berlin with words of peace and an invitation to Frederick William to go to Dresden for the carnival. Flemming's visit was a success—Frederick William, who had been particularly gloomy of late, quite cheered up; Mme Flemming, a fashionable beauty, was kind to Wilhelmine, did her hair for her in the latest manner, and advised her about her clothes. The invitation was accepted.

Augustus was a poor ruler but a picturesque character. His physical strength was so exceptional that he is known to history as Augustus the Strong. It was said of him that he was Lutheran by birth, Catholic by ambition (the Poles were violently Catholic) and Mahometan in his habits. He led an extremely jolly life with a harem of beautiful women whom he collected just as Frederick William collected giants; when he died he left a legitimate heir and 354 bastards. Among his descendants were Louis XVI and George Sand. Historians look with no good eye on Augustus the Strong and his son Augustus III who between them reduced the rich State of Saxony to penury in order to satisfy their craving for works of art. Beautiful Dresden under their rule was the most civilized town in the Empire.

Frederick William could not allow his virtuous Queen to visit such a court, much as she would have liked it, but there was no reason why he should not take Frederick, who was now grown up. The Prince had set his heart on going. He craved the great world which he knew only from books and the colourful imagination of Sophia Dorothea. She was really as ignorant of it as he; the French and English bourgeoisie led more amusing lives than this daughter, wife and sister of kings and her children. Frederick William decided against taking Frederick and set out for Dresden without him. So intense was his disappointment that Wilhelmine thought her brother might fall dangerously ill; she asked Count von

Queen Sophia Dorothea receiving Augustus II in Berlin; painting by Antoine Pesne.

33

The Nymphenbad, Dresden. This formed part of the palace of the Electors of Saxony and the statues are reputed to be Augustus the Strong's mistresses.

Suhm, Augustus's minister to Berlin, if something could not be done. Suhm was very fond of Frederick: he wrote to his master who, as he rather wanted to see the interesting boy, begged Frederick William to send for him. Augustus always put Frederick William in a good temper, no doubt because of his great geniality. ('The ever-cheerful Man of Sin,' Carlyle calls him, 'gay eupeptic Son of Belial'.) So Frederick William not only sent for Frederick but told him to order himself a new coat and tidy liveries for his servants. Father and son lodged with the Flemmings and stayed for a month. Visitors from all over the Empire came for the carnival; every effort was made to amuse them. Frederick saw his first play and, even more thrilling, his first opera; there were balls and entertainments of all sorts. The little Crown Prince found himself treated for the first time as a grown-up person: people talked to him seriously and seemed to be interested in his ideas. Indeed, after a dinner-party where the conversation had turned on philosophy, the Prince signed a letter to

Wilhelmine *Fédéric le Pfilosophe* [*sic*]. Frederick William's temper remained good, although he realized that Frederick was cutting a better figure than he in high society. His drunken boisterousness was out of place at Dresden; he had various misfortunes such as bursting his breeches when dancing with more energy than grace. Augustus's easy manners smoothed everything.

But he could not resist one joke at Frederick William's expense. After dinner, he took his guests to see some rooms in the palace. They were praising the decoration when a curtain was suddenly drawn disclosing a naked woman on a bed. Frederick William was startled into saying that she was very beautiful; but then he rushed from the room and, dragging Frederick with him, left the palace forthwith; he sent Grumbkow to tell the King of Poland that if this sort of thing was going to happen he would pack up and go home. Augustus hurried round to see him and apologized, and the visit continued in cheerful vein. Now Frederick was not as much displeased as his father by what they had seen. He had been making eyes at Countess Orzelska, Augustus's favourite mistress, who happened also to be his daughter and who was in love with Count Rudorfski, another of his children by one of those vaguely Turkish ladies with whom the eighteenth century abounds. As Frederick was a pretty young fellow, Augustus foresaw further cause for jealousy, so he made a bargain with him: he was to abandon Countess Orzelska, and Augustus would give him the naked woman instead, an arrangement which suited Frederick, who finally enjoyed both ladies. Very probably he had never yet had a chance to make love, since he

LEFT: *Ulrich Friedrich von Suhm; engraving.*
RIGHT: *Countess Orzelska; pastel by Rosalba Carriera.*

Wusterhausen.

was not allowed to be alone night or day; in this respect he profited by his visit to Dresden.

Too soon the delightful month came to an end and with it Frederick William's good temper. On their return the Crown Prince seemed more on his nerves than ever; to make matters worse the whole family now went to Wusterhausen. This favourite hunting-lodge of Frederick William's was the abomination of his wife and children. It was small, they were all on top of each other, gloomy and uncomfortable. The only decent room was used as a *tabagie*. There was a smelly moat into which the members of the *tabagie* sometimes threw Gundling when he and they were very drunk (once they forgot that it was frozen over and he bounced most amusingly on the ice). Two bears and four eagles were tethered on the drawbridge, all in a perpetual bad temper, and Frederick William's A.D.C.s had to get past these creatures as best they could several times a day. In this horrible atmosphere, so different from that of Dresden, Frederick subsided into black boredom. When he could get away from the watchful eye of his father he wrote endless screeds to a new friend, Lieutenant von Borsch: '*mon cœur vous adore . . .*' and so on. He told him that the days were so terrible at Wusterhausen that, when each was over, he would like to erase it from his memory as if it had never been. He also wrote to his father, a pathetic note begging him to stop hating him so cruelly; he received a very dusty answer in the third person. Hoping to soften Frederick William he loudly and embarrassingly at a dinner-party told Suhm of his great love for his father—pretending to be drunk he threw himself at Frederick William's feet and covered

36

his hands with kisses. Frederick William was delighted to see him for once behaving like a man—in other words, drunk—but nothing changed. He began to knock his son about systematically—the cane was busy, there were kicks and blows and hair-pulling, all, to add to the humiliation, in front of servants and officers.

Back in Berlin Frederick told Rothenburg that he thought of escaping, to France or England. Rothenburg reported it to his government and was told to put him off at all costs; the arrival of the fugitive Crown Prince in France would have been most embarrassing. The boy looked ill. He became as thin as a rake; doctors spoke of consumption. But Wilhelmine thought that imposed chastity after the delights of Dresden was the cause: 'He was dying of love', she wrote. Whatever the reason, he soon fell desperately ill and seemed really to be dying. Frederick William was overcome with remorse; he hugged and kissed his son, trying to make up for his behaviour at Wusterhausen. 'We don't know how much we love our children until they are ailing.' The Queen, the doctor and Frederick himself tried to prolong this happy state of affairs by pretending that he was critically ill long after he was

A plan of Berlin and its surroundings in 1737. The engraving shows (1) the Berlin State Palace and (2) Monbijou—both of which were pulled down in 1945; (3) the Brandenburg Gate; (4) the Potsdam Gate. Potsdam is only twelve miles from Berlin. (Note that the plan is inverted, with North at the foot.)

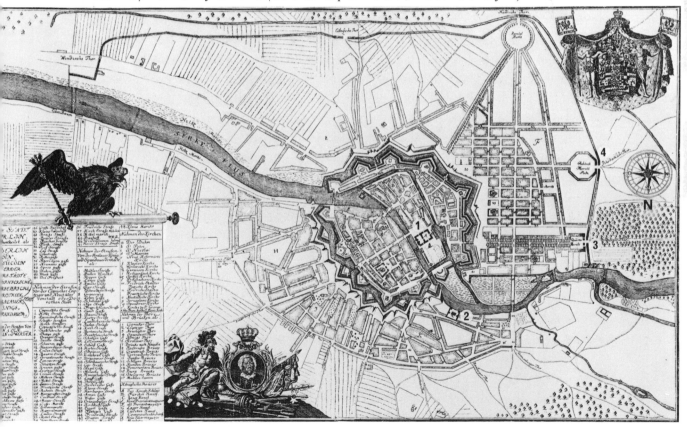

convalescent. At last, reassured, Frederick William went off on a visit to East Prussia and his entourage breathed again. He told Finckenstein that he could allow Frederick a little more recreation, though he must not sin against the laws of God and the wishes of his father, and must still be watched by day and by night.

The absence of the King was a happy time. The Queen gave parties and musical soirées. Frederick was always there, as good as gold, playing duets with his sister—his flute was called *Principessa*, her lute *Principe*; the two young creatures with their angelic looks presented a touching appearance. But the rest of the time he was running wild. His governors had little control over him now; the watching by day and by night was almost impossible to enforce. He had two boon companions, Lieutenants Keith and Hans Hermann von Katte; the three of them were said to have been extremely debauched. Wilhelmine hints that he picked up a disease at this time which worried the doctors and infuriated Frederick William when he found out about it. Keith (no relation of Lord Keith) was a deplorable fellow of Scotch origin, up to any shady business. Katte was a very different sort of person. He belonged to an old, well-connected family; his sister was married to a Bismarck and his aunt was Melusina von der Schulenburg, Duchess of Kendal, the mistress of George I. He was the grandson of a field marshal and the son of a general whose house was decorated with guns taken at Ramillies. Like Frederick, Katte loved music and reading; French was his language and conversation his greatest joy. He was an atheist. (Later, under terrible circumstances, he denied this, saying he had pretended to be one in order to be fashionable.) He was extremely ambitious, though his love for the Crown Prince was genuine. He had charming looks; his fair smooth hair, tied with a black bow, was admired for two hundred years at Wüst, where he is buried, until it was stolen by an English tourist.

On Frederick William's return the horrible family scenes began again: tears and terror. He soon saw that Frederick and Keith were up to no good, and packed off the Lieutenant to his regiment in Cleves. Frederick and Wilhelmine retaliated by teasing their father in many a subtle and unkind way. Gundling was now replaced at meals by a fervent pastor who read and commented on religious texts. The children pretended to think him irresistibly funny, maddening Frederick William by exchanges of naughty looks and repressed giggles. Frederick William, in agony from gout, was often in a wheel-chair, in which he pursued them with even greater fury than usual. Plates, crutches and other objects flew through the air—he caught Frederick and nearly strangled him to death. At meals he made him sit at the bottom of the table, where often he got no food at all; the Queen had to send for 'a box of cold fowls' with which to nourish the boy. Frederick William said: 'You needn't think I shall soon treat you better—on the contrary I shall get worse and worse.'

A marriage in the family, of Princess Frederika Louise, aged fourteen, to the Margrave of Ansbach, who was not much older, made hardly any impact at the court where Frederick and Wilhelmine were the centre of attention. Louise was always the least favourite

38

Baron von Keyserling; painting by Antoine Pesne.

among her singularly united brothers and sisters. She and Ansbach hated each other.

Frederick's two governors now resigned, either because they were revolted by the scenes they were forced to witness, or because they felt they had no longer any control over the Prince. Frederick William replaced them by Colonel von Rochow and Lieutenant Count von Keyserling.[1] The latter was a curious choice since on the face of it he was the sort of person whom Frederick William loathed, a highly civilized young man whose tastes were those of Katte and Frederick himself; indeed he became Frederick's great and adored friend. Frederick William thought he was alert. His great complaint against Frederick at this time was lack of alertness. He told Rochow that the Prince liked only lazy, effeminate pleasures; he rode bent double, made faces and grimaces, hung his head between his ears and looked like an old rag. And then he was so dirty and so dreary. Rochow must try and make an officer and a gentleman out of this poor stuff.

The return visit of Augustus the Strong brought a short respite to the unhappy family. Sophia Dorothea received him in Frederick I's beautiful rooms at Charlottenburg and in her own little palace of Monbijou; he was carried to her in a splendid sedan-chair because two of his toes had just been amputated; in spite of the pain he stood for a long time talking to her. She was in her element—at last she had a chance to show that she knew how to hold a court. The provincial Berliners were astounded by the clothes and general luxuriousness of Augustus's followers. Frederick William and his courtiers were always dressed in field uniform; they looked like sparrows beside the gorgeous Saxons. The daughter-mistress was there, and her affair with Frederick was resumed. According to Wilhelmine they managed many a secret rendezvous. Wilhelmine herself was thrilled by the compliments which Augustus showered upon her; she only realized later that this ancient widower of fifty-eight was considering her as a possible bride. As always when Augustus was there the atmosphere was agreeable; the visit went off perfectly. When it came to an end he was greatly missed.

Now that both the children were of marriageable age Sophia Dorothea was more than ever set on the English marriages. Her confidant was Sauveterre, the new French minister, and she told him everything, even what the King said when they were in bed together. He naturally wrote it all to Versailles, adding that he was amazed by the clumsiness of her *démarches*. Frederick thought himself madly in love with Princess Amelia, whom he had never seen, and he wrote touching letters to her mother.

Meanwhile, Seckendorf and Grumbkow, rolling in Austrian gold, were working hard against the marriages. Reichenbach, Frederick William's minister at the Court of St James's, was in their pay and his dispatches were dictated by them. (When this fact came to light it greatly amused George II.) Frederick William tried to stop Sophia Dorothea's nagging by pretending that he was waiting to hear from London; but then he stole a few

---

[1] He was a Courlander of the same family as the philosopher Keyserling, 1880–1946.

Frederick William and Augustus II at the time of the Prussian King's visit to Dresden; painting by Louis de Silvestre.

Hanoverian giants and refused to give them up, to the detriment of his relations with George II who riposted by kidnapping a Prussian officer and rudely crossing Hohenzollern territory, on his way to Hanover, without a by-your-leave. George I had always sent a civil message on these occasions. Suddenly England and Prussia were on the verge of war, to the delight of other powers. The Pope prayed in public for war between these two heretics, while the Emperor was far from displeased to see his powerful vassals at sixes and sevens. Seckendorf did all he could to fan the flames.

Frederick, now Colonel of the giants, marched them to the Hanoverian frontier; he was congratulated by his father on the perfect order in which they arrived. The two peppery brothers-in-law had second thoughts, and the storm in the teacup subsided as quickly as it had blown up. Frederick marched his giants back to Potsdam.

He was more and more determined to escape. He confided in Wilhelmine, who was horrified—she knew too well that such a venture would have dire repercussions for her and the Queen. One day she saw a beautiful young Frenchman in her mother's ante-room— Frederick in his escaping clothes. Frederick William, who had an uncanny instinct for knowing what his son was up to, told Rochow to keep a very strict eye on the Prince. The boy was now seriously in debt. His pleasures, whatever they may have been, were costing money, and so was the library of books and music that he was accumulating. Frederick William suddenly ordained the death penalty for anybody who lent money to royal minors.

The musician Quantz now came into Frederick's life; Sophia Dorothea induced him to go to Berlin from Dresden and he stayed there until his death in 1773. He was a composer and wrote a musical classic, *On playing the Flute*; he also improved the flute, which was a primitive instrument at that time. Frederick was greatly assisted in his music by Quantz, and he now began to have secret musical evenings in his own apartment. He liked to put on a beautiful embroidered robe, have his hair fluffed up, and then, looking, he thought, thoroughly French, settle down to a few hours of delight. Somebody was always posted to cry *cave* in case Frederick William should appear. One evening Katte dashed in to say that the King was upon them. Frederick just had time to tear off his robe and hide it; the others seized flutes and music and crammed themselves into a cupboard used for firewood. When the King loomed and saw Frederick's hair he smelt a rat (or possibly a Katte—he had his suspicions about the relationship between the two boys) and began to search the room. He soon found the robe and stuffed it into the fire. Then he came upon some French books and while huffing over them he forgot to look in the wood cupboard. He sent off to the town for a bookseller, told him to take them away and get what he could for them. (The bookseller kept them and lent them to Frederick whenever he wanted them.) Quantz and Katte shuddered to think what a narrow escape they had had—Quantz had been especially frightened because his coat was red, a colour which had the same effect on Frederick William as upon a bull.

Early in 1730 King George II seemed to be reconsidering the marriages. He sent Colonel

43

LEFT: *Johann Joachim Quantz. He was paid 2,000* thalers *a year: 25 ducats for every flute solo he composed and 100 ducats for every flute he made for Frederick; engraving.*
RIGHT: *Sir Charles Hotham; painting attributed to J. Richardson.*

Sir Charles Hotham as a special envoy to treat of this matter. Hotham, the head of an ancient Yorkshire family, was one of those agreeable English soldiers who so often succeed abroad. Foreigners are amused to find out that what seems at first sight the real John Bull is civilized, knows how to behave, and talks perfect French. When the Prussians knew Hotham better they were amazed, even impressed, by his knowledge of the arts and literature and also of specialized subjects such as hydraulics, agriculture and engineering. All this was unexpected in a Yorkshire squire. Hotham was welcomed with open arms by the Queen and her children. He took a fancy to Frederick: 'There is something so charming and engaging in the Prince and one day he will be somebody. One hears nothing but good of him.' Even Frederick William liked Hotham at first. He took him off to Augustus's army manœuvres, where there was a typical display of Saxon extravagance, ending with a dinner for all the soldiers, who sat at miles of trestle-tables gorging themselves on beef and a cake containing five hundred eggs and a ton of butter, which had to be cut up by the regimental carpenters.

Back in Berlin, Frederick William gave a dinner-party of men only for Hotham at Charlottenburg. Everybody got drunk and one of the toasts was 'Wilhelmine, Princess of Wales'. Of course this news flew to the palace, and the Queen thought at last her wish had come true; she was beside herself with joy, embraced the Princess of Wales and called her governess, Mlle de Sonsfeld, 'Milady'. This optimism went on for some days; Frederick

William seemed to be pondering over Sir Charles's propositions. But George II stuck to his original offer of both marriages or neither, while Frederick William said that his son was not old enough to marry and furthermore that the English were too fond of meddling in Continental politics and, with their mania for keeping a balance of power, would end by giving France the ascendancy. Then he furiously told Hotham that he had heard from London—the idea there was that once Frederick was married to Princess Amelia, Prussia would become a dependency of Hanover. That, said Hotham, had been put about by Seckendorf and Grumbkow; and in order to prove his point he gave Frederick William a letter from Grumbkow to Reichenbach telling him exactly what to put in his next dispatch. At this, Frederick William flew into a furious rage with Hotham for interfering between himself and his servants. He shouted insults at Sir Charles, flung the letter on the ground, some say he lifted his boot as though to kick His Excellency, and rushed from the room slamming the door. He said later that he knew all about Grumbkow but he supposed he might be allowed to employ the rogues that suited him. His Britannic Majesty having thus been publicly insulted in the person of his envoy, the said envoy had no choice but to pack his bags and prepare to leave Berlin, which he did, in spite of conciliatory messages from Frederick William and the tearful entreaties of Frederick. The affair of the English marriages was over; Grumbkow and Seckendorf had triumphed.

Frederick's signature.

CHAPTER THREE

Escape

The departure of Sir Charles Hotham threw Frederick into despair. The King told him he was not fit for marriage, in other words that he would not be allowed an establishment of his own but must face ever-increasing persecution in his father's house for an indefinite period. While Hotham was in Berlin there had seemed to be hope; now there was none. Frederick William said, 'If my father had treated me as I treat you I wouldn't have put up with it—I would have killed myself or run away.' Frederick loved life and had no intention of killing himself, but he was determined to run away.

A new English envoy appeared in Berlin, Captain Guy Dickens, or, as the children called him, 'Gidikins'. Frederick made a secret rendezvous with him at the gate of the Potsdam palace; he was accompanied by Katte and took Dickens into his confidence. He told him that his plan was to spend six weeks in Paris and then go to England. Dickens passed on the information to George II, who was quite as reluctant to receive Frederick as Louis XV was. The King sent word that the time was not ripe and begged the Prince to put off his journey. Furthermore, he promised that if he did so he would pay his debts as he had done already, more than once. Frederick, who owed 7,000 *thalers*, asked for 15,000, and promised not to escape *from Potsdam*. Meanwhile, Colonel von Rochow got wind that something was going on and he spoke to Katte about it. Frederick's grown-up friends knew the danger he was in, but his behaviour was, as he said himself years later, *furieusement inconsidéré* and Katte's was worse. He threw out dark hints and boasted of the Crown Prince's confidence. He had the money, the maps and Frederick's grey topcoat in his keeping. Lieutenant Keith, now posted at Wesel, and his young brother, one of Frederick William's pages, were in the plot—the latter most reluctantly.

In July 1730 Frederick William went on a tour of Germany to pay neighbourly visits and to inspect his own outlying lands. After some hesitation he decided to take Frederick— it seemed safer than to leave him at home. Frederick saw the journey as a God-sent opportunity for flight since it would bring him near the French frontier. He travelled in a coach with Rochow, General von Buddenbrock and another officer—elderly, distinguished veterans of the wars of Prince Eugene; they were enjoined not to let Frederick out of their sight. The page Keith was in attendance on the King but Katte was left behind, trying

Hans Hermann von Katte; painting by George Lisiewsky, 1730.

47

A view of the main street in Potsdam; etching by F. A. Scheureck.

vainly to get leave so that he could join the party somewhere on the road. It was arranged that when Frederick gave the signal he would come, leave or no leave. They wrote every day by messenger. As the grey coat had been left with Katte, Frederick bought some red cloth and had it made up by the tailor of one of his hosts. Colonel von Rochow was aware of this.

The journey began with Leipzig, Altenburg, Saalfeld, Coburg, Bamberg and Erlangen. At Erlangen, Rittmeister (cavalry captain) von Katte paid his duty to Frederick; he was Katte's first cousin and was there looking for giants. Nuremberg and Heilbronn took the travellers on to Ansbach to stay with Frederick's young sister. Here Frederick got a letter brought by Katte's soldier servant. He had come by way of Erlangen where he asked the Rittmeister how he could find the Crown Prince. Owing to Katte's careless talk the Rittmeister had heard rumours of a dangerous project; he gave the soldier another letter to carry, from himself to Rochow, advising him to be vigilant. The next thing that happened was that a letter from Frederick to Katte, on which he had forgotten to write 'Berlin', was delivered to the Rittmeister. He opened it, read it and sent it to Rochow.

When the travellers left Ansbach they passed by the battlefield of Blenheim. Marlborough had been dead only eight years; Eugene was still alive, and all the senior officers in Frederick William's suite, including of course the Old Dessauer and Seckendorf, had fought in the battle. They took the Crown Prince over the ground and explained every detail of the action to him. He was always to be interested in the battles of Marlborough and Prince Eugene. Then on to Augsburg whence Frederick wrote again to Katte. He said that as they had not been able to meet he thought it would be better to give up the idea of the French frontier and that as soon as Katte got a signal he must go to The Hague and ask for the Comte d'Alberville. He should bring the Count's topcoat and money and remember that if anything went wrong the Count would have taken refuge in some monastery where nobody would think of looking for such a heretic. He told the page Keith to get two good horses; Keith hated the whole business but could not say no to the Prince. Frederick had half hoped to find Katte at Ludwigsburg, where he and his father stayed with Duke Eberhard Ludwig of Württemberg, but there was no sign of him.

The next stop was a little town called Sinzheim. Frederick William did not fancy the inn there and preferred to sleep in the outbuildings of a farm-house. There were two barns, one for the King and the other for Frederick and his three companions. Frederick thought the moment had now come or never. He decided to slip away at dawn with Keith, who had got the horses, and be over the Rhine before anybody could catch up with them. At two o'clock,

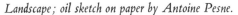

Landscape; oil sketch on paper by Antoine Pesne.

when daybreak was glimmering and his guardians were snoring, Frederick silently dressed, put on his new coat and crept out of the barn. But of course Rochow, not born yesterday, had made dispositions, and he was woken up by his valet who told him that the Crown Prince was outside in a red coat. Rochow went outside. Sure enough, there was Frederick, leaning on one of the carriages while Keith came towards him riding one horse and leading another.

'What's this—what are you doing?' said Rochow. Keith calmly replied that the horses were for him and the other page and he had understood there was to be an early start. 'Not before five. Go back to the stables.'
Frederick strolled towards the King's barn and ran into Seckendorf. Rochow said, 'How do you like His Royal Highness in his red coat?'

Nothing was said to Frederick William and the party got on the road as arranged. Though Frederick's carriage had started an hour before his father's, the King was at Mannheim first. He was seen to be uneasy, quite incapable of making small talk with his host, the Elector Palatine. At last the Elector sent an equerry to look for the Prince, who was not far off and very soon turned up. The King knew all; the wretched Keith had lost his head and made a full confession during the journey. When Rochow arrived Frederick William questioned him and he was obliged to confirm the story. However, nothing was said, except that before dinner Frederick William muttered to his son, 'Still here? I thought you'd be in Paris by now.' But he often made this sort of observation, and Frederick was not sure that it meant the worst.

The next stop was Darmstadt where they stayed with the Prince of Hesse; then on to Frankfurt to embark on yachts which would take them via Bonn and Cologne to Wesel, which was a Hohenzollern possession. As Frederick's carriage approached Frankfurt Rochow told him that he had orders to take him straight to the royal yacht where he was to wait while the King was receiving a municipal welcome. Things were beginning to look nasty, but they were worse than either Frederick or his companions knew. For, in Frankfurt, Frederick's latest letter to Katte had fallen into Frederick William's hands. It had gone by mistake to the Rittmeister, who had sent it to the King. This letter has disappeared but it would have been written in French and in the jaunty, joking tone which Frederick affected with his friend. It threw Frederick William into a blind fury.

He had hitherto bottled up his feelings out of consideration for his hosts; now, further maddened by the letter, he had got the Prince on a Hohenzollern yacht. When he arrived on board there were scenes of the utmost violence. The King drew his sword; General von Buddenbrock threw himself in front of the Prince, saying, 'Over my dead body'. So the cane was brought into play and soon Frederick's face was running with blood. At last Buddenbrock and the others extricated him and hurried him off to another yacht, and the party set sail for Bonn. Frederick was seeing the Rhine for the first time in his life. At Bonn he managed to send word to Lieutenant Keith at Wesel, telling him to fly, which he did,

Mlle de Sonsfeld; painting by Antoine Pesne.

and he had a talk with Seckendorf during which he ate humble pie and begged the General to do what he could for Keith and Katte. At Wesel he had another interview with his father, very much on the lines of the first. He made things even worse by reminding Frederick William that he had taunted him for putting up with his bad treatment. After that he was a prisoner, guarded by two soldiers with fixed bayonets.

Meanwhile, the news had reached Berlin. Frederick William wrote to the Queen's Mistress of the Robes, Mme de Kamecke: 'Fritz has tried to desert and I am obliged to put him under arrest. Please tell my wife without alarming her too much. And spare a thought for a most unhappy father.' He also ordered the arrest of Katte. This would never have taken place but for the suicidal behaviour of the young man. His Colonel gave him a day in which to make himself scarce. In the afternoon a fellow officer met him in the street:

'Still here, Katte?' He replied vaguely that he would be off that evening. When he had not gone the next morning they were obliged to arrest him. Frederick thought the reason was that he was after some girl.

When the King arrived in Berlin, having kept everybody in agonized suspense by lingering on the way, there was a reign of terror. Foreign diplomats describing it to their governments hardly expected to be believed. Frederick William beat and kicked Wilhelmine, shouting that he knew she had had a baby by Katte. He then lurched after the smaller children, who scattered in a fright; he might have killed one of them had not Mme de Kamecke lost her temper with him and cried out: 'Go to the devil, but leave these children alone!' The next day he thanked her for it. Nevertheless, he shut up Wilhelmine in two rooms with Mlle de Sonsfeld. The Queen was made to drink to the downfall of England. A Frenchman who had lent money to Frederick was hanged in effigy (he had fled), and a young girl who used to play tender duets with the Crown Prince was publicly whipped. Frederick William sent for Katte and beat and kicked him before handing him over to the army to be questioned. He wanted to have him put to the torture but Grumbkow drew the line at that. Katte told no more than was known already, adding that he would have followed the Prince but had never really expected him to go.

Frederick was shut up in the fortress of Küstrin, in solitary confinement. His door might only be opened four times a day, for meals and the removal of the *chaise percée*. Nobody was allowed to speak to him. He asked for Holy Communion but Frederick William knew that this was in order to have somebody, even if only a pastor, to chat to; he sent a message to say that the suitable time would be after the court martial. That seemed distinctly ominous. Grumbkow and other officers came to interrogate him; he adopted a bantering tone with Grumbkow, but his answers to the interrogation were brilliant. Try as they might the military lawyers could not get him to admit to having planned desertion; if he had not, the affair was merely a family one between himself and his father; he had broken no law. Frederick William was half pleased, half furious with the boy for being so clever.

There was soon much sympathy for him among his gaolers. The governor of Küstrin began to obey only the letter of Frederick William's rules. The door was not opened but a hole was made in the ceiling of his cell through which came the governor's little boy of seven with books, pens and paper and delicious things to eat. Then the Old Dessauer sent Captain Baron de La Motte Fouqué to keep him company, a charming person, a friend for life.

Frederick William was more miserable and tormented than ever before; he could not make up his mind what to do with the boy. His own violent physical reactions were often accompanied by a perfectly lucid grasp of a situation, and he realized that Frederick had come to a cross-roads; his future and that of his country depended on the path which he would follow, and it was Frederick William's duty, as his father, to put him on the good one. If he failed, would it be right to bequeath the State for which he had slaved and the

Baron de La Motte Fouqué; painting by Antoine Pesne.

The castle at Küstrin.

best army in the world to 'a little French marquis', a frivolous ne'er-do-weel? But in his heart he knew there was more to Frederick than that, just as Frederick knew in his heart that his father was better than a crowned ogre. Recalling this time in later life, Frederick said, 'I never ceased to revere him', and spoke of his sensibility. The Queen, who might have been such a valuable link between the two men, was useless to them; she moaned about the palace, flogging that dead horse, the English marriages. Frederick William's only confidant was the Old Dessauer. He told him that at least his conscience was clear; he had never spared the rod in his efforts to bring up the boy properly. He was shocked to hear from Grumbkow that Frederick was still for ever laughing and teasing. Did he take nothing seriously? He must be made to understand that life is more than little tunes, jokes and French verses.

The military tribunal sat at the end of October 1730. It was composed of a president, Lieutenant Colonel von der Schulenburg, who was a relation of Katte's, Grumbkow, General Count von Schwerin, one of Frederick William's best soldiers who had known and loved Frederick from a baby, another general, and nine officers down to the rank of captain. Katte was sentenced to prison for life. As for the Crown Prince, had he been convicted of desertion the penalty would have been death, but the court declared itself incompetent to try a Prince of the Empire and the case was sent back to the King. But in the tribunal's report the Prince was given his styles and titles which had not been used since the escape, and the escape itself was not called desertion but *retirade, échapade* or *Absentirung*.

The King changed Katte's sentence to that of death. He said Katte was not guilty of a mere juvenile escapade and that he was not an ordinary officer but an officer of the King's Guard. If such as he were unfaithful the whole structure of the State would be in peril. Katte had plotted with the rising sun. Should he get off lightly (a life sentence would only be for Frederick William's life) the King would never be able to trust his Guards again. Justice must be done. Frederick William's severity was probably due to his conviction that Frederick and Katte were lovers. Katte's father, the General, wrote to the King who replied: 'Your son is a *canaille*; so is mine; there is nothing we can do about it.' His grandfather, the Field Marshal, wrote and got a more sympathetic but negative reply. After that, Frederick William refused to see any more petitions. Katte's mother was dead.

On the morning of 6 November Frederick was woken up in his cell by an old officer and some soldiers, all in tears. He thought they had come to execute him and told them to get it over quickly. But then he learnt that Katte had been brought to Küstrin the day before and was about to be beheaded in the courtyard outside Frederick's window. The Prince broke down completely. He implored his gaolers to put off the execution on any excuse, to give him time to write to the King. He would offer to renounce his succession to the throne if only his friend could be saved. In vain. At the appointed hour Katte, in such a cheerful mood that it seems probable he thought the whole thing was play-acting, and that there would be a last-minute reprieve, was led under the Prince's window where 'he saw his beloved Jonathan'.[1] Frederick blew him a kiss and said, in French, 'My dear Katte, I beg your pardon a thousand times.' 'Monseigneur,' said Katte with a low bow, 'there is nothing to forgive.' He then knelt down and prayed, and his head was cut off with a sabre. Frederick was spared the dreadful sight—he had fallen in a dead faint.

---

[1] There are various versions of this scene—this one comes from the letter of an eyewitness to General von Katte.

CHAPTER FOUR

Rehabilitation

Frederick thought his own turn was coming. The King sent him a pastor with whom he had long metaphysical discussions; he was quite prepared for the end. But it is doubtful whether Frederick William intended to kill his son, even at the height of his fury. He is said to have been prevented from doing so by letters he received from other German rulers and from the Emperor Charles VI himself, pointing out that Frederick was a Prince of the Empire and therefore subject to the jurisdiction of that body. They taught Frederick William nothing he did not know already and would not have turned him from his purpose had his mind been made up.

A fortnight after the death of Katte Frederick was suddenly taken from his dungeon and put into the administration of the town of Küstrin. He was to learn about local government from Councillor Hille, a cultivated and learned man. The rules for his existence were strict; he was not allowed to dine out or have guests; all the same, with the fear of death removed, a little house of his own and two jolly young A.D.C.s to talk to, Frederick's spirits soared and poor Katte soon seemed forgotten. As all the posts on the Council were occupied he put in for the Navy. Why not?—the Oder flows into the sea. The Councillors were delighted with his jokes and to see that the Prince was as merry as a grig; they were soon under the spell of his charm. Hille and Frederick laughed together, though Hille was strict and firm with the Prince; he had nothing of the courtier and told Frederick some home truths. The poetry the boy was always writing was quite good for a Crown Prince but would not be much for an ordinary bourgeois, he said. He discovered that Frederick knew the French translation of Aristotle by heart but nothing whatever about German history—his ancestors might have got their lands by playing cards for all he cared. Hille taught him about industry, trade and agriculture. He explained that until Silesia could be stopped from stealing its trade Brandenburg would never flourish—there were not enough outlets. Frederick took note of this and other geographical facts such as the inconvenience to the Hohenzollerns of the kingdom of Prussia being surrounded by Poland. Prince Eugene received an account of the Crown Prince's conversation at this time; he said his neighbours would probably have trouble when he came to the throne.

Frederick William, having taken the very sensible step of putting Frederick to work out

Frederick as Crown Prince; painting by Georg Wenzeslaus von Knobelsdorff.

of his sight, remained on the usual bad terms with him. The liaison between the two of them was ensured by Grumbkow. Frederick always thought that he had advised the King to do away with him, but this is improbable. Grumbkow was a rogue but he was a civilized person; the Emperor, who paid him, was against Frederick being put to death, and there is no reason why Grumbkow should have been for it. Frederick teased and insulted him but the General gave as good as he got, and seems to have been rather fond of the Prince, whom he always referred to as 'Junior'. Frederick's Maréchal de Cour said that the whole *boutique* regarded itself as being under Grumbkow's protection.

Frederick William heard that Frederick believed in predestination. The villain—did he indeed? And who taught him this heresy? Frederick sent a list of the books in which the doctrine can be found. Aha!—books don't fly of their own accord—who procured them? Duhan, most likely. So Duhan was exiled, with no pension. Now Frederick is said to be ill—predestination, no doubt, but he won't die—weeds never do. Frederick William forbade oysters, capons and other delicacies; Frederick decided to drop predestination as hardly worth martyrdom. But the sad doctrine suited him. In 1760 he wrote: 'God, like a gardener, sows people as they are: narcissus, jasmin, marigold, carnation, violet—leaves them all to grow without interfering here on earth.' Frederick was penniless. He asked for summer clothes; Frederick William replied that no true German would think of wanting such a thing; it was a decadent French conception. He asked for books and was told to read the Bible—too many books had got him where he was. Soon he was fearfully bored at Küstrin, where the company of his *boutique*, the Maréchal de Cour and the two A.D.C.s, was beginning to pall. In every letter to his father he begged to be allowed to leave, but Frederick William said only when he was reformed and not play-acting. 'And I shall know when that is.'

Schulenburg went to see the Prince, to sound out his ideas on a possible marriage. Frederick, whose great desire now was to achieve his own establishment without marrying, said that if the King insisted he would obey, but then he would leave his wife to go her way while he went his. 'The King will find out and make your life a misery, apart from the fact that you will ruin your health.' 'You don't know what is to become of me?' Schulenburg thought presently he would be given a regiment. 'The only impossible thing is for me ever to live with the King again.'

Wilhelmine and Mlle de Sonsfeld had been shut up together in the palace at Berlin for six months and given just enough nasty food to keep them alive. Wilhelmine's spirit was not broken and presently her durance became less vile. In May 1731 the Austrian spy who was the concierge of the palace informed her that she was going to be married to the Duke of Saxe-Weissenfels, a drunkard whom she knew and loathed. If she refused she would be shut up for life and Mlle de Sonsfeld would be whipped. Guy Dickens actually heard Frederick William saying that if Mlle de Sonsfeld did not further the marriage he would send her to the prostitutes' prison. As the infinitely respectable Mlle de Sonsfeld was so

The Porcelain Room at Charlottenburg. The original K'ang Hsi period china was destroyed in 1943, when the palace was badly damaged. This collection has been acquired since.

well-connected that she was called 'Everybody's Aunt' this might have seemed funny except that, with Frederick William, you never could tell. However, she bravely urged the Princess to refuse, and so did the Queen, who still hoped for the Prince of Wales.

The King and Queen were at Potsdam. Grumbkow asked to be received by Wilhelmine and arrived with other dignitaries. After a pompous preamble he announced that the Margrave of Bayreuth, of the House of Brandenburg, was to be the bridegroom—adding that as she had never seen him she could not dislike him. If she refused she would go to a fortress and Mlle de Sonsfeld would be punished; but if she accepted Frederick would be rehabilitated. So she accepted. The Queen was furious and vowed eternal hatred for her.

Then the King held a review of his army at Berlin to which princes came from all over the Empire. Frederick begged to go, but in vain. Wilhelmine was at the window to see the guests arrive; an unknown young man got out of his carriage. 'Who is he?' The Prince of Bayreuth. Next day, at the review, he was presented to the Queen, who was most dis-agreeable, but Wilhelmine hid in the lady-in-waiting's coach. However, she met him at dinner and was unable to conceal her tears, though he was tall, handsome and noble-looking. Bayreuth told the Queen that if Wilhelmine hated him he had better go away. The King announced the engagement officially and then hugged Mlle de Sonsfeld; but the supper party at which this occurred was most melancholy. As usual, the King felt that he was in the wrong; got drunk; and then fell ill. The Queen forbade Wilhelmine to speak to her fiancé and was furious with her for winking at him. The King made him drunk to see what he was like. Bayreuth, finding the atmosphere decidedly difficult, asked the King for a regiment and went off with it to the provinces until the wedding in November. Before he left Berlin he spoke affectionately, even lovingly, to Wilhelmine, who was pleased; but of course the Queen interrupted them. She had become hysterical, still hoping for news from London. She told Wilhelmine to live with her husband as a sister so that the marriage could eventually be annulled; she was as cruel to her as Frederick William at his worst. Wilhelmine now had but one idea, which was to get away from home for ever.

On 15 August, Frederick William's forty-third birthday, Frederick's Maréchal de Cour was told to inform his 'subordinate' that the King was coming to see him. 'When I look into his eyes I shall know whether he is reformed or not.' Grumbkow was present at the interview and wrote a detailed account of it. As soon as he saw his father the Crown Prince fell at his feet. The King told him to get up, and then at some length recapitulated their relationship to the time of the escape: 'I always hoped you would own to your misdeeds—but in vain. You became more and more obstinate. I did what I could; I even tried kindness but I never could get the truth out of you. When I paid your debts you didn't tell me what you owed but went off and borrowed money from a Frenchman. That is the road to ruin. You didn't trust me.' Here Frederick once more fell at his father's feet. 'Did you mean to go to England?' 'Yes.' 'You never thought of your mother, or that I should have certainly suspected her of being in the plot, or of Wilhelmine whom I should have shut up for life,

61

Wilhelmine; painting by Antoine Pesne.

or of the war that would have broken out with Hanover where I should have put the whole country to the sword. Was it you who tempted Katte or he who tempted you?' 'I tempted him.' 'I'm glad to know the truth. How do you like it here? Better than Wusterhausen, no doubt. I'm afraid my company isn't good enough for you—I'm a German Prince—I can't make jokes in French; but you hate everything I like. . . . May God in his mercy help you, Fritz—as for me, I forgive you.' By this time they were both in floods. Frederick William dashed to his carriage and, having taken the Prince in his arms before a gratified crowd, he drove off. Frederick told Grumbkow that for the first time in his life he felt his father loved him, in a way.

After this the rules which made Frederick's life so dull were relaxed. He was allowed to visit farms and estates to see how they were run, to receive guests, and even to dine out, though he was forbidden to see any women. He went to dine with a Colonel de Wreech at a beautiful house called Tamsel about six miles from Küstrin. The Colonel's wife, all lilies and roses, was ten years younger than her husband. Tamsel belonged to her; it had been built for her grandfather by Greek workmen brought back from the Turkish wars. Frederick fell in love with her, wrote her some bad poetry and touching letters. She became pregnant; tongues wagged. Grumbkow asked Junior straight out if he was the father but Junior said, 'Untrue'. Frederick William heard the rumour and seems not to have been displeased. The baby did not live very long. When Frederick left Küstrin he sent his portrait to Mme de Wreech hoping that she would sometimes look at it and say, 'He wasn't a bad fellow; he left me because he loved me too much and often infuriated me with his inconvenient passion.' Six years later he wrote to Voltaire: 'When I was very young an adorable person, a little miracle of nature, inspired me with two passions: one was love, the other poetry. The love was a success; the poetry a failure.'

Wilhelmine's wedding-day was 20 November. There were fêtes and festivities, though the Queen still sulked. Wilhelmine had become fond of Bayreuth, and with her natural high spirits she enjoyed the whole thing very much indeed. One evening she was happily dancing when Grumbkow said, 'See who is standing by the door.' She looked and looked again; it was her brother. She flung herself into his arms but he was as cold as ice, which seemed unfair, considering that she had consented to the marriage entirely on his account. This unexplained coldness, which extended also to the Margrave of Bayreuth, lasted for a day or two, after which they were on their old loving terms.

The King took Frederick to the Queen and said, in French, 'Here is Fritz back again, Madame.' But Sophia Dorothea, always jealous and touchy, was displeased to think that he had come back on Wilhelmine's account and not on hers, and she was as disagreeable to him as to the bride and bridegroom. The King, who had been looking forward to a happy family reunion, said to Wilhelmine, 'The fact is, all our troubles are due to your mother and her intrigues.'

Frederick had grown and filled out during his exile; he looked more of a man. Frederick

Wilhelmine's husband, the Margrave of Bayreuth; painting by an unknown artist.

Mme de Wreech; painting by Antoine Pesne.

William's generals, headed by the Old Dessauer, went in a body and begged the King to forget the past and give his son a regiment. Perhaps nothing loath, the King allowed him to put on his uniform again and sent him to Ruppin as Colonel of a regiment that was quartered there. He had two small houses; always passionately fond of gardening, he could make a garden of his own for the first time: '*Amalthée—mon cher jardin de Ruppin*'. Here he grew melons, meditated and played the flute, and here a fellow officer, the architect Knobelsdorff, designed the first of his many buildings for Frederick—a sad little *temple d'Amalthée*. For company he had men of his own age, some of whom, like Keyserling, were already great friends. Keyserling had been under a cloud at the time of the escape, but Frederick had managed to get him back again. Above all Frederick could read as much as he wanted to: 'the dialogue with dead people, so much more fascinating than the living'. He wrote a great deal of French poetry which, with the flute, was his favourite hobby. At this time a new, long association began. General von Schwerin, who loved and understood the Prince, sent him a private from his regiment called Fredersdorf, hoping that he might suit. He suited, and remained with Frederick as his soldier servant until his death in 1758. He was tall, handsome, clever, silent and polite; and was a talented flautist. As the King refused to allow Frederick any musicians or musical instructors at Ruppin this was a great advantage: he played duets with Fredersdorf. When Fredersdorf was away, as in later years he often was, on confidential missions, Frederick wrote to him almost daily—gruesomely intimate letters about his servant's health—and clearly worried about him. Some of these letters have a decidedly erotic flavour and some are fatherly in tone. Whatever the relationship between the two men may have been, they were certainly very close to each other.

The sad little temple d'Amalthée *by Knobelsdorff, still to be seen in the gardens at Ruppin.*

CHAPTER FIVE

Marriage

Frederick now had to face his future. Most young German princes went on the Grand Tour before settling down, but he knew that it was hardly worth asking Frederick William to permit this. He hesitated to stir up his father who at last seemed relatively well-disposed towards him, but he bombarded Grumbkow with requests to intercede for him. Like Voltaire, he passionately longed to see Italy; like Voltaire, he never did so. The alternative was marriage. He had no wish for a wife, but he wanted an establishment of his own; and it was not the custom to give that to a young, unmarried prince. Grumbkow and Seckendorf, having successfully buried the English connection, now put forward their master's candidate, the Empress's niece, Princess Elizabeth of Brunswick-Wolfenbüttel. She was eligible, the right age and a Protestant. So Frederick William made no objection and wrote to Frederick to announce his engagement. He added that as soon as he had a son he would let him travel.

Frederick had never seen the Princess but he worked himself into a passion of hatred for her, which he poured out in letters to Grumbkow. He always begins by asking after the General's dear health. He submits, of course, to his father's wishes but he feels sorry for the hideous creature because now there will be yet another unhappy princess in the world. Grumbkow must get her educated—Frederick would much rather be cuckolded by a clever woman than driven mad by a fool. She must learn Molière's *École des Femmes* by heart. Why, he would almost rather marry ugly Mlle Jette, who has no ancestors, than a stupid princess. (Mlle Jette was Grumbkow's daughter.) He knows what an old womanizer Grumbkow is—no doubt he would agree that a flirt is better than a prude. How Frederick hates the heroines of novels! He likes women only while he takes his pleasure—after that he despises them; he is not the wood out of which one carves good husbands.

Grumbkow went to Brunswick and reported on the Princess to Frederick. He said he would not raise false hopes by over-praising her but that she was really not bad at all. After that Frederick refers to her as 'the abominable object of your desires'. He is sunk in melancholy; he cannot bear the idea of an idiot whom he will dread showing in public. The King, as a Christian, should consider what he is doing in making another ill-assorted marriage— he should think of the Ansbachs, who hate each other like fire.

Under his banter and mockery Frederick was really miserable. He spoke of suicide. A

The marriage of Frederick and Elizabeth Christine of Brunswick-Wolfenbüttel;
engraving.

member of his staff wrote to Grumbkow to ask if he could not stop the marriage; Grumbkow said he had no intention of having his head cut off for taking Frederick's side. There was good in the boy but he needed some more chastisement, which seemed to suit him.

The betrothal took place in March 1732. An interesting and charming guest at the ceremonies was Francis, Duke of Lorraine. He had been brought up at the Austrian court and was like an adored son to the Emperor, while the eldest Archduchess, Maria Theresa, had been in love with him from childhood. It was understood that they would marry in due course. He and Frederick made friends. When Frederick put the ring on Princess Elizabeth's finger his eyes were seen to be full of tears. He wrote to Wilhelmine: 'The person is neither ugly nor beautiful; not without *esprit* but badly brought up, shy and awkward. . . . There can be neither love nor friendship between us.' (When Wilhelmine saw her she said she was rather pretty, like a child, but with bad teeth.) His letters to Grumbkow were terrible: 'I will keep my word and marry the lady; but then it will be, *bonjour, Madame, et bon chemin*' (good day, Madame, and good luck to you). Presently he was to go to Brunswick which would be no great excitement as he knew what his dumb lady would say to him. She has sent him a china snuff-box which arrived broken; what can that portend? However, he told Wilhelmine that he did not dislike the dumb lady as much as he pretended to— Wilhelmine must help her to dress better—but that he wanted the King to realize that he was making a huge sacrifice in order to please him.

Just before the date of the wedding, Augustus the Strong died after a drinking-bout with Grumbkow who, for his part, was never the same again. This death opened the question of the Polish succession: Louis XV wanted his father-in-law Stanislas, who had already been King of Poland (1704–09), to go back there, whereas the Emperor's candidate was the son of Augustus. Charles VI, casting about for allies against the French and anxious now to please the English, told Frederick William to break off Frederick's engagement and marry him to Princess Amelia. Frederick William was furious at such a dishonourable suggestion—indeed he never forgave the Emperor for doing all he could to stop the English marriage in the first place and then, when it suited him, trying to humiliate a young woman on the eve of her wedding. Frederick William had become fond of Princess Elizabeth. As for her, she had fallen in love with Frederick and loved him all his life.

So the Brunswick wedding duly happened. Frederick William gave his daughter-in-law the palace of Schönhausen, near Berlin, where she lived while Frederick went to the wars. His father had sent 10,000 men to help the Emperor against the French who were besieging Philippsburg on the Rhine. The Austrians were commanded by Prince Eugene, and Frederick was enchanted to think that he would fight his first battles under the tutelage of that legendary hero. But he soon realized that Eugene was old and had lost his magic. There was no engagement; Philippsburg fell and Frederick learnt nothing except that the Imperial army was in poor shape. He said that though his body was with the Austrians, his wishes were for a French victory.

At the siege of Philippsburg he acquired a French friend, the Comte de Chasot. He had killed a member of the powerful Boufflers family in a duel and had fled to the Imperial ranks with a statement, signed by his colonel, that honour had demanded the duel. Frederick invited him to dinner, enchanted to meet a real Frenchman from France. The party was in full swing and Chasot, a jolly soul, was having a great success, when his horses arrived, sent after him by his fellow officers. Prince Eugene said: 'You'd better sell them and we'll give you some that speak German.' Prince Liechtenstein bought them there and then—for much more than they were worth. The Prince of Orange said: 'It always pays to sell horses to people who are dining well.' Chasot stayed on with Frederick, not to fight against his own country but to chat and play the flute.

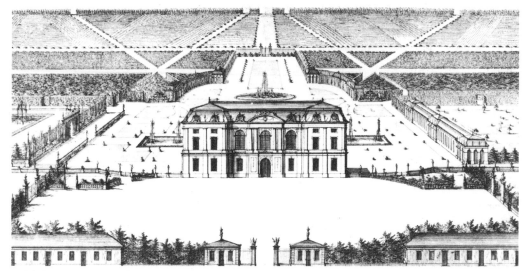

Schönhausen; engraving by J. G. Merz.

More valuable than Chasot was Hans Karl von Winterfeldt whom Frederick also now met for the first time. Five years older than he, an officer whom Frederick William had already singled out for special jobs, a brilliant, single-minded, reliable German soldier, he had no airs and graces and peace-time accomplishments, and spoke no French. Frederick loved him deeply and unchangingly. 'He was my friend and a good man, a man of soul.'

On his way home Frederick went to Bayreuth to see Wilhelmine. It was rather a horrid surprise to her when he told her, most disagreeably, that she had better stop playing at queens and lead the life of a country lady—then she would be able to pay her debts, which he had no intention of doing. She cried. He offered to console her with a little music. Frederick often teased Wilhelmine but he always loved her best in the world. They spoke of their father's possibly approaching end—he was seriously ill. Frederick, who was longing to succeed him, said how much he admired the behaviour of his father-in-law, the Duke of

LEFT: *The Comte de Chasot; painting by the school of Pesne.*
RIGHT: *General von Winterfeldt; painting by an unknown artist.*

Brunswick, who had shown such politeness towards his son by dying. (At about this time the Prince of Wales was fervently praying that George II would be drowned on his way to Hanover.) Wilhelmine liked to think of her mother as a dowager. 'It will be a furious blow to her.'

At Potsdam, finding his father in a ghastly state, Frederick was very kind and loving to him, but began to make dispositions for his death, which seemed inevitable. He intended to take advantage of the weakness of the Imperial army and to invade Silesia there and then. But the King recovered. He was turning from his old loyalty to the Emperor whose behaviour over the English marriages rankled and who had also double-crossed him by promising Jülich and Berg to both him and Count von Sulzbach. Frederick William was always helping the Emperor in various ways but seemed to get nothing in return; he decided to send no more troops for the next campaign. The war was nearly over, and in October 1735 Louis XV and Charles VI arrived at a settlement by which Stanislas Leczinski was to rule over Lorraine while the Duke of that ancient province, the fiancé of Maria Theresa, was given the Grand Duchy of Tuscany. He minded passionately, and so did the Lorrainers, who now became to all intents and purposes French. Augustus of Saxony was then elected King of Poland. In concluding this treaty Charles VI did not even consult Frederick William in spite of the fact that anything to do with Poland concerned him vitally.

In the summer of 1735 Frederick went to Prussia on a tour of inspection. At Frederick William's accession it had been a miserably poor, wild, empty country where the old German gods still seemed to hang about among the ruined castles of the Teutonic knights.

Frederick William was colonizing it with religious refugees, mostly from Salzburg where the Protestants were much persecuted. He organized every detail of the immigration and administration himself: the design of the towns, the crops to be grown, the extermination of vermin—from bears and wolves to squirrels. Huguenot immigrants were taught German and obliged to speak it. Frederick always affected to despise Prussia. He loathed the Gothic past and anything that reminded him of it, and he said there was not a single thinking person in the whole region. However on this occasion he took trouble to please his father— he even sent home samples of the peasants' bread—and though in some of his letters he declared that he was bored to death among the savages, he was truly very much impressed by the contrast between Frederick William's lands and the surrounding Poland. In Prussia, order, prosperity and hundreds of children; in Poland, a desert.

At the Prussian capital, Königsberg, Frederick paid his respects to Stanislas Leczinski who had taken refuge there, having been thrown out of Poland for the second time in his life. Frederick William had resisted a great deal of pressure from both Austrians and Russians to give him up—he even made him a small allowance. The ex-King and Frederick got on very well. They had long discussions on a subject which was always to fascinate Frederick, the immortality of the soul. Stanislas, a highly civilized, amusing, cynical man, was a tepid Roman Catholic; his holy daughter, the Queen of France, tried without much effect to keep him on the right road. Frederick hated and despised the Christian religion which had wrought such devastation in Germany during the Thirty Years' War; his views on God were to be contradictory all his life. Like Voltaire, whose influence over him was already considerable, he believed in a Superior Being but not in one who bothers about individuals. In the bottom of his heart he seems to have believed in immortality; but he liked to startle people with a mixture of Bayle's metaphysics and Voltaire's jokes.

When he returned to Brandenburg after his tour of Prussia, Frederick was on better terms with his father than ever before; both realized that, as long as they lived apart, they could get on perfectly well. 'Keep away from Jupiter,' said Frederick, 'there is less danger of thunderbolts.'

CHAPTER SIX

Out of a Rembrandt into a Watteau

Frederick's two little houses at Ruppin could not accommodate a Crown Princess, so Frederick William bought a property for him at near/by Rheinsberg. When he went campaigning the house was handed over to Knobelsdorff to be rebuilt according to Frederick's ideas, that is to say in the delicious, light and airy taste of the day. It was said that going from Wusterhausen to Rheinsberg was like stepping out of a Rembrandt into a Watteau. The young couple began their life together there in 1736. Remusberg, Frederick called it (there was an improbable local legend that Remus had died there and was buried on an island in the lake), and here he surrounded himself with congenial souls, more like guests than courtiers. He was happy for the first time in his life. He, who had been so bored at Wusterhausen that he wished to erase the time there from his memory, was never bored again. He had his regimental duties at Ruppin; the rest of the day belonged to him.

There is no more agreeable and fruitful environment for intellectual work than a well/run country house. The worker can spend as much time as he likes in his own apartment; when he comes downstairs for meals or for a promenade he finds cheerful company, intelligent conversation and music or theatricals in the evening. At Rheinsberg the worker was Frederick; he spent many hours alone in one of the two round towers that he and Knobelsdorff had preserved from the old house; here he had his library.

Frederick had a touching desire to find out the causes of all he saw around him, and he thought that the best way of doing so would be to study literature and philosophy. In later life, having found out that *le fond des choses* is not so easily determined, he spoke ironically of his young ambitions; nevertheless, at Rheinsberg he acquired a solid grounding in European thought from Classical times. He was also preparing himself to be a king. 'Good intentions, love of mankind, and the hard work of a solitary can perhaps be beneficial to society and I flatter myself that I am not among its idle, useless members', he wrote to Schaumburg/Lippe, thanking him for a huge man he had sent him for Frederick William. The only thing he wanted at Rheinsberg was books, more books and the money with which to buy them. He borrowed money from German princelings saying that, if he died, the repayment would be a true source of pain to Frederick William. He read six or seven hours a day, and sometimes all night. Every evening there was a concert except when the

Frederick with his wife at Rheinsberg. Detail from a painting by Georg Wenzeslaus von Knobelsdorff.

household got up a play, generally by Racine or Voltaire. On Sunday Frederick did not go to church with the others; he galloped over to Ruppin loudly declaiming a sermon by one of the great French preachers which he would then deliver, in French, to his soldiers. He knew all Bossuet by heart. German was never spoken at Rheinsberg where half the inhabitants, including the cook, were French.

The household consisted of about twenty people. The Crown Princess had six ladies-in-waiting and a chaplain. The ladies, all Prussian, were no doubt rather provincial but seem to have been bright and gay; it was noticed however that the Prince had no mistress among them. At this time he did not object to female society; indeed he said that conversation languished without it. Three of the men were already attached to Frederick: La Motte Fouqué, Keyserling and Chasot (the French deserter); these soldiers stayed with him all their lives. Fond as he was of Keyserling and Chasot, his feelings for Fouqué were on a different level. He was about forty, a good, serious man; he never asked for anything; on the contrary, he said that Frederick did far too much for him, with the result that he received more favours than anybody else. In 1739 he quarrelled with the Old Dessauer and had to leave Brandenburg; Frederick took care of his children and sent them 'to the school behind my house'—the next year he became King and the two men were never separated again. Fouqué was one of his most valued generals. Too many of Frederick's friends died young or were killed in battle but Fouqué lived to a ripe old age. The other pearl of great price at Rheinsberg was Frederick's secretary, Charles Étienne Jordan. He was also a French refugee, aged thirty-six, a Protestant pastor, rather rich, a widower with one daughter. To console himself at the death of his wife he had travelled and had been to England and the Netherlands. Frederick always said Jordan was the friend he had loved the most: 'wise discreet Jordan, more lovable than Erasmus'; 'good Jordan of my soul'; 'so tender-hearted he would weep to think of the horrors in America'. On succeeding to the throne Frederick wrote: 'I am your friend and brother more than your King.' He was the only person to whom Frederick said *tu*. Jordan never lodged at Rheinsberg but lived in the town with his little girl.

The Crown Prince and Princess and most of these friends were painted by Antoine Pesne, a Frenchman who had been brought to Berlin by Frederick's grandfather Frederick I on Pesne's return from the Italian journey always undertaken by painters in those days. He was an old fellow now, fifty-three, with a wife, Anne du Buisson, whom he had married in Rome. She, her father, three brothers and two sisters were all flower painters; the whole family lived together and Frederick persuaded them to settle at Rheinsberg where they were happy. Pesne was a dear. Knobelsdorff, Frederick's architect, a Protestant from Silesia, had also gone to Italy to study art but he despised the 'servile and perfidious' Italians and all their doings since the Emperor Constantine. Everything had to be Greek; so vases, colonnades and statues multiplied in and around the house. The only typical courtier among these people was Baron Bielfeld, who wrote an account of the life at Rheinsberg. The others,

Charles Étienne Jordan; painting by Antoine Pesne.

honest and busy, were all truly devoted to the Prince and got on well together.

The atmosphere seems to have been idyllic, and the idyll was to last four years, a long time at Frederick's age. When they were old, both he and his wife regarded it as their happiest time. Of the Crown Princess we know little except that she was dull, with a tendency to fussiness bordering on hysteria and that she used to gaze into Frederick's eyes hoping to forestall his slightest wish. Frederick said he 'paid his tribute to Hymen' but there was no sign of a baby and this was a grief to Frederick William. He sent a splendid green velvet bed but with no result. He loved his daughter-in-law and never burst out at her. From time to time he summoned Frederick; at first he would be loving and hold Frederick under his charm, then the irritation exacerbated by physical agony took over. 'If he can't bear the sight of me why not leave me in peace at Remusberg?' In remorse after one of these meetings Frederick William gave Frederick his stud farm, which brought a good income; Frederick was touched and delighted.

In 1738 two members of fashionable cosmopolitan society visited Rheinsberg. They were an older and a younger man, travelling to England after having visited Russia together. Lord Baltimore, aged thirty-eight, was in the household of the Prince of Wales; scandalously debauched (according to Lord Lyttelton who had met him at Lunéville), he was a frequenter of foreign courts and his finances were not in too good a state. His friend was a handsome young Venetian, Algarotti; of the same age as Frederick, he had that Italian polish—a combination of the manners, tact and intelligence of an ancient race, a childlike *joie de vivre* and an easy sexuality—that operates so powerfully on the less sophisticated northerner. These were the first people of their kind whom Frederick had ever met; perhaps they confirmed him in an already latent homosexuality; he was certainly entranced by them and fell in love with Algarotti—so had Lord Hervey, Voltaire, Mme du Châtelet, Lady Mary Wortley Montagu and many another. When Frederick knew him better and the glamour had worn off he said he was agreeable and many-sided but a wheedler with an eye to the main chance. But he was always fond of him. Lord Chesterfield called him 'a led wit of Lord Hervey's . . . a consummate coxcomb', and Voltaire, 'the most lovable of Italian amateurs; highly agreeable conversation'. Algarotti wrote books, now forgotten, on philosophy. The visitors stayed only a few days at Rheinsberg, but the Italian was soon to reappear.

All his life Frederick loved to write and receive letters—the post-bag was a joy to him. He signed his letters *Fédéric*, which seemed more French and therefore more civilized than *Frédéric*—beautiful *Friedrich*, rich in peace, was never used. As soon as he was settled at Rheinsberg he wrote his first letter to Voltaire. It reads like a child's homework—one feels he copied it out over and over again in his desire to please and possibly impress the man who had been his guiding star from childhood. No sparkle, no originality, not a joke. Also the Prince had to be careful, much as he longed to see Voltaire, not actually to invite him to Rheinsberg. Until Frederick William and his cane went to a better world that would have

76

Count Algarotti; pastel by Jean Étienne Liotard.

been rash indeed. Voltaire replied, hailing the advent of a Prince-philosopher; if the tumult of affairs and the wickedness of mankind did not change his divine nature Prussia could expect to have a Golden Age. He too was guarded in his hopes for a meeting; he had heard of the cane. Frederick sent Keyserling as his ambassador to Cirey; after this he and Voltaire wrote to each other until Voltaire's death.

His other correspondents at Rheinsberg were his father, to whom he sent amusing accounts of local doings; 'Maman' Camas, his mother's lady-in-waiting and the wife of an old soldier; Grumbkow; and distinguished foreigners of all sorts. His letters always have a point of interest but they are at their most serious, least affected by the fashionable flippancy, in his correspondence with Ulrich von Suhm, formerly Saxon minister to Berlin, who had befriended him when he was a boy. Suhm was now representing Augustus III at the court of the Empress Anne of Russia. He and Frederick wrote on all subjects from metaphysics to European politics. Frederick wished to be informed about Russia, always a subject of preoccupation with him. Suhm replied, stressing its enormous size, that if Russia were highly populated like other European countries it would be master of the world. He says it is invincible in defence—the soldiers are first-class, utterly obedient. He loves St Petersburg for its beauty and the clear, cold air. He thinks highly of Biron, the Empress's lover— Frederick says so does Keyserling who was at school with him and that he, Frederick, would not mind accepting a loan from him, though not from the Empress. He can't get enough books (this was always his cry until his succession)—could he borrow some from Russia if he promised to return them? He would also like thirty skins of black sable. To Frederick's grief Suhm died at Warsaw on his way home in 1740. He said the Prince was the most lovable and truly good person he had met during his pilgrimage through life.

Frederick now applied himself to literary composition at which he laboured for the rest of his days. His collected works begin with an essay (1736) on the state of Europe, drawn mostly from information given him by Grumbkow. Here are his conclusions. Germany, fatally divided into small states and cursed with a language which is only a series of bar-baric dialects, is a field waiting to be tilled. Italy is also divided: an ancient garden run to seed which, since all the alleys, statues and vases still exist, could easily be refertilized and could flower again. Full-blooded England, happy and rich, though without a single painter, sculptor or musician, mistress of groaning Scotland, tyrant of Ireland, makes little impact on the Continent. Austria, a noble old dame in fusty purple, has an internal malady likely to become dangerous at the death of the Emperor. Holland has subsided into cheese-making. France, light-hearted, funny, lovable from birth, can't help being rich and strong ('If God made the world for me he put France there for my entertainment'). Russia is a chaos, organized only yesterday and thrown into the path of history by a demiurge. Frederick notes that France and England will always be on different sides and that he can ally himself to whichever of them suits his book. As for Austria, it is necessary as a barrier against the Turks, but that is no reason why it should dominate Germany.

A watercolour, painted in the nineteenth century, of a room at Rheinsberg.

LEFT: *Antoine Pesne; self-portrait.*
RIGHT: *Georg Wenzeslaus von Knobelsdorff; painting by Antoine Pesne.*

This analysis shows that, like Louis XV, Frederick was uninterested in the world outside Europe. He also wrote the celebrated *Anti-Machiavel* to show that armed aggression is immoral and honesty the best policy for a ruler, sustaining the argument with such vigour that even Voltaire thought he had gone too far.

Frederick had never been strong, and at Rheinsberg he had his first serious attack of the disease which was so soon to kill his father. It took the form of appalling internal cramp; he thought he would die. He said it came from thickened blood in the little veins at the bottom of the stomach causing the bowels to contract so that, instead of performing their worm-like action, different parts of them tightened, filling with wind and pressing on the diaphragm. Two months later he was still shaken, and thereafter he was never really well again.

In May 1740 Frederick William was dying at Potsdam. His torments were atrocious; sleep was out of the question. His bed was covered with carpenter's tools; night and day he made little wooden boxes; the hammering could be heard in the town. He was in a frightful temper, hitting out to right and to left. He said he expected to scream with laughter in the tomb at the mess Frederick would make of everything. When it seemed that he was sinking, Frederick was sent for and he galloped over from Rheinsberg. But on his arrival at Potsdam he saw a crowd outside the palace, and there was his father, up and dressed, inspecting a smithy he was building for an English blacksmith. Frederick was slightly unnerved; if he went to his father unexpectedly he generally received a few blows; but the King opened his arms and Frederick burst into tears. Then they retired into the palace and Frederick William expounded his views on foreign policy. He said there would always be more to lose than to gain by war with Russia; that Austria would never willingly allow the expansion of Prussia and that France should be played off against England. Never start a war light-heartedly, he said, it doesn't always stop when you would wish it to.

Frederick and Wilhelmine wrote to each other most feelingly at this time; there is no doubt that they felt both affection and pity for their father. He was very much interested in his own approaching death. He spoke of his funeral: 'Naked I go—well, not quite naked, I shall have my uniform on'; and he asked that they should sing 'Fight the good fight'. He ordered his horses to be brought into the courtyard and told the Old Dessauer to choose one. That Prince, blinded by tears, did so. 'But he's no good at all—you must have this one.' Finally: 'I die happy to leave such a worthy son and successor.'

The dead King's face was a mask of torture.

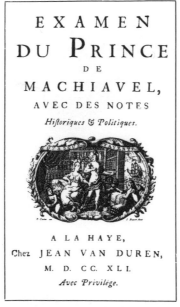

The title-page to Frederick's work, the Anti-Machiavel.

CHAPTER SEVEN

The Throne

Frederick left Potsdam at once for Charlottenburg.

That night, Knobelsdorff galloped over the wooden bridge at Rheinsberg. 'Get up, Bielfeld; the King is dead.' Bielfeld sleepily replied that he had heard this before and that Frederick William always recovered. 'They are embalming him; he won't recover from that.' Bielfeld, in getting out of bed, knocked over a table on which he kept some small change. He began to pick it up—Knobelsdorff said, 'Funny bothering about the ha'pence when it's going to rain ducats!' A lady-in-waiting was sent to tell the new Queen, who appeared looking beautiful in a black and white *négligé* to receive the homage of the little court. Then they all dashed to Charlottenburg. Here the Queen was given a note from her husband telling her to go to the palace at Berlin 'since your presence is still necessary. See nobody.' The separation had virtually begun, although for the next few years the King and Queen sometimes stayed under the same roof and he always took her with him when he went to Rheinsberg. But in 1744 he gave Rheinsberg to his young brother Prince Henry and Wusterhausen to Augustus William; presently he built himself Sans Souci which the Queen never saw. She confided in nobody, and her behaviour was so perfect that it is impossible to know what really happened; she had evidently not expected so sudden a break. At the beginning of their marriage Frederick's letters to her were chatty, affectionate and intimate; they ended 'I pray you never to forget me', 'I belong to you', or 'I am yours most tenderly'. But after his accession they became shorter and colder and ended as one would to the barest acquaintance or even a tradesman. She lived in the palace at Berlin during the winter and at Schönhausen in summer, receiving all the honours due to a Queen. The foreign diplomats told their governments that any politeness to her was well received by Frederick. She is said to have become disagreeable. '*Bonjour, Madame, et bon chemin.*'

Frederick to Algarotti: 'My fate has changed—I await you with impatience—don't leave me to languish.' Keyserling, too, wrote to him saying, 'Come quickly'. The new French minister, Valory, says that Keyserling was often closeted with Frederick for hours on end, Frederick forbidding him to go near the window as he did not want him to be seen and talked about.

There was to be no coronation, superstitious oil or other mumbo-jumbo. At Berlin

Frederick when King; painting by Antoine Pesne.

Monbijou; painting by an unknown artist.

Frederick took the oath on the balcony of his palace and remained there for half an hour, gazing at his people, deep in thought. He had to go to Königsberg to receive homage and attend essential ceremonies. When Frederick I was crowned there he took 1,800 carriages and 30,000 horses. Frederick II had no escort. He went in a small travelling carriage with Keyserling and Algarotti. During the journey he slept on Algarotti's shoulder—they called themselves *Auguste* and *Mécène*. And then to work. He immediately sent Truchsess as minister to Hanover (where Uncle George had gone to be in at Frederick William's death) and Camas, the husband of his 'Maman', to Paris. He told the former to make a great deal of Camas's appointment. 'Say, as though you were jealous of him, that he is one of my intimates and has certainly not gone to Paris to string beads.' Camas was to tell Cardinal Fleury that the new King would soon set Europe on fire. Fleury was a man of peace who, with the co-operation of Sir Robert Walpole in England, had succeeded in settling several European disputes during the last few years.

Frederick knew where he was going. There was no improvisation : every step he took had been carefully prepared. He kept all his father's officials, even those whom he suspected of having advised severity after the desertion. He would probably have kept Grumbkow had he not recently died from the effects of his carousal with Augustus the Strong. There was no rain of ducats for his Rheinsberg friends, but they received appointments according to their worth. Good Jordan became 'respectable inspector of the poor, the sick, orphans, lunatics and modest dwellings'; Keyserling was A.D.C. and colonel of a cavalry regiment; Frederick William's old friend Schwerin became Commander-in-Chief and Count Heinrich von Podewils First Minister, with nothing much to do, as Frederick intended to govern himself. His only political confidant was his father's Chef de Cabinet, Eichel, a mysterious person about whom little is known. For the rest of his life he never left Frederick and never had a day off; he arrived in his office at 4 a.m. He was devoted to Frederick, who could do no wrong in his eyes. The ambassadors never saw him. Life at Berlin was always to be difficult for them because there was nobody with whom they could intrigue, no possibility of bribery, and nobody, except invisible Eichel, who knew more than they did themselves. Frederick used to say that, as his horse carried him and all his ministry, anybody wishing to know his secrets would have to corrupt it. Queen Sophia Dorothea retired to her own little palace, Monbijou, where Frederick visited her every day when he was in Berlin, but he never discussed politics with her and she had no influence whatever.

Duhan was recalled from exile by a letter in Frederick's own hand, and in due course was made Director of the Liegnitz Academy. 'You ask about your functions: they are to draw your salary, to love me and to be happy. Your faithful pupil, Fédéric.' The philosopher Wolf was also invited to return. The Berlin Academy, founded by Frederick I and shut as a measure of economy by Frederick William, was reopened and Frederick asked the French philosopher Maupertuis to come and be its President. The father of Katte was made a Field Marshal. The Potsdam Grenadiers were reorganized—the officers remained and the regiment was always to be noted for its splendid-looking men; some of the brighter giants, such as the Irish Kirkman, became palace servants, but the tallest, most cretinous, were disbanded; the roads of Europe were covered with huge weak-kneed loons trying to find their way home.

Torture of civilians was abolished. Frederick, perhaps because he had so much of it to

LEFT: *Prussian soldiers being flogged and running the gauntlet; engraving by Daniel Chodowiecki.*
RIGHT: *Pierre Louis Moreau de Maupertuis; engraving after a painting by R. L. Tournières.*

bear, always hated the idea of inflicting pain. He thought the habit of torturing prisoners before execution 'a horrible and very useless cruelty'. Somebody once asked him why he never wore spurs: 'Try sticking a fork into your naked stomach and you will soon see why.' The flogging of soldiers, however, was considered essential to prevent desertion, and it continued. (It was used in all European armies except the French.) All religions were tolerated and a few years later Frederick built a Roman Catholic cathedral in Berlin. The press was given total freedom and there was no censorship of books. 'I do what I like, and the people say what they like.' He was fanatical on the subject of freedom of expression— more fanatical as he got older. He thought it was one of the things that really mattered. As there was a shortage of food after a cold summer the granaries were opened and wheat was sold at a reasonable price. Most of these measures were put into effect in one week; Frederick thought that each day seemed twenty-four hours too short.

When Voltaire heard of these liberal and enlightened doings he wrote to Frederick as 'Your Humanity'. The meeting for which Frederick so greatly longed was imminent. In July 1740 he left Berlin for those outlying parts of his kingdom which were in the Rhineland; he arranged to join Voltaire either in or near Brussels. He spent a few days at Bayreuth but his visit there was spoilt for Wilhelmine by the presence of the despised Ansbachs—Frederick naughtily making more of Louise than of Wilhelmine. She was in a melancholy mood just then; having come to love Bayreuth and to appreciate his many good qualities she had found out that he was infatuated with one of her ladies. Very soon husband and wife were friendly again but this was a bad moment and Frederick's teasing cast her down. When she was sad she had a sure resource, the study of French literature. That and music were ever the consolations of Wilhelmine, of Frederick and, when he was grown up, of their much younger brother, Henry.

On leaving Bayreuth Frederick and Algarotti decided as a joke to go incognito to Strasbourg. It was the only time the King ever set foot on French soil; the venture was not a success. His alias, 'Comte Dufour, a nobleman from Silesia', was unconvincing because of the large suite he brought with him. Maréchal de Broglie, the governor of the city, very nearly had him arrested as a suspicious character. Soon Frederick was recognized by the uncle of one of the giants and the cat was out of the bag. Broglie sent to ask the King if he wished to be received with the honours due to him or if he would rather remain incognito. So Frederick went to call on Broglie; the two men seem to have disliked each other thoroughly, and this was to have unfortunate consequences. Frederick accepted Broglie's invitation to go to the play but then he changed his mind and left Strasbourg in a hurry. Feeling that he had behaved in a stupid, boorish way he fell into a great rage against the French race and nation. He wrote to Voltaire describing his adventure in terms more than insulting to Broglie and the other officers whom he met at Strasbourg. It was the first time he had written such a letter to Voltaire, though later one of his ways of teasing him was to be by denigrating everything French.

86

At Wesel Frederick fell ill. It seemed pointless to travel as far as Brussels, so he asked Voltaire to meet him in his Duchy of Cleves. Voltaire arrived there on 11 September, under a harvest moon. Frederick wrote to Jordan: 'I have seen that Voltaire whom I was so curious to know but I had my fever upon me and my brain was as confused as my body was weak. One needs to be in good shape to keep up with him—his table talk is so dazzling that you could write a brilliant book simply by recording it.' Voltaire says in his memoirs, 'I became fond of him; he had wit and charm, and besides he was a King.' It is doubtful if he ever had much real affection for Frederick; but the King could be useful to him. The two men enjoyed each other's company because they laughed at the same things, but after this first meeting, which lasted for three days and had a honeymoon quality, there was always an uneasiness between them.

Voltaire was not the only French philosopher who went to see Frederick during this journey. Maupertuis, now at the height of his fame, was at Wesel. Four years ago he had gone to Lapland, to measure a degree of longitude; he came back with the interesting news that the earth is flattened at the poles; thereafter he was known as the 'Flattener of the Globe'. He was a tall, handsome, pompous man of forty-two—*joli garçon*, Frederick said, though not such good company as Algarotti—and he appeared to be a great friend of Voltaire's. He had been—perhaps still was—the lover of Voltaire's mistress Mme du Châtelet and in truth Voltaire had a well-concealed hatred for him. However, at this time he made a great case of having recommended him to Frederick as President of the Berlin Academy.

Frederick had not only gone to the Rhineland to meet philosophers; he had business. He owned a small enclave situated in the middle of a principality administered for the Emperor by the Bishop of Liège. His few subjects there were not very fond of joining the Prussian army or of paying Prussian taxes and the Bishop seemed to encourage their bad citizenship. Frederick intended to put an end to this nonsense. He sent 2,000 soldiers to the Bishop with an ultimatum composed by the peace-loving Voltaire, who had become quite over-excited by his new friend's display of force. The Bishop complained to the Emperor, who wrote a furious letter to Frederick about the unheard-of violent doings in the Reich. Frederick observed that Charles VI was only the ghost of an old idol; he neither answered the letter nor received the Emperor's envoy, but he suggested to the Bishop that he might like to buy the property in question. The Bishop did so and the matter was settled without further reference to Vienna; Frederick got a comfortable sum in ready cash with which to improve the equipment of his army. It was generally felt that the lion cub had shown his teeth, and Frederick's neighbours began to wonder what his next move would be.

They had not long to wait.

CHAPTER EIGHT

Check to the
Queen of Hungary

Frederick was still far from well and still had a recurring fever when, in October 1740, Wilhelmine visited Berlin. She had not been there, nor seen her mother and younger brothers and sisters, since her marriage in 1732. She was horrified to find Frederick looking so ill. On the 20th his treaty with the Bishop of Liège was signed and then he took his sister and some friends to Rheinsberg for a rest; he had a high temperature and they were all worried about him. During the night of the 25th Fredersdorf woke him up with the tremendous news that the Emperor Charles VI was dead. It was like a magic medicine; Frederick's temperature went down at once and another sort of fever took possession of him.

26 October 1740

My dear Voltaire,

The most unexpected event in the world prevents me from chatting as I would like to. The Emperor is dead. My pacifism is shaken. . . . My affair with Liège is wound up but the new situation is of far greater consequence for Europe; the old political system is in the melting-pot; Nebuchadnezzar's rock is about to crush the statue of the four metals and destroy everything. I am getting rid of my fever because I need my machine to take advantage of these circumstances. . . . Adieu, dear friend, never forget me and be sure of the tender esteem with which I am your very faithful friend. Fédéric.

After three hundred years of Imperial power the Habsburg family was now no more. Charles VI, having lost his only son, was survived by two daughters. He had succeeded his brother Joseph I, who had also had two daughters, and there was no male Habsburg left. Their hereditary lands were subject to the Salic law and women could not inherit them. The Emperor Leopold, father of Joseph and Charles, as though he had foreseen the situation which now arose, had entailed the succession on the daughters of Joseph before those, as yet unborn, of Charles, should the brothers die without male issue; but as soon as Charles became Emperor he changed this compact in favour of his own daughters. His fixed idea in life was that the elder, Maria Theresa, should succeed him and that her husband should be elected Emperor. He made enormous sacrifices in order to get an agreement to this effect, known as the Pragmatic Sanction, ratified by the German Electors and the Great Powers. Prince Eugene, now dead, used to tell him that the signatures he so eagerly canvassed were quite worthless and that all Maria Theresa would need to consolidate her position

Maria Theresa, Archduchess of Austria, as a young woman; painting by A. Möller.

The Emperor Charles VI with his family; painting by N. B. Belau.

was 100,000 highly trained soldiers and a full treasury. This was more than Charles VI could achieve but, before he died, he had collected all the necessary signatures for his Pragmatic Sanction except that of the Bavarian Elector, Charles Albert. He was the husband of the Emperor Joseph's younger daughter and himself had the best hereditary claim to the purple through a Habsburg great-grandmother.

At the death of Charles VI, Maria Theresa, Archduchess of Austria, became Queen of Hungary; her husband, Francis of Lorraine, was Grand Duke of Tuscany; they counted on the German Electors to make them Holy Roman Emperor and Empress and on the other European princes to recognize the fact according to their promises. Maria Theresa, now aged twenty-three, was beautiful in a doll-like way—perfect complexion, golden hair, dark blue eyes and white, regular teeth; her demeanour was royal with a deceptive look of calm stupidity. She was neither calm nor stupid; besides a keen native intelligence, she had energy, courage, tenacity and a talent for making other people do their work. Her education had been extremely sketchy; she spoke most of the European languages, including Latin in which to communicate with her Hungarian subjects; but she had no knowledge of affairs and, oddly enough, she had never learnt to ride. She was without a sense of humour and during her lifelong struggle with Frederick, whom she never met, she probably minded his jokes and teasing and brazen lack of hypocrisy more than his aggression. Her husband, Francis, was as typically French as she was German. His mother was the daughter of Monsieur, Louis XIV's brother, and of Madame, whose letters from Versailles are such a joy. In them she often bewailed the unhappiness of her daughter with the adorable but unfaithful Duke of Lorraine; with such a father and his Bourbon blood Francis was not bred to be a good husband. He was brought up at Vienna and from an early age he charmed not only his future bride but also Charles VI, whose letters to him show how completely he had taken the place of the dead son. There was never any question of another husband for Maria Theresa, in spite of the fact that the head of the House of Lorraine was by no means a brilliant match for such a personage. He counted as royal, but only because one of his ancestors had been King of Jerusalem. The Austrians are conscious of these things. Francis, like his wife, was ignorant of politics but he had a talent for finance.

Charles VI died at a bad moment for the success of his plans. Maria Theresa was practically unknown in her father's dominions and her marriage was not popular. The Emperor had intended to have Francis elected King of the Romans when he had a son and had acquired some military prestige. But at present the young couple only had two daughters, and Francis had done particularly badly in the recent war against the Turks. The Emperor left an empty treasury and the little cash he had was seized by his widow. The army was in a poorer way even than when Frederick had seen it; most of the generals, including Seckendorf, were in prison for having failed to win battles. Nobody in Vienna wanted to be governed by a young woman at such a critical juncture, and Maria Theresa knew that people were saying it would be better to have Charles Albert. Her father's ministers were dried-up, ancient creatures, all over seventy; even if they were not ready to betray her they regarded her situation as desperate. Thomas Robinson, the English Ambassador, wrote of them: 'The Turks seemed to them already in Hungary, the Hungarians themselves in arms [against Vienna], the Saxons in Bohemia, the Bavarians at the gates of Vienna and France the soul of the whole.' However, Maria Theresa summoned them to a council, and with a brilliant display of royal authority she touched their old hearts and won them round. Francis, who never left her, was amiable to everybody, and by degrees public opinion came down on their side. The only danger now seemed to come from Charles Albert, should he be backed by the French. Neither Maria Theresa, nor her husband, nor her ministers looked nervously towards Berlin. Frederick had been most friendly to Francis when they met and had kept in touch with him by letter. It was often said that he owed his life to the late Emperor's intervention after the escape. The many snubs which Charles VI had administered to Frederick William, his bad faith over Jülich and Berg and the fact that he had prevented the English marriages were forgotten. Frederick was supposed to be the protector of the young couple. 'He is like a father to us.'

Death was thought to be getting very uppish in 1740. Having gathered Frederick William and Pope Clement XII he waited only eight days after reaping the Emperor to pounce upon the Empress Anne of Russia. Keyserling's school-friend Biron ruled the country for three weeks, until a *coup d'état* sent him to do a stint of twenty-two years in Siberia; after that for quite a long time the Russians were too much occupied with their own affairs to trouble about the rest of Europe.

Berlin was now the centre of wild activity. The King spent most of the day with his generals; troops were at the ready, and depots of arms and provisions were being laid in the direction of the frontier with Silesia. The foreign courts were naturally anxious to know what all this was about. Maria Theresa, serene in the knowledge that her husband's great friend would do nothing disagreeable to her, nevertheless felt a mild curiosity and sent Marchese Botta to see what he could discover. Less trustful than his mistress, he thought Silesia was the target, and during his audience with the Prussian King he ventured to remark that the roads there were terrible. Frederick said he had heard they were rather muddy. Botta said he hoped the King would never underestimate the Austrian army—the Prussian troops looked splendid but the Austrians had seen the wolf.

Guy Dickens boldly asked Frederick why his soldiers were marching about in such a

The Empire, showing Prussian and Austrian territories, in 1740. Prussia dark tint, Austria light tint.

LEFT: *Thomas Robinson, later first Lord Grantham; painting by an unknown artist.*
RIGHT: *The Marquis de Valory; engraving.*

sinister way. 'Do I ask you what you intend to do with your navy? Certainly not. I hold my tongue and pray you won't get a thrashing from the Spaniards.'[1] When Dickens mentioned the possibility of a guarantee for Jülich and Berg Frederick said he was not interested in the Rhine country, 'but on the other frontier the Maritime Powers would not interfere'.

Cardinal Fleury had two envoys in Berlin, the Marquis de Valory and the Marquis de Beauvau, both completely at sea, though Beauvau warned Fleury that Frederick hated the French and longed to humiliate them. Fleury now sent Voltaire to see what he could find out. Voltaire wrote enthusiastic letters to Paris: 'There may be greater kings but there are few more amiable men. What a miracle that the son of a crowned ogre, brought up with the beasts of the field, should understand the graces and subtleties of Paris. He is made for society.' Frederick took time off from preparing his war to prove that his court was indeed, as Voltaire called it, the modern Athens. He showed him the pictures he was buying, mostly Watteaus (pronounced by Voltaire, behind his back, to be fakes); he played the flute; he chatted for hours on end with his philosopher. They exchanged tender notes calling each other *coquette* and *maîtresse*. The atmosphere at Frederick's court was now homosexual. A male party was given by Valory, the fat French minister, where *tendre Algarotti* and *beau Lugeac*, Valory's secretary, behaved oddly indeed; it was immortalized by Voltaire in a poem.

Voltaire rather spoilt the *ambiance* by demanding the expenses for his journey. Frederick, who knew quite well that he had come to spy, thought this went too far. 'As court jesters go,

[1] The War of Jenkins's Ear was in progress.

this one is rather dear.' Valory says that Voltaire was too free and easy with the King and passed too quickly from excessive reverence to excessive familiarity. He certainly did not mind what he said about him, and in a letter to Maupertuis he called Frederick a respectable, singular and lovable whore. However, the atmosphere was friendly to the end of the visit, though the mission was a failure, and Voltaire left Berlin no wiser than when he had arrived.

The reader has certainly guessed by now that Frederick's warlike preparations were no joke and that his objective was the beautiful province of Silesia, one of the richest of the Habsburg possessions. But Maria Theresa still regarded Frederick as a loyal vassal. To do him justice, he felt a certain shame when he thought of this, and in his *Histoire de Mon Temps* he speaks frankly about it. He says he went to war in order to acquire reputation and to increase the power of his country. He chose Silesia because the French, the English and the Dutch would have no reason to stop him and because it would be a great addition to his domains with its agricultural and industrial riches and largely Protestant population. (The poor, on the whole, were Protestants and the rich Catholics.) Besides, he said, his family had a claim to it. There was a sort of claim which Frederick had not bothered to investigate; he was uninterested in it as in all German history. He told Podewils to cook up some legal nonsense—'that's the work of a good charlatan'—and then issued a proclamation: 'Having, as is well known, interests in Silesia, I propose to take charge of it and keep it for the rightful owner.' He gave a masked ball in Berlin on 13 December and the next day he set out at the head of his troops. The only person who told him that he was committing a sin and a folly was Jordan, but then he was a pacifist. The King told him to be sure and let him know what people were saying in Berlin.

Extracts from Jordan's letters, 14–20 December 1740:

Everybody here is waiting for an event of which few can determine either the reason or the object. I am charmed to see that many of Your Majesty's subjects are in a state of pyrrhonism—a catching disease. Those who, like theologians, are always in the right, tell me that Your Majesty is awaited with a religious impatience by the Protestants while the Roman Catholics hope to see a reduction in their taxes. Some critics think that this venture is in direct contradiction to the last chapter of the *Anti-Machiavel*.

Beauvau says, 'Can't imagine who put it into his head to invade, but it's not such a bad idea.'

The Queen of Hungary has died in childbirth.

Everybody says, without knowing why, that Your Majesty's rights are incontestable.

All say it's a Protestant crusade.

Frederick to Jordan, Ottomachaw, 14 January 1741:

My dear M. Jordan, my sweet M. Jordan, my calm M. Jordan, my good, my benign, my pacific, my most humane Jordan, I announce to Your Serenity the conquest of Silesia.

St Cecilia by Rubens. In 1754 d'Argens offered to buy some Lancrets for Frederick in Paris, but the King said that his taste had changed and he would prefer paintings by Van Dyck or Rubens. Frederick bought this in 1756 for the gallery at Sans Souci.

He had met with practically no resistance. He arrived at the frontier in drenching rain—the roads, as Botta had truly observed, were terrible—and found it touchingly undefended. Two local barons called on him to protest against the invasion; Frederick kept them to dinner, fascinated them, and the next night stayed with one and dined with the other. Maria Theresa's Irish Governor of Silesia, Wallis of Carrighmain, shut himself up in Glogau with about 1,000 men, reinforced its defences, burnt down its suburbs, to the great disgust of their inhabitants, and awaited the siege. Browne, her general of Irish descent, having done all he could with the tiny force at his disposal, retreated to Moravia. The native population seemed, on the whole, to welcome a change. The Habsburgs had not exactly maladministered Silesia nor had they persecuted the Protestants, though they had some difficulty with their children's education. But there was no loyalty to the Empire. Frederick rode into Breslau with a small bodyguard, lodged in the house of the Cardinal Primate, who had fled, and gave a ball there. A few Catholic dowagers stayed at home but on the whole it was well attended.

Rather late he remembered the rules of international behaviour and sent an envoy, Count Gotter, to Vienna. He had an interview with Francis of Lorraine—Maria Theresa was behind the door, listening. Gotter said his master was at her entire disposition; would support her rightful claims with his last man and his last ducat; would also ensure the election of Francis as Emperor, if he could have the whole of Silesia. Francis kept his head and said that, even if the Queen wanted to do so, she had no authority to give away bits of the dominions entailed on herself and her heirs. Gotter said in that case he must go back to Berlin. Francis asked if Frederick was already in Silesia and Gotter admitted that he was. At that point Maria Theresa put her head round the door and said that Francis must come away—she refused to treat with the King of Prussia while he was in her dominions with an army. The Austrian courtiers told Gotter what they thought of him and his master, and he seemed to feel a certain shame.

At the end of January Frederick was back in Berlin, having taken Silesia in seven weeks. Horror and indignation at the invasion was felt all over Europe—Frederick said the general view was that only a man who did not believe in God would dare to attack Austria—but nobody was prepared to send help to the Queen of Hungary. In Vienna she was the only person who was not paralysed. Although in an advanced state of pregnancy she acted with the energy of rage. She had riding lessons. She brought Marshal Neipperg out of prison, where her father had put him for delivering Belgrade to the Turks, and gave him the command of her troops in Moravia; somehow she managed to raise enough money to equip them—possibly from the English secret service funds. She inspired her subjects with her own courage; confidence began to creep back. That spring she had a piece of luck: she gave birth to the greatly desired son, the future Emperor Joseph II.

In February 1741 Frederick returned to Silesia taking Jordan, Maupertuis and Algarotti for chat. Valory, of whom he was getting very fond, was also there. Glogau fell without any

Elizabeth Christine, Queen of Prussia; copy of a painting by Antoine Pesne.

trouble. In April Neipperg and his army advanced into Silesia and on the 10th battle was joined at Mollwitz, not far from Breslau. On the night before his first battle Frederick had thoughts of death. He wrote to Augustus William, his heir, now known as the Prince of Prussia, whom he had left at Breslau with Jordan, 'I recommend to you, in dying, those whom I have loved the most in life: Keyserling, Jordan, Wartensleben [once a Captain of the giants, now Frederick's A.D.C.], Hacke who is a very honest man, Fredersdorf and Eichel in whom you can have confidence.' He asked the Prince to give souvenirs to all their brothers and sisters, especially Wilhelmine. 'Do not forget a brother who has loved you very tenderly.' To Jordan: 'If my destiny is over, remember a friend who always loved thee tenderly.'

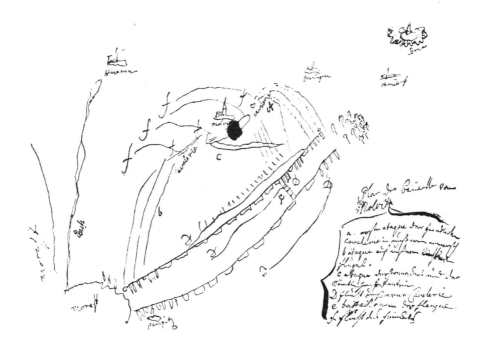

A sketch of the Battle of Mollwitz drawn by Frederick and enclosed in a letter of his to the Old Dessauer.

Unlike many great generals, Frederick never could sleep before an engagement or when campaigning if things went badly; he used to spend the night reading, generally Racine, and writing poetry. Before Mollwitz he had two wakeful nights because the day after he wrote his letters there was a blinding snowfall which made it impossible to fight. He knew that Neipperg had a superior force and that if he won the battle he would be in a position to cut the Prussian communications. Frederick was nervous and anxious. On the morning of the 10th the snow had stopped falling and lay hard and deep. Frederick marched his army in five columns to the enemy's camp. Neipperg, who had not known that the Prussians

Field Marshal Count von Schwerin; painting by an unknown artist.

were so near, was taken by surprise, but Frederick, instead of attacking at once, as he would have done later in life, carefully disposed his army in battle order. The operation was ill conceived and badly carried out. The Austrian cavalry, under continuous fire, made a premature charge which put the Prussian cavalry to flight. The inexperienced Frederick, carried hither and thither in the uncontrollable mass of horses, thought the day was lost. Field Marshal von Schwerin, who wanted to be left to fight in his own way, urged him to leave the battlefield, saying that if he stayed he would probably be captured. So Frederick rode away accompanied by Maupertuis, a French valet and a few soldiers. At midnight they arrived at the little town of Oppeln; the gates were opened by Austrians. Frederick said, 'Good-bye friends, I am better mounted than all of you', and galloped off, leaving the others to their fate. It was not very terrible. Maupertuis was taken as a prisoner of war to Vienna, where high society made a fuss of him, and Francis, learning that he had lost a Graham watch, gave him his own, also a Graham.

As for Frederick, some soldiers sent after him by Schwerin soon told him that the battle was won, and he rejoined his army at daybreak, having ridden over fifty miles. Frederick William's infantry, his methods and his friend had turned Frederick's defeat into victory. Ten years later Frederick, who never made excuses and never suffered from delusions, described the Battle of Mollwitz to the Comte de Gisors: 'Our soldiers were willing and disciplined but few of them had seen active service. I was a complete novice and the only person who could guide me, Field Marshal von Schwerin, was not on speaking terms with me. Without him I should have been done for; he alone repaired the mistakes and won the battle.' At the beginning of his reign Frederick had trouble with Schwerin and the Old Dessauer, who had dandled him on their knees and who, furthermore, were universally recognized as the best living European generals; they were not always able to accept his orders without argument. In a very short time, however, they learnt their place. Frederick always held a review of his troops on the anniversary of Mollwitz and in old age would say to the men, 'Try and be as good as your grandfathers were.' As for his running away, it gave a great deal of pleasure and gave rise to many a good joke; Voltaire said Frederick never felt gratitude to any living creature but the horse which bore him from Mollwitz.

At the news of Mollwitz, Maria Theresa wept. Robinson told the English Foreign Secretary, 'Vienna is in flat despair but without the strength to be desperate.'

Frederick having raised the wind, Europe was now in a ferment. Charles Albert of Bavaria claimed the Empire; the Pope, Piacenza and Parma; Philip of Spain and Charles Emmanuel of Savoy, the Milanese. The French made no claim but their activities were portentous. They were directed at giving Louis XV the position hitherto occupied by the Emperor: that of overlord and mentor to the German states. This vast scheme originated with the Comte de Belle-Isle, the grandson of Fouquet, Louis XIV's minister, imprisoned for treasonable activities. Fouquet's son, Belle-Isle's father, had lived in voluntary exile,

LEFT: *Maréchal Duc de Belle-Isle; pastel by Maurice Quentin de La Tour.*
RIGHT: *The third Earl of Hyndford; painting by an unknown artist.*

but when the Comte de Belle-Isle grew up old Louis XIV received him at Versailles and made him Captain of the Musketeers attached to his person. People said that Mme de Maintenon had not forgotten Fouquet's generosity to her first husband, Scarron. Belle-Isle was wounded at Blenheim and again at Lille, where he nearly died; after that he was given a regiment. He became a general under Louis XV and got the *Saint-Esprit* for gallantry at Philippsburg. As governor of Metz he greatly beautified that town, laying out new streets, quays and gardens. Belle-Isle had cosmopolitan relations through his wife, a Béthune: she was connected with John Sobieski; one of her uncles was a Radziwill and another a Jablonowski; so he knew Europe and its problems better than most French people.

A tall thin man of fifty-six, Belle-Isle was Ambassador Extraordinary to the Reichstag (or Diet) of German princes, assembled at Frankfurt to elect the new Emperor. His mission was to induce them to postpone their deliberations, and eventually to elect Charles Albert. Germany could then be divided into four parts: Bavaria, Saxony, Prussia and Austria, all in the French sphere of influence. Bavaria was an old ally of the French—Charles Albert's father had fought with Louis XIV against Marlborough and Eugene and the grandmother of Louis XV was a Bavarian princess. Charles Albert was a good, sweet man greatly loved by all who knew him and esteemed by posterity as the builder of beautiful Amalienburg. But he had little political sense and was very poor; he could easily be put

LEFT: *Cardinal Fleury; painting by Hyacinthe Rigaud.*
RIGHT: *Charles Albert; engraving by C. H. Muller after F. Lippold.*

into French leading-strings. This was Belle-Isle's scheme and his alone. Cardinal Fleury
knew that it was against nature and impracticable, but he was now ninety and had lost
influence of late to the belligerent young sparks of the young King's little set. Louis XV was
pacific by nature; he lived for the arts and really believed what Frederick was always saying,
that 'peace cannot fail to make art and science flourish'. He had all the territory he wanted,
internal troubles of a religious nature and a weak economy. But Belle-Isle and his arguments
were very convincing.

After Mollwitz, victorious Frederick established his headquarters near the battlefield
and here, in a tent which seemed about to be carried away by every gust of wind, with only
one candle and no heating, he received the ambassadors of foreign powers, by night. His
days were spent training the cavalry which had let him down. Belle-Isle, touring the
German courts in order to canvass votes for Charles Albert, was at Dresden when he heard
of Mollwitz; he immediately went to call on Frederick. It is supposed, though not certain,
that he expounded his plans for Europe there and then, but in any case Frederick was not
so stupid that he could not guess what they were. The last thing in the world he wanted
was French supremacy in Germany; he would much have preferred to see Francis as
Emperor. However, he enjoyed the company of Belle-Isle, who was exactly the kind of
man he liked: a brilliant, amusing, civilized soldier, accustomed to the ways of courts.

Frederick was susceptible to good manners and he often liked those who possessed them. Belle-Isle was fascinated by him. He wrote to Fleury:

> He was born with a first-class intelligence, which pushes him towards great designs; he is full of fire; has a keen and penetrating sense of what men are like, quick to pounce on and take advantage of their foibles; never asks advice and indeed could not do so safely since he is surrounded by people in the pay of Austria. He has no heart whatever.

After a few days Belle-Isle went back to Charles Albert and then to Frankfurt.

George II sent Lord Hyndford to Frederick—a blustering, hectoring, rude man whom Frederick could not bear. This war was beginning to worry the English, who counted on the Austrians to keep France occupied while they were avenging Jenkins's ear on the Spaniards. But now Frederick was keeping the Austrians occupied; furthermore, the Prince of Anhalt-Dessau irritated George II by sitting on the Hanoverian frontier with a large force. The English wanted the war to stop, whatever the cost to Maria Theresa. Hyndford asked Frederick whether, if he were allowed to keep Silesia, he would support the election of Francis. Frederick replied that he had always said he would. Hyndford said something about a magnanimous peace. 'Do not, my lord, talk to me of magnanimity. A prince must consult his own interests. I am not averse from peace; but I expect to have four duchies and I will have them.' But he refused to say which duchies he meant. (They were Liegnitz, Brieg, Jägerndorf and Wohlau.)

Then Mr Robinson from Vienna was told to go and see Frederick. He was a prosy man whose talk was like a public speech—his English friends often had difficulty in keeping their countenances when he got going. He was in love with Maria Theresa—enthusiastic proclaimer of her charms, said Frederick, who was overcome with mirth when Robinson told him that if he could see her he too would fall in love. *L'infatigable Robinson*, as Frederick called him, had a most trying time between these two young people. Maria Theresa loathed his advice and received him only when she hoped for English gold, and Frederick covered him with sarcasms. After Maria Theresa had been preached at by him for weeks, she empowered him to offer Gelderland and Limburg to Frederick if he would drop all claims to Silesia. But Frederick said that in the first place most of Gelderland belonged to him already and, to go on with, he was amazed that the Queen could consider violating the Barrier Treaty (by which the Low Countries were inalienable). And then who would guarantee her offer? Robinson had an answer but was cut short. Who observed guarantees in these days? England and France had both guaranteed the Pragmatic Sanction but they didn't seem to be flying to the help of the Queen of Hungary. Frederick added that his ancestors would rise in their tombs if he should abandon his righteous claim to Silesia. (Robinson often heard from the Queen that her ancestors would rise in their tombs if she let Silesia go.) He went back to Vienna and told Maria Theresa that she must make peace. She burst out at him: 'Would to God your cursed ditch did not exist and that you were a part of Europe;

then you might understand the danger of upsetting the Empire—to touch one part of it is to undermine the whole. Silesia is essential for its defence.'

In June, Maria Theresa, pregnant again, her little Archduke, lively as a squirrel, in her arms and her husband at her side, set forth to be crowned Queen of Hungary at Pressburg according to tradition. She was greeted by Count Palffy, doyen of the nobles who were all-powerful in that land. When the coronation ceremonies were over the reason for the riding lessons became apparent. She mounted a beautiful black horse and, riding astride like her Imperial ancestors, followed by old Palffy in tears and the rest of the Hungarian nobility, she galloped up a hill overlooking the endless plain. Here she drew a sword and shook it to north, to south, to east and to west amid the acclamations of the crowd: 'We will die for our King, Maria Theresa.' Francis was not there to share her triumph—the Hungarian magnates refused to have anything to do with the foreigner. But Thomas Robinson was. More in love than ever, he described the scene, adding, 'The tattered robes of St Stephen became her as well as her own rich habit, if diamonds, pearls and all sorts of precious stones can be called clothes.' She looked marvellous at the state banquet; her beloved husband was by her side once more, the hot weather gave her a colour and her golden hair hung in fat curls round her face.

While the Queen was still in Hungary the French sent a large army commanded by Belle-Isle to support the Imperial claims of Louis XV's cousin, the Elector Charles Albert. Together with the Bavarians they took Linz and arrived almost at the gates of Vienna. At the same time another French army threatened Hanover. George II and the other German Electors were becoming increasingly doubtful about the Pragmatic Sanction and were turning to Charles Albert. The Italian states relapsed into a neutrality on the whole favourable to France. The horrified Robinson wrote from Pressburg to the Foreign Secretary, 8 September 1741: 'It is upon this great moment that depends the fate, not of the House of Austria, not of the Empire but of the House of Hanover, of Great Britain and of all Europe.'

Vienna prepared for the worst; the rich sent away their valuables and joined with the poor in saying that the whole thing was the fault of Francis and that they would be far better off with Charles Albert. The only person who might have raised their morale was the Queen, and she was not there. Even the Hungarians were less enthusiastic about her now that the ceremonies which had so touched their hearts were over. At one moment Maria Theresa nearly gave up; she said there seemed to be nowhere on earth where she could be confined in peace. But nothing could daunt her for long. She had her ancestors in their tombs solidly behind her, and that most valuable of allies, the certitude of final victory. She now adopted a bold and original policy. Against the tradition of her family and the advice of her ministers, and to the horror of the Austrian nobility, she decided to mobilize the Hungarians and ask them to raise an insurrection in her favour. The Austrians said that if such a thing were allowed it would certainly turn against them and be used for Hungarian independence, as had happened in the past. The very names of Hungarian regiments made Austrian blood run cold: Pandours, Tolpatches, Hussars, Uscocks, Slavonians, Warasdinians. Dressed in their wild uniforms, mounted on their wild horses, they seemed to portend a dread invasion from the East. In fact they were never much good against regular troops but had great nuisance value as guerrillas.

Maria Theresa had her own way. In black from head to foot, wearing St Stephen's crown, she summoned the Hungarian Diet and addressed it in Latin. She told of the invasion of Austria; she spoke of her children; she wiped away a tear. 'Forsaken by all, we place our sole resource in the fidelity, arms and long-tried valour of the Hungarians.' There was an outburst of loyalty; the Diet voted to raise and equip an army and even accepted Francis as co-Regent. At the end of the session he cried: 'My blood and life for the Queen and kingdom', while the little Archduke was produced and shown to his future subjects. It was clever of Maria Theresa to surround herself with such a wealth of feminine accompaniments and to lay them at the feet of the chivalrous Hungarians; they were deeply touched and never betrayed her. From that moment the tide slowly turned in her favour.

A gold quarter-repeating watch made by George Graham.

CHAPTER NINE

Diplomats' Nightmare

During the months which followed Mollwitz, the various ambassadors who had to deal with Frederick lived through a nightmare. His own objectives were so clear and logical that the said ambassadors must have been rather dense, since none of them seems to have guessed what he was up to. He simply wanted to keep Silesia while preventing French supremacy in Germany. The French, for their part, wanted to see the collapse of Austria while limiting the growing power of Prussia. A secret Franco-Prussian treaty was signed (5 June 1741) and never published; it was the uneasy alliance of rulers who were fighting the same enemy for different reasons.

As the presence of Belle-Isle was considered essential at Frankfurt where the Reichstag was about to assemble, the French and Bavarian troops were all under the command of Charles Albert. The French general was Maurice de Saxe, one of Augustus the Strong's bastards and a member of Louis XV's little circle of friends. The main Austrian army was held down by Frederick in Silesia and only 6,000 men were available for the defence of Vienna. But instead of marching straight there, as everybody, and especially the Viennese, expected, Charles Albert laid siege to Prague. Beautiful Prague, situated on steep hills which in places are almost like cliffs, was easy to defend. The Hungarian hordes were not yet under way and Maria Theresa felt obliged to make overtures to the French and the Prussians. Naturally, as allies, they divulged her propositions to each other and equally naturally decided to reject them. But while the French really rejected them, Frederick only pretended to do so. One day Valory accidentally dropped a dispatch from Versailles telling him on no account to let Frederick have the mountain fortress and county of Glatz, considered as the key to Silesia, which, by the Franco-Prussian treaty, was to go to Charles Albert. Frederick put his foot on the paper and Valory never saw it again. Then Frederick rounded on Valory: 'When are you going to deliver Glatz into my hands?' 'I thought I had delivered it into Your Majesty's feet.' They both burst out laughing. Valory was beginning to have doubts. He tried never to let the King out of his sight, a fact which Frederick soon cottoned on to; fat, breathless Valory was taken for many a wild gallop when he was longing for his siesta.

All this time Frederick was busy training and reorganizing his troops. He raised a

The Prussian army in Breslau, 1742.

LEFT: *Maréchal Général Comte Maurice de Saxe; pastel by Maurice Quentin de La Tour.*
RIGHT: *General von Zieten; painting by Anna Dorothea Therbusch.*

regiment of Hussars on the Hungarian model and gave it to Zieten, who turned out to be the most dashing of all his commanders. Zieten had never fitted into ordinary regimental life; he was now over forty and still only a major, but he distinguished himself during an engagement against Hungarian irregulars in the company of Frederick's friend Winterfeldt, and from that moment he never looked back. He became a colonel and very soon a general; he and his merry men performed legendary feats in the practical joking, fancy-dress style of warfare.

On 9 October 1741, Frederick, saying he must inspect various outposts, sent Valory to dine with the young Princes of Anhalt-Dessau. He then sneaked away, alone except for the head of his Intelligence, Colonel von der Goltz, to meet 'the English fraud' Hyndford, Neipperg and another Austrian general. After a long, naughty preamble in which he declared his deep respect for the Queen and almost brotherly love for Francis, he gave the Austrians every detail of the French positions in Bohemia and pointed out the best way of attacking them. As payment for this piece of treachery the Austrians were to surrender the town of Neisse, but only after a sham siege. Frederick wanted the French to think he was still on their side. He would exchange a few harmless shells with the garrison; the town would fall and the Austrians would leave him in peace for the winter except, perhaps, for a little imaginary fighting here and there. In return he would never molest the Queen again. He graciously suggested that she might care to keep Glatz, though he said the French had specifically guaranteed that he should have it. Could he lend the Queen 50,000 *écus?*—he would be so glad to be of use to her. Frederick refused to sign any document; the Austrians must believe his royal word; and he stressed that if this highly secret agreement should leak out he would be obliged to go back on it—that was a condition. He knew that Maria Theresa's court was a hotbed of gossip and felt reasonably sure that this clause would soon operate. Francis thought that Frederick, after an extraordinary lapse, was once again his friend and he wrote soliciting his vote at the Reichstag. Frederick replied with a cordial rigmarole of which he said that he himself did not understand one word. He wrote to Belle-Isle: 'Louis XV is the arbiter of Kings and Maréchal de Belle-Isle the instrument of his power.'

The 'siege' of Neisse duly took place; Neisse duly capitulated to Frederick. Valory, a soldier himself, thought there was something very odd about the operation. It was unusual to invest a strong place without engineers—and then no sooner had it fallen than they appeared, busily fortifying it for the Prussians. However, the King showed him a despairing letter from Lord Hyndford, which he himself had dictated, saying that as he could make no headway with Frederick he was giving up and going home. Valory felt remorseful about his suspicions. But soon there were more curious occurrences and he wrote to Belle-Isle that he could not bear to formulate the dreadful things in his mind.

Of course the whole story came out. Everybody in the secret had told somebody else, and the London clubs were soon buzzing with it. Frederick and Valory had a furious interview: 'If that's what the Queen says she'll pay for it!' While they were on the subject he might as well tell Valory that he had no intention of going to the help of the French and Charles Albert, who were still besieging Prague. 'I like to fight wars in my own way.' Things were going badly for them. Charles Albert was a hopeless commander-in-chief and the French officers refused to obey him; all were at sixes and sevens, and meanwhile Neipperg was on his way to relieve the city with terrifying Hungarians. The Chevalier de Belle-Isle wrote from outside Prague telling his brother to come at once and take command or all was lost. Belle-Isle got as far as Dresden and there was met by Valory who was appalled by the state he found him in. He had sciatica and literally could not move, while one of his eyes was so swollen that it seemed to be falling out of his head. He was in no condition to command an army. The two men were beside themselves with worry, but there was nothing to be done; they had to wait for Belle-Isle to get better. A messenger arrived from the French army with a note for the Marshal. It seemed to be in the writing of a child of five—there was no punctuation and no attempt at spelling.

> Monseigneur you wished for Prague to be taken it is taken the Governor [General Ogilvy] has surrendered to me and I am writing from his room I can never tell you the courage of the troops and above all the good conduct of M. de Chevert. Maurice de Saxe.

The messenger enlarged. Saxe had found a flaw in the fortifications and crept through it with Colonel de Chevert and a handful of carefully chosen men. At the city wall they found three ladders on the near-by gallows which, tied together, reached to the top of it. Now comes the celebrated *Histoire du Grenadier*, known in all French nurseries. Chevert asks for a volunteer to go up the ladders. Grenadier Pascal offers and the following dialogue ensues:

You [*tu*] will be the first to go up.
Oui, mon colonel.
When you reach the top the sentinel will shout '*Wer da?*'
Oui, mon colonel.
You won't answer.
Non, mon colonel.
He will shoot at you.
Oui, mon colonel.
But he will miss you.
Oui, mon colonel.
You will then kill him.
Oui, mon colonel.

Pascal went up and all happened according to plan except that the sentry, having missed him, made off in the dark to give the alarm; but by then Chevert, young Broglie and other sparks from Versailles were already over the wall and had got the city gate open. French troops poured in and General Ogilvy had to surrender. That night a ball was going on and at daybreak it was French, not Austrian, officers who armed the young ladies to their homes. Saxe had the army in perfect control; there was no looting and the shops of Prague were open the next day as usual.

Maria Theresa wept. Belle-Isle was cured. Frederick, probably none too pleased, wrote him fulsome congratulations and offered him sixteen squadrons of Dragoons. 'Sending help now we don't need it any more', said Belle-Isle. Frederick became very loving with Valory again and asked how he could have suspected him of collusion with the Queen. 'What about Neisse?' 'You seem to have taken Prague without firing a shot. Perhaps you have an understanding with her?'

But he wrote to Voltaire: 'Trickery, bad faith and duplicity are unfortunately the dominating characteristics of most men who lead their countries and who ought to provide them with an example. The study of the human heart in these circumstances is humiliating and makes me regret my beloved retreat, the arts, my friends and my independence.' At this time, careful though he had to be with money, he could not resist buying the collection of antiquities which Cardinal de Polignac had made in Rome.

The French success at Prague brought the German Electors down on their side of the fence. To the amusement of Frederick, who thought it very funny to see how his uncle had to twist and turn in his double role of King of England and Elector of Hanover, George II voted for Charles Albert in return for Hanoverian neutrality. He had really believed in the Pragmatic Sanction and was the hardest nut to crack—the other Electors were won over by various forms of bribery and on 24 January 1742 Charles Albert was unanimously elected Emperor as Charles VII. It was a not very expensive success for France and a triumph for Belle-Isle.

Wilhelmine went to Frankfurt for the coronation and found many an old enemy,

Prince Charles of Lorraine; painting by E. Philipkin in the nineteenth century after Frans van Stampaert.

including Seckendorf, who had left Maria Theresa for the new Emperor and who was appointed governor of Philippsburg. The ceremonies were sumptuous but people began to see that Charles VII was a poor creature; for one thing, although only forty-six he was so ill with gout and stone that he could hardly stand. The cruel joke *Et Caesar et nihil* went from mouth to mouth. Wilhelmine cleverly saw that he was a bad bet and got her husband out of an agreement to back him up with troops.

On the very day of the election Maria Theresa's army took Linz and, on that of the coronation, Charles VII's own capital, Munich, fell to Mentzel, the hideous Colonel of the Pandours. To make a diversion Frederick invaded Moravia, reluctantly supported by the French and the Saxons. Maurice de Saxe had left Prague to command the troops of his half-brother Augustus III who was bankrupt, a condition to which he was accustomed and which never prevented him from buying enormous diamonds and works of art at the exorbitant prices of those days. Frederick said of him, 'The conquest of ten countries would not make him leave the first act of an opera.' Maurice de Saxe did not appreciate Frederick's way of marching his allies about and starving them while his own army went ahead and 'ate the land'; he soon left him to his own devices and proceeded to enjoy a series of country-house visits, falling thankfully into the Schloss of any nobleman who cared to invite him. Before long he and the French withdrew their troops.

Maréchal de Broglie, he whom Frederick had so much disliked at Strasbourg, was now commanding in Prague. Frederick went to see him there and again expressed an exaggerated loathing for him; he could not hear his name without falling into a terrifying rage or pronounce it without a string of dirty words. He told Valory that he intended to fight the Austrians by himself without the aid of the French. This was the real truth. No doubt he took a poor view of Broglie, as did many of the Marshal's own officers, and this served Frederick as an excuse for not collaborating with him. Altogether his was an unlucky appointment. He was seventy and had had a stroke. The French officers, at the beginning of the campaign, thought they would march on Vienna under the orders of Frederick, who was the hero of all young soldiers. The leadership of Saxe had suited them perfectly; now they found themselves shut up in Prague with an old dodderer, no battles, no glory, bored, uncomfortable, and with a most unreliable postal service to Versailles. They complained vociferously.

Frederick was making overtures to Vienna but always increasing the ante. After what had happened at Neisse, Maria Theresa was naturally rather unwilling to make any more concessions, especially as she had assembled a large and well-equipped army to be led by her beloved Charles of Lorraine, her husband's brother and her sister's husband. In May 1742 this army advanced from Moravia and arrived in the neighbourhood of Frederick's headquarters in Bohemia. On 17 May the Prussians and Austrians met at Chotusitz and here the first battle Frederick ever fought in his own way took place. Mollwitz had been his father's victory, but at Chotusitz Frederick's long consideration of the art of warfare, his

A miniature of Augustus III set in diamonds.

carefully trained cavalry and his brilliant leadership came into their own. With the eyes of the world upon them and the advantage of slightly superior numbers the Austrians were determined to win and made a dashing start. But Frederick cut their army in half by burning a village and then forced their cavalry into boggy ground, making it useless. After four hours of desperate fighting Charles of Lorraine was obliged to sound a retreat. Then, to the dismay of Valory, who could hardly believe his eyes, Frederick remained on the battle-field, allowing the Austrian army to get away intact, and busied himself with burying the dead; he bought nine acres of ground for the purpose which, for a hundred years, bore heavier crops than the surrounding fields. 'None of our friends is killed', he told Jordan; 'dear Rothenburg, who is wounded, will recover.' But Rothenburg, who was now Frederick's closest friend, never fully recovered.

Two days after Chotusitz Broglie, who had been joined by Belle-Isle, responded to a dispatch from Frederick asking for co-operation, by defeating the Austrian general Prince Lobkowitz at Sahay. The news of these two defeats came to Maria Theresa just after she had given birth to the Archduchess Maria Christina. More shaken than usual by this confinement, she felt in despair; she wept. Hyndford told her, not for the first time, that she had no choice now but to negotiate with Frederick. He said that nobody on earth could blame her, whatever treaty was signed, if later on she decided to reconquer Silesia. Frederick at present could beat her beautiful new army whenever he chose; if she went on being so obstinate she would lose Bohemia as well as Silesia. Maria Theresa dried her tears and became extremely angry. Never, never, she said, would she give up Bohemia, not if the King of England in person, followed by the whole of his Parliament, came and ordered her to do so. But over Silesia, most reluctantly, she gave way. It now remained to be seen if Frederick would insist on the whole of his conquest or accept Upper and Lower Silesia. The Austrian proposition was sent in writing.

On 4 June Belle-Isle went to see Frederick who, saying that his troops needed a rest and were short of rations, had settled them down on the banks of the Sasawa. Belle-Isle had been to Versailles, where he was made a duke and ordered to go and replace Broglie at Prague. He had arrived in time to command at Sahay, felt uneasy at Frederick's curious behaviour after Chotusitz, and decided to go and find out his plans. Frederick, with Maria Theresa's propositions in his pocket, came out of doors to meet the Duke, laughing and congratulating; he hugged his friend. As they walked towards the tent he took off his cloak and threw it over Belle-Isle's shoulders saying that on no account must he catch cold. Belle-Isle was full of praise for Chotusitz, and the King inhaled the incense but without mentioning Sahay, except to ask in an airy manner why Belle-Isle had not pursued Lobko-witz? Of course, Belle-Isle could not resist asking why the King had not pursued Prince Charles. Frederick replied evasively that he could not do much before July when, if Belle-Isle liked, they could join forces and march on Vienna. He described an imaginary peace plan (very different from the one he had in his pocket) in which the French would have

115

The sword-hilt from the emerald set of regalia made in 1742 for Augustus III. The pendant was mounted by J. F. Dinglinger and the onyx carved by C. Hubner.

this and the Saxons that, and then he launched into a diatribe against the Queen, whose wicked obstinacy would set Europe ablaze. They must all act together in order to control her. After this interview, Belle-Isle, utterly charmed as usual by Frederick, told Valory that in another month everything would be all right. The next day, when he went to take his leave, Frederick carelessly mentioned the fact that Prince Charles and Lobkowitz had joined forces and were marching on Prague. Belle-Isle knew that Prince Charles would never have dared take this step if there had been any danger of Frederick's falling on his rear. The French were isolated in the middle of Europe without communications and without an ally. He fainted dead away.

It may seem strange that the French should have been so roundly beaten at the diplomatic game of which they are the acknowledged masters, but it must be remembered that they play it according to the rules. Frederick, not to put too fine a point on it, had cheated.

On 11 June Frederick and Maria Theresa signed the Treaty of Breslau by which Frederick got Upper and Lower Silesia. There was no comfort for his allies the French and the Bavarians—they were not mentioned. Maria Theresa wept for her lost province and, as usual, Robinson was at the receiving end. At Versailles old Cardinal Fleury wept and so did the many people whose relations were now trapped in Prague. Louis XV, however, let it be known that the news of the treaty must be accepted with calm and without undig-nified recriminations against the King of Prussia. As for Valory, Frederick said he made killingly funny faces when he realized that the dreadful thoughts he had been unwilling to formulate had fallen short of the dreadful truth. He took leave of the King, saying he must go and see what use he could be in Prague. When Frederick heard this he did look vaguely uncomfortable and begged Valory to go back to Berlin with him, but in vain.

Frederick trotted home at the head of his army, all his objectives having been attained. He had won a beautiful province about one-third the size of England, with inhabitants who were notably good and clever. He came to like them the best of his subjects, and they, except for the Catholic dowagers of Breslau, returned his affection. The French had been taught a sharp lesson and might think twice before meddling in German politics again. The Austrians were weakened and so was the new Emperor—indeed, ill and penniless, his country occupied by the enemy, he had nowhere to lay his head. The Emperor's ally and brother-in-law Augustus III had demonstrated his impotence. Uncle George had been made to look a fool. Above all the young King of Prussia had acquired reputation. Nevertheless, Frederick was in a vile temper. He may have had doubts as to the eventual wisdom of his behaviour and he possibly felt remorse when its consequences became apparent.

After they had been abandoned by Frederick the French were shut up in Prague for five months, besieged by Prince Charles and Prince Lobkowitz with 70,000 men.

It may be of interest here to examine the French army in the eighteenth century. It was the

The central scene shows the deputies of Lower Silesia swearing an oath of fealty to Frederick in Breslau, 1741; engraving by J. D. Schleuen.

Occupation de Bresslau sous comandement du Mareschal de Schwerin, et du Prince d'Anhalt, le 10 Aout en 1741

Einnahme der Stadt Bresslau durch die Königl. Trouppen unter Anführung des Feldmarschalls von Schwerin u. des Prinzen Leopold v. Anhalt Dessau der 10. Aug. 1741

Acte de l'homage fait a Bresslau par les Deputés de la basse Silesie le 7 Nov en 1741

Solenne Erb Landes Huldigung von Nieder Schlesien an Se Kön Maj geschehen auf dem Fürsten Saal zu Breslau d 7 Nov 1741

Prise de Troppau au Nov. en 1741
Eroberung der Stadt Troppau im Nov. 1741.

FRIDERICUS BORUSSORUM REX SUPR. SILES. DUX

JUSTO VICTORI
FIDES SILES. IN GRATISO AXIOCT MDCCXLI

Prise de Freudenthal au Nov. en 1741
Eroberung der Stadt Freudenthal im Nov. 1741.

Olmütz, la Capitale de Morav se rend aux trouppes du Roi par capitulation du 27 Dec en 1741. Les autres viles de cette province suivent cet exemple excepté la fortresse de Brunn

Die Hauptstadt Olmütz in Mähren gehet mit Accord über an die Kön. Trouppen d 27 Dec 1741 welcher auch die andern Städte ausser der Festung Brunn in kurzer Zeit folgen

only one in Europe composed entirely of its own nationals, with no mercenaries. For this reason its soldiers were better treated than any; there was none of the flogging employed in every other army (though later it was introduced by Louis XVI); the ambulances, commissariat and surgeons were incomparably the best. Frederick always had French surgeons for his own soldiers. When properly led the French troops were unrivalled—between the death of Saxe and the coming of Napoleon they were improperly led. The reason for that, not far to seek, was that the high command was reserved for the great nobles. The best officer of his generation, François de Chevert, was a country gentleman; he could never rise above Lieutenant-General. Frederick, too, observed this rule whenever possible, but he was lucky enough to have two excellent commanders in his own family, as well as others among the rulers of neighbouring principalities: Holstein, Hesse-Darmstadt, Brunswick, Württemberg, Anhalt-Dessau and his three sons and, in due course, a grandson.

On 7 December 1742 Belle-Isle led the French out of Prague. A Franco-Bavarian army under Maillebois and Seckendorf had been sent to relieve them, but arrived in Bohemia exhausted after long marches on short rations and was unable to dislodge Charles of Lorraine, who held an almost impregnable position in its path. It retreated to Munich. Everybody thought that the French in Prague would be forced to a shameful capitulation; the Austrians were already gloating over the guns, the equipment and the prisoners of war which they expected to gather in. But when Belle-Isle arrived there with Valory, after

LEFT: *François de Chevert; painting by J. H. Tischbein.*
RIGHT: *Prince Lobkowitz; engraving by an unknown artist.*

leaving Frederick, he transformed the spirit of the soldiers. Broglie refused to relinquish his command; the orders from Versailles on the subject were not clear; indeed, Louis XV, to please the powerful Broglie family, had made him a duke. (Frederick said he could have understood it if Maria Theresa had done so.) His officers sent a deputation to Belle-Isle saying they would take orders only from him. 'Then I order you to obey M. de Broglie.' However, to everybody's relief he soon went off to join Maillebois. Belle-Isle, who was never out of pain from his back and leg, made things so disagreeable for the besiegers with constant sallies that they scorched the earth round Prague and retired ten miles from the city. He put the whole town—citizens, officers and privates—on the same rations, their food consisting of cavalry horses and the maggoty biscuits which his excellent quarter-master had laid in. (Army biscuits in those days were always maggoty but one ate them all the same.) The gilded youth as well as the men would take anything from Belle-Isle, and discipline and morale were perfect. But a particularly severe winter, lack of fuel and of suitable clothes were causing many casualties and when it became clear that he could not be relieved before the spring, Belle-Isle decided upon a retreat. He asked Prince Charles if he could leave with the honours of war. The Lorraine brothers would have been inclined to agree but Maria Theresa would hear of nothing but total surrender.

So Belle-Isle gave out the news, to citizens and spies, that he was going on an important foraging expedition. 'Good luck to him', said the Austrians, who knew that there was nothing left to be eaten in the countryside, frozen like iron. They never for a moment thought he would be so mad as to take the difficult road through forests and mountains with an army, in that weather. He sallied forth in a carriage with eight horses, accompanied by the Count of Bavaria, who had been governing Prague for his half-brother, the Emperor; also in the party were the beautiful Countess and their newly born baby. (The Countess was the illegitimate daughter of the Emperor and thereby her husband's niece.) They were unmolested. Belle-Isle's force consisted of 14,000 able-bodied men, and he took all his equipment, and provisions for twelve days, leaving 4,000 sick and wounded in Prague with François de Chevert. The officers gave up their horses to pull the guns and went on foot. By day Belle-Isle, in agony from his sciatica, was driven in a light sleigh in which he seemed to be everywhere at once, comforting and encouraging the men. He himself read the maps, decided which way to go and saw to every detail. By night he lay sleepless for five or six hours in the coach with the Bavarias and the baby; the soldiers built a wall of snow to protect it from the terrible wind. Two of Belle-Isle's young officers were to become famous: the Marquis de Montcalm and the Marquis de Vauvenargues. Vauvenargues's health never recovered. It is said that of the three great winter retreats of modern times—the other two being the Swedes' from Norway after the death of Charles XII and Napoleon's from Moscow—Belle-Isle's was the only one in which the troops came away in perfect order with all their guns. Not so much as a kettle-drum was left on the road; but many corpses were. Thousands of men were dispatched by the cruel cold, the lack of food, and

the Hungarian irregulars, waiting to pounce on dead and dying and strip them of their clothes, attacking over and over again in the hopes of taking the treasure wagons. Those who lived were nearly all frost-bitten. Finally, it was not much more than half the army that struggled back to France. Belle-Isle, worn out and heart-broken, could not face Versailles; he went to Metz to take up his governorship and to be consoled by the company of his little boy, the Comte de Gisors, whom he worshipped. Some weeks later he had an audience with Louis XV; he looked ghastly and had to be half-carried by two men.

When the Austrians found that Belle-Isle had slipped through their fingers they were furious, and Maria Theresa wept. Robinson speaks of the agony of her mind. She had set her heart on revenge, on thousands of French prisoners of war and, above all, the guns and the booty. Lobkowitz called on Chevert to surrender, but Chevert demanded a safe conduct to Eger and wagons for the sick — otherwise he threatened to burn Prague to the ground. Lobkowitz, who owned a lot of property there, gave in to all his terms.

In May 1743 Maria Theresa went to Prague and was crowned Queen of Bohemia.

The coronation of Maria Theresa as Queen of Bohemia, in Prague;
engraving by M. H. Rentz.

CHAPTER TEN

The King's Friends

Now that he was at peace Frederick set to work to gather congenial friends round him. First of all there was his family. The ten surviving children of Frederick William were exceptionally united; Frederick had a strong family feeling and was devoted to his brothers and sisters. Most of them were now grown up; all the sisters but two were married and had gone away—their rare visits to Berlin were always an excitement and Frederick wrote to them regularly. The two youngest lived with their mother; they were Princess Ulrica, who was soon to marry the future King of Sweden, and Amelia, who remained a spinster. The King's brothers were more like sons to him—Augustus William, the Prince of Prussia, was born ten, Henry fourteen and Ferdinand eighteen years after him; he was strict with them and of course they chafed under his rule. The Prince of Prussia, a good-natured, not very interesting fellow, was already surrounded by all the elements of Berlin society which were hostile to Frederick. It is evident from the King's delightful letters to this brother that he loved him but he kept an eye on the entourage. Ferdinand was never of much account, but Prince Henry, now seventeen, was a great character, to be a pleasure and a pest to Frederick all his life. Their relationship was complicated by Henry's acute envy of his brother. When he was a boy he sometimes refused to speak to Frederick for months on end. Frederick complained bitterly of his *extrême froideur*, said they lived together like a dreary old married couple and begged him to try and overcome his too evident antipathy. Henry became less openly rebellious as time went on, but there was always a degree of jealous hatred in the love and admiration he certainly felt for the King. They had the same gifts, the same marvellously logical intelligence and the same energy; no doubt Henry felt that only a wretched accident of birth relegated him to a back seat and the oblivion of history. They shared all their tastes—Henry was nourished on French literature and was happy alone at Rheinsberg as long as he could read and study. An Englishman who knew him well said he was 'French to the bone'. To look at he was a caricature of the King.

The Queen was still not entirely discarded and many of her fourteen brothers and sisters were almost as dear to Frederick as his own. He arranged a marriage between the Prince of Prussia and her sister Louise; his sister Philippine, his favourite next to Wilhelmine, was married to the Duke of Brunswick; Duke Ferdinand of Brunswick became Frederick's

123

Frederick with his brothers Augustus William, Henry and Ferdinand;
painting by C. F. Rusca.

LEFT: *Field Marshal Duke Ferdinand of Brunswick-Wolfenbüttel; painting by Antoine Pesne.*
RIGHT: *The Marquis d'Argens; engraving by E. J. Desrochers after T. van Pee.*

best general; Duke Frederick Francis and their first cousin, the Duke of Brunswick-Bevern, also served in the Prussian army. Two of the brothers were in the Austrian interest (the Brunswicks were first cousins of Maria Theresa) and one of them, Anton Ulrich, married Anna Leopoldovna, Regent of Russia, and was the father of the unlucky Ivan VI.

The old Rheinsberg set was much in evidence at Frederick's court, especially Jordan, Knobelsdorff, Chasot and Keyserling, who was engaged to be married to a beautiful person, one of the few women whom Frederick really liked. He wrote a play for the wedding festivities, which were brilliant and went on for days. Keyserling was happy and in love but his friends were worried about his health. Maupertuis had not yet returned to Berlin after his adventures at the wars, but Frederick had a new French courtier, the Marquis d'Argens. From now on he was a leading member of the King's coterie and was to be the recipient of some of his most brilliant letters. D'Argens, eight years older than the King, was from Provence. He had been disinherited by his father for running away with an actress, had wandered all over Europe and had for a time been attaché to the French embassy at the Porte; he earned his living by writing poor novels and works of philosophy. Jordan got to know him while Frederick was at the war; he was in the household of the Duchess of Württemberg (probably his mistress), with whom he was having a series of ringing quarrels. Jordan, seeing at once that he would amuse Frederick, made him leave her and join the household. D'Argens was one of those people who live for the theatre; he helped Frederick very much with the Comédie française de Berlin of which he became director. He also loved pictures; as a very young man he had been to Rome where he was so much absorbed in art that for a whole month he never looked at a woman.

All these people were solid friends on whom the King could rely and who never let him down, but they were rather provincial. Algarotti and Voltaire had given him a taste for more sophisticated companions, and he wanted stars. He wrote to Algarotti saying that his apparition at Berlin would be like that of the *aurora borealis*, but, never able to resist teasing the Italian, he added, 'You would be specially welcome if you came for my sake and not that of Plutus.' It was too much for Algarotti, who cheekily replied that, far from being attracted by Plutus, he had found his last visit to the King in Silesia very expensive indeed. Frederick was furious and, though Algarotti wrote a grovelling apology, five years elapsed before they made it up. Algarotti spent most of this time in Dresden, no doubt, Frederick said sarcastically, as military adviser to Augustus III.

It might be assumed that among the letters congratulating Frederick on the Treaty of Breslau there would not have been many from France. There was one, however, and that the most fulsome of all. Frederick the Great, said Voltaire, has made a good treaty and his virtuous soul is becoming that of a statesman. If the French are not quite pleased with him, if they think he has abandoned their army, it is because they never know what is best for them. Frederick has outdistanced the 'Good Old Man' (Fleury). Philosophers think that the hero of the century will be the pacificator of Europe and Germany. Frederick is no longer the ally of France but that of the human race. And so on.

Frederick modestly begged Voltaire not to overdo the praise. He said he had been obliged to abandon Broglie because he and his army had to be bolstered up the whole time—besides, Maria Theresa had offered him more than France ever could. Other excuses he made for his behaviour, of which he was certainly ashamed, were that his treasury was empty, that he had begun to see that the best conducted battle was a lottery and that he was tired of hearing from Valory that, as the French were good at everything and the Germans good only at fighting, it was obvious that when they were allied the fighting had better be done by Germans.

Now the great question was how to get Voltaire to Berlin. Mme du Châtelet, fearing that she might lose him for ever, was more and more unwilling to let him out of her sight, while he himself, with much to occupy him in Paris, did not seem anxious to undertake a long journey. So he had to be prised out in some cunning way. Frederick sent copies of the letter hailing him as Frederick the Great to the Good Old Man he had outdistanced, to all the French ministers, and to Louis XV's patriotic mistress Mme de Mailly, with a view to making Paris too hot to hold Voltaire. He succeeded. Voltaire, wildly protesting that he was not the author, was obliged to take a little holiday. He went first to Brussels and presently joined Frederick who was taking the cure at Aix-la-Chapelle. In order to pacify Fleury he sent him an account of his political conversations with the King; Fleury was so anxious to know Frederick's thoughts and intentions that he pretended to believe

Voltaire's denial of the letter. As usual Frederick gave nothing away; he asked a great many questions about the reaction at Versailles to the Treaty of Breslau. Were the French exhausted in men and money and utterly discouraged? Voltaire had the honour to deny this suggestion, which came from Milord Hyndford.

After a few days Frederick parted from his philosopher, more anxious than ever to possess him, and went back to Potsdam to play with what he called his dolls: the re-decoration of Charlottenburg, where Pesne was painting the ceilings; the unpacking of Cardinal de Polignac's antiques, which arrived in perfect condition, and putting the last touches to Knobelsdorff's opera-house. Frederick William had vainly warned Frederick in his will against raising such a temple to the devil; he opened it with a good deal of pomp on 7 December 1742, the very day on which Belle-Isle left Prague. It was a beautiful and supremely comfortable building with room for a thousand carriages to park outside. Seats were not for sale: the audience was invited by the King. The first performance was of Graun's opera *Cleopatra e Cesare*, written for the occasion and sung by a company which Graun had been collecting in Italy for two years.

Frederick began to write the *Histoire de Mon Temps*; a highly readable work, it gives portraits of his fellow rulers and a clear account of his policy towards the Europe he found at his accession. His main preoccupation now was observing the conduct of the said rulers. He told Voltaire that he had infected Europe with warfare as a coquette gives a painful keepsake to her admirers; he himself was cured but he watched the events resulting from his own actions with a slightly uneasy interest. The Maritime Powers (the English and the Dutch) were gathering forces in the Low Countries to invade what seemed to be a defenceless France; the Spaniards were attacking Maria Theresa in Italy; fortune's plaything, the Emperor, sent Seckendorf to ask Frederick if he could manage a small loan and if he would use his influence with the other German princes to give him a little support, even if only moral. But the Emperor was written off as unlucky and nobody wanted to be associated with him.

In January 1743 Cardinal Fleury died. As he was ninety it would perhaps be exaggerating to say that the French reverses in Bohemia had killed him, but they probably hastened his end. He had ruled France for eighteen years and nobody had anything but praise for him; even Frederick said that he had been a good shepherd, though he added he was forgotten in a week. Louis XV announced that he would now govern by himself like his great-grandfather at the death of Mazarin—the difference was that Louis XIV had Colbert, Louvois, Condé and Turenne, while the ministers and most of the generals available to Louis XV were mediocrities. Fleury's death left a vacancy at the Académie française which Voltaire longed to fill, but the fact that he was generally considered to be the greatest living writer was more of a handicap than a help, since the thirty-nine members of the Académie were not anxious to be put in the shade by him. Another drawback was the doubtful quality of his Christian belief. The Bishop of Mirepoix, tutor to the Dauphin,

The opera-house at Berlin designed by Knobelsdorff; engraving by G. G. Fünck.

the minister Maurepas and other influential figures were against his election on religious grounds. So Voltaire circulated a statement in Paris and Versailles: he adored the religion which had made one family of the human race—it alone had been his support during thirty years of sorrow and calumny. He also wrote grovelling letters to those who, like the Bishop of Mirepoix, stood in his way. In vain. A dull cleric was unanimously elected to the vacant armchair. On top of this blow to his pride and check to his ambitions, his new play *La Mort de César* was withdrawn by order of the police.

Frederick gloated. He was ever on the look-out for a situation which would force Voltaire to leave Paris and, he hoped, come and live in Berlin; it seemed to have arisen. He wrote, unkindly indicating that he had seen Voltaire's letter to the Bishop and asked how Mme du Châtelet liked his unfaithfulness to her with the Virgin Mary? (He always made fun of Voltaire's religious tergiversations: unfairly, because while he himself could safely mock at the Church, Voltaire lived in a country where persecution was still a reality.) He urged Voltaire to leave his inconstant, bigoted, cowardly, effeminate compatriots who disdained him so humiliatingly, and come to a King who knew how to appreciate him. Voltaire, who did not mind what he himself said about the French, but who never liked hearing this sort of thing from Frederick, replied that neither the public nor Louis XV was responsible for his recent disappointments but only the mitred ass (Mirepoix). But, he added, Frederick's magnet was too strong to be resisted any longer: 'I will leave Minerva for Apollo.'

The real reason for this sudden decision was very Voltairean and typical of the times. Louis XV had given him a large sum of money to go and spy on Frederick and if possible to bring him back to the French alliance. *La Mort de César* had been seized by the police with Voltaire's own connivance, to make his flight from Paris seem inevitable. Frederick told Jordan that he knew Berlin was only a last resort but that in any case Voltaire would make them all laugh, and he told Voltaire: 'There is no ass of a Mirepoix here; we've got

The library at Charlottenburg. Along the top of the bookcases, which are the originals and still house the library of the 'Philosopher of Sans Souci', are copies of the antique marble busts that Frederick acquired from Cardinal de Polignac. The ceiling, by Antoine Pesne, was destroyed during the Second World War.

a cardinal [of Breslau] and several bishops, some of whom make love before and others behind—good fellows who persecute nobody.'

He met Voltaire in the gardens of Charlottenburg; they were delighted to see each other. They went for a walk and then looked at the Polignac marbles and all the embellishments to the palace; afterwards there was a concert with Frederick playing the flute. Supper was extremely jolly; Valory, back again and more in favour than ever, was the only foreign envoy there. The King had given Voltaire a room next to his own; here, after supper on the first evening, they had the only serious, political conversation of the whole visit. Frederick said he supposed that Louis XV would never forgive him for having made a separate peace. Voltaire replied that great kings did not think of vengeance, only of the national interest—the interests of France and Prussia were identical. 'But the French are treating with the Queen of Hungary.' 'The Austrians may say so, but they said the same about you last year. Why don't you support France and the Emperor against the common enemy who hates you?' 'Perhaps, but I can't do anything unless the princes of the Empire back me up and that's why I'm going to Bayreuth next week. I want to be sure that the Palatinate, Hesse, Württemberg and Cologne can provide troops for the Emperor. I don't want to fight again but I should like to be the pacifier of the Empire and humiliate the King of

England who always interferes in Germany.' Voltaire said that everybody knew the Queen wanted to retake Silesia; Frederick replied that she would have a job to do that. Then they spoke of Russia, and Frederick said he had advised the Empress Elizabeth to send the little dethroned Ivan (his wife's nephew) with his mother and father to sub-Arctic Russia.[1]

At this point in the conversation a servant told Frederick that the musicians were ready and he carried Voltaire off to the concert with many expressions of love and friendship. But only three days later: 'My situation begins to be thorny; somebody has implanted suspicion.' Frederick had already found out that Voltaire was there to spy but he still longed to possess him. He was not alone. Voltaire's presence was a bright light wherever he went; its rays had been cast in many different societies: Paris, London, Brussels, Lunéville, The Hague and rural Champagne, and had never failed to dazzle. He had a charming way of entering into the lives of people he liked, knowing, remembering everything that interested them and, when they were absent, keeping in touch with them by letter. Although he had a foolish love for kings and grandees of all sorts, he was faithful and affectionate with more modest folk and decidedly at his best with them: his middle-class manners never quite stood up to court life and at Versailles he used to embarrass people by not knowing how to behave. In Berlin, however, the atmosphere was less rarefied and he did very well. He made friends with the two Queens and with Frederick's brothers and sisters. Whenever he had an evening free he was eagerly snapped up by some royal or distinguished person; all begged him to settle there for life.

Voltaire sent the King a political questionnaire: the answers were bad jokes and rubbish. Then Frederick wrote him a letter setting forth the misdeeds and absurdities of the French, but he added: 'All the same this nation is the most charming in Europe and even if it is not feared it deserves to be loved. A king worthy of it will be sure to win back the ancient splendour that Broglie and the rest of them have rather eclipsed.' Voltaire said that Frederick felt about France as he (Voltaire) and his friends felt about Jesuits, abhorring the order but loving the individual members. He asked if the King would take him to Bayreuth and Frederick said yes, but he must arrange to be in good health. He knew that Voltaire's illnesses were always nervous and sometimes diplomatic: he was generally well when he wished to be.

The visit to Bayreuth was a success. Frederick went off to talk to the German princes about the future of Charles VII and left Voltaire with Wilhelmine. Her little palace was like a French country house, the company was charming and she gave a series of fêtes to entertain the great man. His feathers, which were constantly ruffled by Frederick, were smoothed down by the sister who was so much like him that she might have been Frederick

---

[1] She soon followed this horrid advice; the unlucky Brunswick and his wife were sent to Kholmogory, a place ghastly beyond belief, where they both eventually died. Frederick's wife begged him to intercede for them but he said he quite understood the Empress: 'She shuts them up in order not to be shut up herself.'

in petticoats. When he left her Voltaire went back to Berlin for a few days and then made for Paris to put his affairs in order before settling in Prussia for ever. On the way he stopped at Brunswick to see the Duchess, and here he had his usual success. He wrote to Maupertuis, ostensibly to say how much the dear earth-flattener was missed at Berlin, but really to boast about his own reception there. Voltaire has been to see the Academy where Dr Eller thinks that he has made people believe that he can change water into elastic air. The King has put on the opera he has composed, specially for Voltaire—the opera-house is the most beautiful in Europe. Charlottenburg is a delicious place to stay in—at Potsdam one might be in the country house of a French nobleman except for the terrifying Grenadiers. Jordan still resembles Ragotin in Scarron's *Roman comique*, but a good-natured, discreet Ragotin with a large income. D'Argens is the Chamberlain with a golden key and 200 *louis* a month. Chasot, who has been known to curse his destiny, is blessing it now: he is a major with a big battalion which must be worth a lot of money. He deserves it, having saved the King's baggage in the last battle. Voltaire could also enjoy all this bounty if he chose to, but a greater sovereign, Mme du Châtelet, calls him to Paris. He has also spent a few days at Bayreuth where Her Royal Highness spoke much of Maupertuis—it is a delightful retreat. Brunswick where he is now has a different sort of charm. He has had a celestial journey flying from planet to planet and it will end in tumultuous Paris where he will be sad indeed if he does not find unique Maupertuis, whom he admires and loves for life.

Mme du Châtelet said that Voltaire had quite lost his head over these silly little German courts.

Ragotin being released from the chest in which a maid had locked him up. One of a set of fourteen illustrations to Paul Scarron's Roman comique*; painting by J. B. Pater. Frederick had these paintings bought in 1766 by Girard and Michelet, Berlin dealers, for the Neues Palais.*

A corner cupboard of cedar wood with bronze fittings by J. A. Nahl, Berlin, about 1745, after a design by Knobelsdorff. The Berlin porcelain includes a shepherd and shepherdess by F. E. Meyer; a Gotzkowski teapot; a cherub from the service of the Potsdam palace; Fama, also by F. E. Meyer; two figures by C. W. Meyer and two plates from the Charlottenburg service.

CHAPTER ELEVEN

The Second Silesian War

Maria Theresa's position had greatly improved since the days when Father Palffy seemed to be her only prop and stay. It must be said that this was entirely due to her own efforts: she alone had animated the Austrians and roused the Hungarians. In control of Bohemia and Bavaria, she was able to force the Emperor to conclude a treaty of neutrality, by which he kept his title but renounced his claim to the Habsburg territories. Prince Lobkowitz was doing well against the Spaniards in Italy. The English were still financing her and seemed about to engage in full-scale hostilities against the French; they had been fighting for some months but war had not actually been declared.

Frederick sent his great friend, Frederick Rudolph von Rothenburg, to Versailles, supposedly for a change of air (his wound still troubled him), but really on a secret mission. He had many links with France, as his wife, who hated Berlin, and other members of his family lived there; the Rothenburg who had been French minister to Frederick William was his uncle. Frederick Rudolph had served in the French and Spanish armies and was a Roman Catholic convert. While preparing a new treaty between Prussia and France he was also to buy pictures for Frederick and it was probably at this time that the King acquired Watteau's *Enseigne de Gersaint*. The treaty, secret as usual, was signed on 5 June 1744. Louis XV's new mistress, Mme de Châteauroux, who had helped Rothenburg, sent Frederick her portrait by Nattier and he wrote her a civil letter.

Prince Charles Edward, the Young Pretender, hitherto little known and unconsidered, suddenly found himself rocketed into a position of importance. He had fought well with the French at Dettingen against George II, and they decided to back his claim to the English throne. He was given Maurice de Saxe, 18 French men-of-war and 15,000 soldiers, and appeared off the Isle of Wight. Of course he was driven away by the usual storm but he had succeeded in startling the English. The result was that they allied themselves with Maria Theresa, whose cause suddenly became the Cause of Freedom (in other words, their own), and sent a large army to the Netherlands. There they were faced by Louis XV himself with Maurice de Saxe. The French troops, greatly inspired by the presence of their King, were soon carrying all before them—they took Ypres and Menin and seemed about to overrun the Low Countries. At this point Charles of Lorraine with a huge army surged into Alsace;

133

The Empress Maria Theresa; painting by Martin van Meytens.

LEFT: *Count von Rothenburg; painting by the school of Pesne. In 1725 after studying at Frankfurt-on-Oder he went to Lunéville and imbibed a good deal of French culture before joining the French army. He is reputed to have met Frederick in 1734 at the siege of Philippsburg. He bought many paintings for Frederick in Paris.*
RIGHT: *Field Marshal von Daun; engraving by J. I. Nilson after Martin van Meytens.*

Louis XV, leaving Saxe and a small holding force to contain the English, marched off to meet the Austrians. But at Metz he fell ill, and became rapidly worse until his life was despaired of.

There was great anxiety in Paris. The English army vastly outnumbered that of Saxe and must have defeated him had it taken the offensive; the Austrians were reported to be behaving with horrible cruelty in Alsace; the French burghers were appalled to think that these allies might soon be at their very door. The survival of their young King seemed closely connected with their own safety; the churches were thronged day and night with people praying for his recovery. Their prayers were answered and the clouds dispersed as quickly as they had gathered. Louis got better, Saxe easily consolidated his positions, and Frederick, who had mobilized with a speed of which only he was capable, was reported to be at the gates of Prague. By the time the rumour was confirmed he had taken the city (16 September 1744). Prague had changed hands three times in three years.

Charles of Lorraine left Alsace with all possible speed to go to the help of his sister-in-law's kingdom of Bohemia. It was a sad time for him: while he was on the march his young wife died in Brussels after a terrible confinement which also killed the baby. Frederick raged against the French for not pursuing Prince Charles, delaying him and damaging his army. But the Prince de Conti was holding another Austrian army on the Rhine and it is hardly surprising that, after what had happened in 1742, the French should have been chary of venturing into the heart of Europe at the behest of so uncertain an ally as the King of Prussia.

Seckendorf took Munich from the Austrians and the Emperor was able to go home at last, to the rejoicing of his people. With her usual energy, Maria Theresa hastened to Pressburg bearing gifts for Palffy: her own horse, 'worthy of being mounted by none but my most faithful subject', a sword and a ring. Once more the charm worked, and soon a new army of 44,000 men hastened to the defence of Bohemia, which had almost entirely fallen to Frederick. His position there was not happy. He had forgotten about the lateness of the season—he himself says (in the *Histoire de Mon Temps*) that he ought to have stayed in Prague until the spring—but he wanted to cut a dash in the eyes of the French. He over-extended his lines of communication in order to take Tabor and Budweis. The Hungarian irregulars swarmed round his army and stole his mail, so that he had no idea what was happening elsewhere. He was isolated, with winter coming on—the terrible Continental winter, so much worse, it seems, in those days than now—and an extreme shortage of provisions. Prince Charles, or rather his much cleverer colleague General Daun, refused to give battle and wore out Frederick's army by forcing him to march it here and there, in increasingly bad weather, to protect his stores of food. Finally, he was obliged to retreat into Silesia, having lost, mainly by desertions, nearly half his men. The situation might have turned to disaster but for the brilliant conduct of Winterfeldt, now a general. Frederick said that Daun's strategy had been extremely clever and that he had learnt a good deal from it for future use.

Maria Theresa triumphed. She shed not a tear for her losses in Italy and the Netherlands; so great was her loathing of Frederick that she only wanted one thing in life: to see him humbled and to deprive him of his conquests. Perhaps unduly elated—Valory said, 'It takes very little to raise the hopes of the Austrians'—she had visions of retaking Silesia there and then. She embarrassed George II by tearing up the Treaty of Breslau and telling her faithful Silesian subjects that they would soon be freed from the Prussian tyrant. She did cause Frederick a certain anxiety. He left the Old Dessauer, who was now seventy but more active than any of his own sons, to keep the Austrian army at bay on the Silesian frontier, while he himself went to Berlin to raise money for a new campaign with which he had not reckoned. At dead of night Knobelsdorff took all the royal silver to the mint; Frederick even thought of selling Emden to the English.

1745 was one of those years when there is never a dull moment. It began with the kidnapping of the Maréchal Duc de Belle-Isle. He had gone to Germany on behalf of Louis XV to sound the intentions of various princes and to see whether Seckendorf was not playing a double game between the Emperor and Maria Theresa. The disposition of his troops seemed quite mad for such an experienced old soldier, and the King of France drew his own conclusions. On the road, Belle-Isle decided to spend the night in a village which he supposed to be in Hesse-Kassel. Unfortunately, it was in one of those small enclaves, so common in Germany at that time, which happened to be Hanoverian. Here, helpless from sciatica, he was carried off like a log, separated from his doctor, taken to England and given rooms in Windsor Castle. The local aristocracy was delighted with its new neighbour, but the attitude of the press was hostile.

The *Penny Post*, 18 February 1745, summed up his career:

'Our Hero' visited the German courts where he bribed ministers, persuaded princes and made boldly great promises which he constantly broke, urged sophisticated Arguments, published false News, being all things to all men, purely that he might ensnare that poor Country, pretending to secure the Peace of Germany by the ravages of French armies and to defend Protestant consciences by the French dragoons and Jesuit Missionaries. Some electors were forced, others inveigled to the election of a Bavarian Emperor. The King of Prussia was divided from the Protestant Cause chiefly by the arts of Monsieur Belle-Isle. . . .

Belle-Isle's movements, however, were followed with interest:

April 24: has taken Frogmore House near Windsor for which he is to pay £600 p.a. July 8: visited the Physic Garden at Chelsea. July 29: entertained by the Duke of Newcastle at Clermont. August 13: went to Dover and embarked for Calais. Distributed grand presents. On arrival told the French King of the polite treatment he had received. Prisoners to be returned.

In January the Emperor Charles VII died. He had been a tragic failure. No doubt if he had been of the stuff of Maria Theresa the House of Bavaria might have superseded the House of Austria, but he had assumed a role for which he was unsuited. His downfall dated from the time when, instead of taking his Franco-Bavarian troops to the conquest of Vienna, he turned round and besieged Prague. After that everything had gone wrong, and his health had deteriorated until, at forty-five, he had become an old and dying man. He took leave of his ugly wife in the most touching terms and exhorted his seventeen-year-old heir to renounce all pretensions to the Empire and to make an arrangement with Maria Theresa by which he could keep Bavaria. The Emperor's body was exposed in the dress of a fifteenth-century Spanish king, an ancient custom, although no Emperor after Charles V had ruled over Spain. A terrestrial globe was carried before his remains and the word 'Invincible' written on his coffin.

When the ceremonies were over the new Elector of Bavaria signed a treaty with Maria Theresa by which she recognized the legality of his father's election; and in return he engaged to vote for Francis of Lorraine at the Reichstag. The only other possible claimant to the Empire was Augustus III, but that charming man liked pictures better than power. Maria Theresa gave him a sum of money with which to add to his collection and promised that he should have some land belonging to Frederick as soon as he had been brought low by a new alliance between Saxons and Austrians. Frederick always thought that George II was a party to this project and liked him none the more for that. The Saxons were marvellous soldiers and, had they been led by Maurice de Saxe, would have been a serious danger to

Frederick; but luckily for him the Count had turned his back on Germany and only loved France. His mistresses and his friends were all French; he was in high favour with Louis XV, who called him his cousin, made him Marshal General of the French army (a rare honour) and gave him the royal château of Chambord. So the Saxon army was led by Austrians who, from now on, were outclassed by Frederick and his generals.

In May Maurice de Saxe, in the presence of Louis XV, won the spectacular victory of Fontenoy against the English; he then took Ghent, Oudenarde, Bruges, Dendermonde, Ostend and Nieuport. The French, led by him, were invincible. The English commander was the Duke of Cumberland, 'a great ass', said his first cousin, Frederick; 'Those animals [the English] have been beaten three times because they allowed themselves to be attacked in their positions; they always fall into the same errors for which they have been blamed by Caesar, Condé and Turenne—they are incorrigible animals and deserve to be damned.'

On 23 July Charles Edward made his last attempt to re-establish the Stuarts on the

Plan of the Battle of Hohenfriedberg, 1745; engraving.

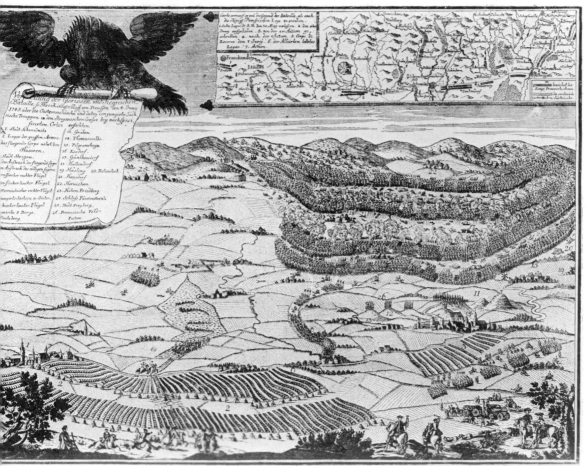

English throne; he landed in Scotland; Cumberland and his troops were recalled from the Low Countries to deal with him.

Frederick never gave Valory the satisfaction of seeming pleased, for once, with his allies the French; he said their victories in the west were of no more use to him than the taking of the Great Wall of China would be. But of course they made things easier for him—indeed he could not have retained Silesia without their help. On 4 June he won the Battle of Hohenfriedberg, a clash of 70,000 men on each side, and at the end of September that of Soor against an army twice the size of his own. The Austrian morale at Soor was not good and Lobkowitz himself shot three officers for cowardice. Frederick said that now he knew he could beat the Austrians anywhere. Prince Charles made one more attempt to turn the tables at the end of November, was outmanœuvred, saw that more fighting would be useless and made for home. So did Frederick. On his way he found that the indomitable Dessauer had defeated a Saxon army outside Dresden. 'O God,' the old man had prayed, before the battle, 'be on our side this day but if thou wilt not, be neutral.' Frederick met him on the battlefield where people were still looking for their dead in the snow; he took off his hat and embraced the Old Dessauer. They entered Dresden together as conquerors. Augustus III had fled to Prague; Frederick stayed in the Lubomirski palace and behaved most genially. He paid calls on Augustus's children, gave parties, went to the opera and to the Protestant church, and was much fêted by the Saxons, who were amazed that such a great warrior should be so kind and affable. On Christmas Day the Peace of Dresden was signed. It gave Frederick the duchies of Upper and Lower Silesia and the county of Glatz. He was to evacuate Saxony and recognize Francis of Lorraine as Holy Roman Emperor. Once more Frederick was out of the conflict with all his aims achieved, while practically every other country was still at war.

Maria Theresa's armies were doing badly on all fronts, but she had one satisfaction which outweighed her defeats. In September her husband had been elected Holy Roman Emperor and she herself had placed the crown on his head. It made little difference to him, as the new Empress allowed him no say in the conduct of affairs. She loved him; they had sixteen children; she minded when he began to be unfaithful to her; but she was the ruler. Francis administered his own Duchy of Tuscany extremely well and had a surprising talent for finance, but for some reason she had no faith in his judgment—or rather she knew that she alone was right. As the French say, *elle possédait la vérité*, an unattractive trait but one that is sometimes valuable in a sovereign. Frederick spoke of her as the Queen of Hungary to the end of her days, just as Louis XV called him 'le Marquis de Brandebourg'.

Frederick's return to Berlin was melancholy. He was ecstatically received by the citizens and this gave him no satisfaction; few leaders can have disliked public acclamation as much as he did. Jordan and Keyserling had died during his absence; his beloved tutor Duhan de Jandun lay dying and Frederick was only just in time to say good-bye to him. Jordan had

The Emperor Francis I, Maria Theresa's husband and father of her sixteen children; painting by unknown artist.

written, 'If I die, if I live, I shall die or I shall live full of gratitude for all the favours with which Y.M. has honoured me.' Frederick replied that he would be back very soon; it was not soon enough. Jordan and Keyserling were his greatest friends — Keyserling perhaps more than a friend. 'I loved him more than myself.' He wrote to 'Maman' Camas: 'I had been so longing to get home, but now I dread Berlin, Potsdam and Charlottenburg, which will only remind me of those I have lost for ever.' He begged her to see what could be done for Keyserling's baby girl. To d'Argens he wrote: 'A true friend is a gift from heaven. Alas I have lost two whom I shall miss to the end of my life. . . . To my way of thinking friendship is necessary to our happiness. It does not matter whether we have the same ideas, that one should be gay and the other sad. . . . But without decency and honesty there can be no real community.'

Frederick, who made such a cult of friendship, was always to be unlucky. Most of the people he loved died young or were killed in battle; all except Prince Henry and the Duchess of Brunswick died before he did. After losing Jordan and Keyserling he made new friends who were not always as decent and honest, erudite and cultivated, as they had been. D'Argens was a stand-by but he had not seen Frederick through the vicissitudes of his youth. Except for Wilhelmine no woman counted for him. He did not hold a court, in the usual sense of the word, at Potsdam; only, occasionally, at Berlin. The Queen, who must have hoped against hope that he would take her back on his return from the war, was never again invited to stay under the same roof. He seldom wrote to her, but sent messages through her lady-in-waiting.

A contemporary enamel box with plans of battles in the Seven Years' War.

Frederick; painting by J. G. Glume.

OVERLEAF: L'Enseigne de Gersaint, *the sign painted for the shopkeeper Gersaint, by Antoine Watteau. In 1744 Rothenburg negotiated for the sale of this painting and from 1755 it hung, cut in two, in the music room of the new wing at Charlottenburg. In 1760 it was damaged by Austrian and Russian soldiers. It now hangs at Charlottenburg again.*

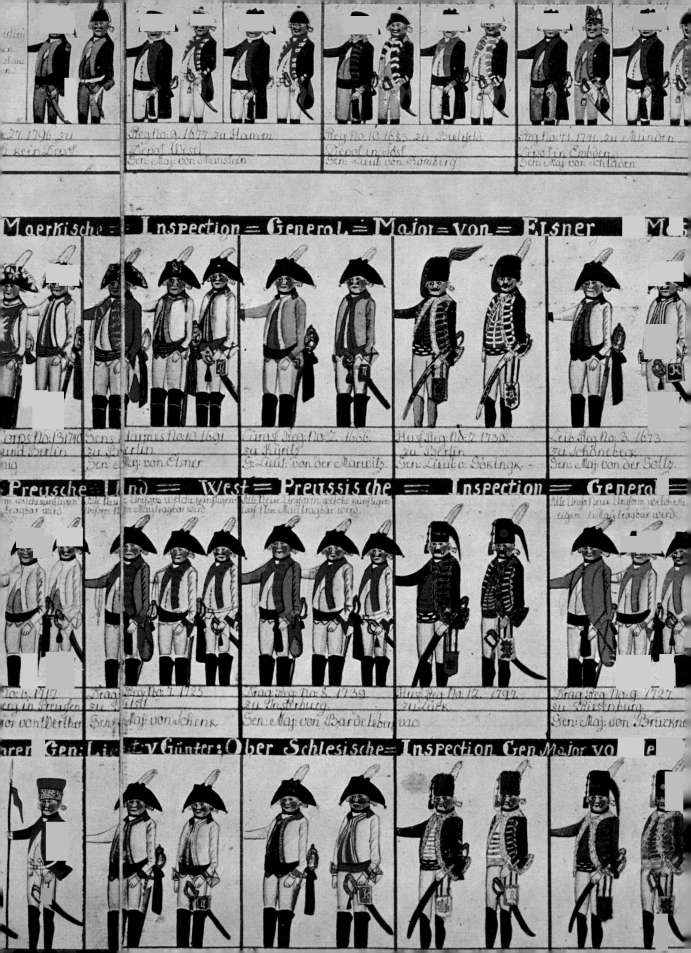

27. 1796 zu | Reg. No. 9. 1677. zu Hamm | Reg. No. 10. 1683. zu Bielefeld | Reg. No. 11. 1741. zu Münden
kein Depot | Depot Wesel | Depot in Soest | Depot in Emden
| Gen: Maj: von Manstein | Gen: Lieut: von Romberg | Gen: Maj: von Schladen

Maerkische = Inspection = General = Major = von = Elsner = M

Corps No. 13. 1740. und Berlin nig | Gens. Namens No. 10. 1691 zu Berlin | Cüras: Reg: No. 7. 1666. zu Fürth | Hus: Reg: No. 7. 1730. zu Berlin | Leib Reg: No. 3. 1673. zu Schönebeck
| Gen: Maj: von Elsner | G: Lieut: von der Marwitz | Gen: Lieut: v. Söringk | Gen: Maj: von der Sölly

Preussche = Und = West = Preussische = Inspection = General

No. 6. 1719. berg in Preussen | Drag: zu | Reg: No. 7. 1725. zu Insterburg | Drag: Reg: No. 8. 1739. zu Wasterburg | Hus: Reg: No. 12. 1797. zu Lück | Drag: Reg: No. 9. 1727. zu Rastenburg
ior von Werther | Gens: | Maj: von Schenk | Gen: Maj: von Bardeleben | vac | Gen: Maj: von Brückn

ten Gen: Lieut. v Günter: Ober Schlesische = Inspection Gen Major vo e

CHAPTER TWELVE

Thoughts on Warfare

For the first time since he came to the throne Frederick felt that he was going to enjoy a long period of peace. He knew that, given the turbulence of the times, he might well be faced with a defensive war; but he was determined never to take the offensive again. He had wanted Silesia; he had got it; his object now was to make the new Prussian State happy and prosperous and a power to be reckoned with. He must see to the administration of a larger, richer land than that which he had inherited. Law reform was urgent. As he never delegated the work of government, but saw to everything himself, he was busy from four or five o'clock in the morning until the evening hours of relaxation.

His mind was still much exercised with thoughts of warfare and he set them down in two long essays. As he grew older he was more and more obsessed by its horrors: 'Admit that war is a cruel thing—what a life for the unhappy soldiers who receive more blows than bread and who mostly retire with scars or missing limbs. The peasant is even worse off—he often dies of hunger—you must admit that the obstinacy of the Queen of Hungary and myself makes many people wretched.' (To his reader Catt during the Seven Years' War.) Yet of course he must have enjoyed what he did so supremely well.

In *Discours sur la Guerre* he tried to analyse his feelings. It is very difficult to consider the subject objectively, he said. Caesar loved war because it flattered his vanity; Calpurnius because it filled his purse; a poor countryman loathes it because it ruins his land and a pedant who sees only the surface of things spits fire and flame at the very word war. They are all in the wrong. It is hardly necessary to say that a man who is governed by vanity or cupidity will be incapable of any good action. Caesar's wish to deliver his people from the yoke of Pompey was laudable until it became obvious that he had delivered them in order to oppress them. But vanity must not be confounded with ambition and love of glory—real ambition is a desire to be distinguished from others by virtuous deeds and that is how a decent man seeks glory. Admittedly, if one only considers the horrors of warfare human nature must take fright. Severed limbs lying about; ferocious soldiers bathing in blood; towns in flames; widows and orphans without hope—any sensitive person must be penetrated with sorrow at such sights. But cruel as they are, they must not be allowed to stop recourse to arms. Warfare is the first defence of the oppressed; the revenge of faith betrayed; men risking their

Some of the uniforms worn by the Prussian army under both Frederick and his successors. Detail of a drawing by von Muhlen.

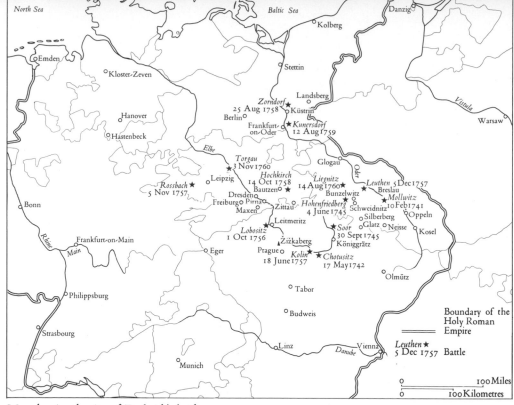

North Sea

Baltic Sea

Danzig

Kolberg

Emden

Kloster-Zeven

Stettin

Landsberg

Zorndorf
25 Aug 1758 ★
Küstrin

Hanover

Berlin

Frankfurt-
on-Oder

★ *Kunersdorf*
12 Aug 1759

Warsaw

Hastenbeck

Elbe

Torgau
★ *3 Nov 1760*

Glogau

Leipzig

Hochkirch
14 Oct 1758

Liegnitz
14 Aug 1760 ★

★ *Leuthen 5 Dec 1757*

Breslau

Oder

Rossbach ★
5 Nov 1757

Dresden

Bautzen ★

Bunzelwitz

★ *Mollwitz*
10 Feb 1741

Bonn

Freiburg Pirna

Maxen

Zittau

★ *Hohenfriedberg*
4 June 1745

Schweidnitz

Silberberg

Oppeln

Frankfurt-on-Main

Leitmeritz

Glatz

Neisse

Kosel

Main

Lobositz
1 Oct 1756 ★

★ *Soor*
30 Sept 1745

Eger

▲ *Žižkaberg*

Königgrätz

Prague

★ *Kolin*
18 June 1757

★ *Chotusitz*
17 May 1742

Olmütz

Rhine

Philippsburg

Tabor

Budweis

Boundary of the
Holy Roman
Empire

Strasbourg

Linz

Danube

Vienna

Leuthen ★
5 Dec 1757 Battle

Munich

0 _____ 100 Miles
0 _____ 100 Kilometres

Map showing the sites of Frederick's battles.

lives for the peace of their fellow citizens, the support of the State and the advantage of their master. What are the tears of a few widows if the State has been saved by the death of those for whom they weep?

People who hate war say that it gives rise to crime. But those who fight are only the same men with the same characters as those who live in peace. Is there a single day, in peace-time, when one does not hear of crimes? War has advantages for society—not that these should be an excuse for indulging in it lightly. The study of its art furthers such skills as medicine and mechanics and there are no other circumstances in which a man has to be so fully stretched in order to obtain his objective. We don't know much about Plato but he seems to have con-fined himself to the search for truth; Demosthenes had eloquence; Socrates and Seneca were resolute and Locke reasoned correctly. But a good general must be gifted in many different ways—besides which, whereas in peace there is time to reflect, during an action decisions must be taken at once and if the result is disastrous the general is covered with shame. This sharpens his wits.

Wars feed a quantity of men who would otherwise starve and a lot of worthless creatures are not only prevented by military discipline from troubling the State but are given the chance of being useful to it. People like the Vandals, Celts, Picts and Saxons who used to go ravag-ing about can now be channelled into armies. The nobility would go to pieces if there were no wars; if poor they would be obliged to till the soil; if rich they would be idle. In peace-time people fall too easily into decadence—the great example is Rome. That city, which once ruled the world, can now produce only a few miserable *castrati* hopping about the boards of the opera. Laziness and luxury harden the heart towards the poor and lead to jealousy among the rich. But war begets virtues: resolution, mercy, greatness of soul, generosity and charity.

His *Instructions militaires du Roi de Prusse pour ses Généraux* was written, like all his works, in French. Army orders were always issued in French as well as German, a language which some of his generals did not know. In the *Instructions* Frederick spoke of the composition of his troops which made them difficult to lead. Half of them were foreign mercenaries, out for what they could get, given to looting if they had a chance and ready to desert whenever it suited them. So strict discipline was essential and they must be better fed than the enemy's soldiers. In order to prevent desertion a general should put sentries in the cornfields, never camp near a forest, never let the men know in which direction he is going to move, never march by night if he can help it. The troops must not be short of beer. When the army is in winter quarters do not pay the men. If there is an outburst of desertion there is sure to be a reason, and this must be looked into—the men are probably being unfairly treated.

When setting up winter quarters in enemy territory, a river is no protection, as it will freeze; nor is a mountain, because where a goat can go so can a man. When the army is settled, everything must be put in order: boots, blankets, tents, harness. The heavy repairs of guns, wagons and so on must be done by the local people. An occupied country must provide recruits in time for them to be trained for the next campaign. The greater part of an army is composed of lazy folk; if the general is not always seeing that they do their duty this machine, which is artificial, will soon run off the tracks. The general must be at work all and every day—he won't fail to discover many abuses. Soldiers themselves will not put up with unsatisfactory comrades—the French Grenadiers in particular have never allowed weaklings in their ranks. Marauding is the source of all trouble.

But it is by no means enough to have good troops, and the King is now going to speak of generalship. To establish the body of an army one begins by the stomach. Always put the main magazine in the rear of your army—if possible in a fortified town. During the wars in Silesia and Bohemia the King had his largest magazine in Breslau because the provisions could come down the Oder. The best places for magazines in Brandenburg are Magde burg and Spandau. It is essential to have honest commissaries. There are two ways of filling the magazines with corn. One can order noblemen and farmers to provide it, paying them the rate fixed by the *chambre des finances* or taking it off their taxes, or, if the country is not rich in grain, one can get it from middlemen; but they are seldom honest and one should never use them except in dire necessity. If there is a navigable river it must be used—this is the best way of keeping an army properly provided. But in Bohemia and Moravia one must use wagons and they must be drawn by horses—oxen are no good. The general himself must see that the horses are properly looked after. [There is a whole chapter on the care and feeding of horses.] As well as provisions the army must transport iron ovens and bread must be baked at every stop. Biscuits are useful but the men will not eat them except in soup. In cases where the peasants have fled, leaving their houses empty, one has no duty towards them; the soldiers' wives can bring in anything they find in the way of vegetables and livestock.

A profound knowledge of the country in which one is going to fight is most necessary. Something can be learnt beforehand from maps—the towns, the rivers, the roads. Always go to the nearest height, map in hand, and study the view. Never neglect an opportunity of talking to old inhabitants, especially shepherds and gamekeepers. You must know where there are fords, and which rivers or marshes dry up in summer. Villars was beaten at Malplaquet because what he thought was a marsh on his flank was a dry field. [The opposite of this was to happen to Frederick himself at the Battle of Prague.] Find out how many columns of troops the road can take. All this is fairly easy in the plain and much more complicated in the mountains where one must know the gorges and defiles. Never camp away from water. One can send officers to find out these things but it is far better to do it oneself. Full use should be made of the lie of the land: cemeteries and sunken roads can be excellent defensive positions.

Forces must never be divided. Eugene lost Denain because Lord Albemarle was cut off from the main army; Frederick himself ought to have lost Soor for the same reason, but was saved by the brilliance of his generals and the courage of his troops. He describes various ways of making the enemy think that one is going to attack in a certain place and then doing so elsewhere; also of forcing the enemy to make detachments, as Luxembourg did when he beat the English at Neerwinden in 1693. Frederick urges his officers to study Turenne's last two campaigns.

There are several sorts of spies: one, amateurs who get caught up in this trade; two, double agents; three, spies in high places; four, those whom one forces into this horrible profession. The ordinary people, peasants, priests and so on, who go into the enemy camp are useful only for finding out where it is. Their reports are generally so hazy that they only add to one's uncertainties. The statements of deserters are no better. One uses double agents to give false information to the enemy. For many years Eugene paid the Head Postmaster at Versailles and got the orders before the French generals themselves.[1] Luxembourg did the same with one of the King of England's secretaries. The King found out and made the traitor send all sorts of false information to Luxembourg so that, if the French had not fought like tigers, they would have lost Steinkirk.

In enemy territory, if you are driven to it you can do a hard and cruel thing. Get hold of a rich bourgeois with much property, a wife and children; by threatening to burn his houses and chop up his family you can force him to take one of your soldiers disguised as a servant with him into the enemy camp. Frederick was once obliged to do this and it was successful. He would add that one must be generous, even extravagant, in paying spies. The poor brutes risk their lives and deserve their reward.

The country in which one makes war can be one's own, or neutral, or the enemy's. If the

[1] No doubt this was the spy whom Mme de Maintenon speaks of in her letters; he was never caught.

King only wanted glory, he would always fight at home where every peasant is a spy and a guerrilla. After Hohenfriedberg the Silesian mountain people brought in quantities of Austrian prisoners. In a neutral country things are fairly even, each side trying to win over the population. In a Protestant country like Saxony one is the protector of that religion and one must try and inspire poor, simple folk, who are easily taken in, with fanaticism. If the country is Catholic one preaches moderation and tolerance, blaming the priests for the sad rift among Christians. In enemy countries like Bohemia and Moravia one must play for safety. Most of the troops will be needed to guard the convoys. One will never win the affection of the people except for a few Hussites. The nobles and priests are all traitors and though they may seem well-intentioned their interest attaches them to the House of Austria.

The King should not fight with his troops except in an emergency but he must always be prepared to do so. He must have an eye to every detail, even an overloaded horse.

The big guns are decisive. Turenne had seventy – what would he say to the two hundred we have got?

Frederick had the gift of never forgetting a face. He knew hundreds of his men by sight and knew all about their behaviour both during and between battles. 'Why is that excellent soldier in irons?' 'He was found committing bestiality with his horse.' 'Fool—don't put him in irons, put him in the infantry.' To the soldier: 'I'm very sorry you will lose your horse.' But he dreaded any sort of relationship with the men; he forced himself to regard the army as a huge impersonal machine, the slave of the State as he was himself. He once said to the Old Dessauer: 'Don't you think it's amazing that you and I should be quite safe among 60,000 men who all loathe us, all larger and stronger than we are, and armed? Yet they tremble before us!' After a battle he said to one of the men, 'You fought very well today.' 'And why should we not? We are fighting for our land, our faith and for you.' Frederick burst into tears. He despised sentimentality and avoided such scenes. As for the men they probably loved as much as they hated him; they were certainly proud to fight under the greatest commander of the age. At the end of his life his old soldiers looked back nostalgically to their youthful campaigns with him and worshipped him.

The spectacle of Frederick's battles was terrible. Sir Andrew Mitchell, who hardly left his side during the Seven Years' War, used to write home saying he knew not if he would be able to go on enduring 'the horrour'. The imagination boggles at the idea of the cavalrymen at full gallop, lashing out at their foes with razor-sharp sabres, slashing off their limbs and crippling their horses; of the artillery 'cutting a path' with shells through the enemy's infantry, and of the infantry struggling up to the guns, hacking and bashing the gunners and putting their horses out of action. It was perhaps a mercy that the notorious 'fog of war' soon blotted out the appalling sights. Owing to the powder which was used the battlefield was covered with thick black smoke after the first volleys were fired. It then became very difficult to see what was going on; many unexpected turns of fortune were due to this fact.

CHAPTER THIRTEEN

Sans Souci

Having finished the war, disposed of his wife and organized his time to suit himself, Frederick built a new house at Potsdam in which to lead his new life. He and Knobelsdorff together designed a little pink and white palace situated on the top of a slope and called it 'Sans Souci'. Its originality lies in its position: the falling ground is terraced and the terraces are glassed over, so that the house seems to stand above a cascade. Frederick was tired of trying to grow the Mediterranean flowers and fruit he loved so much in north Germany and he hoped to cheat nature with his greenhouses. The glass which he used, set in tiny panes, is as different from modern glass as stone is from concrete; the whole effect is extremely pretty. But the palace does not stand high enough above the terraces, and seen from below it seems cut in half. This was Frederick's fault. Knobelsdorff wanted to put it up on steps but Frederick insisted on being able to walk straight out of his window into the garden. He had his way.

He moved into Sans Souci in May 1747, and thereafter it was his chief residence. Frederick also busied himself with Potsdam, which became one of the most elegant and charming small towns in the Empire and which still, happily, exists today. He went to Berlin less and less, though he was always there for the Christmas celebrations, when he held a court and attended parties given by members of his family. His only suit of plain clothes came out at this time; it was seldom renewed; the rest of the year he wore his uniform. The efforts he had made to be elegant when young were short lived—he always looked shabby and rather dirty; the only jewels he liked were snuff-boxes, of which he had about fifteen hundred; his pockets were lined with chamois leather so that the boxes should not be scratched.

The King's time-table when he was at home did not vary from now on; many people have described it and their accounts tally. He was woken at 4 a.m.; he hated getting up early but forced himself to do it until the day he died. He scolded his servants if they let him go to sleep again, but he was sometimes so pathetic that they could not help it; so he made a rule that, under pain of being put in the army, they must throw a cloth soaked in cold water on his face. He was much loved by his servants, whom he always addressed as *Mein Kind*—he never punished them, even if they stole from him, or, as once happened, brought him poisoned chocolate. The man who did that looked so ghastly that Frederick asked what was

Overdoor painting of Sans Souci in the music room at Sans Souci, by C. S. Dubois (see page 164).

The upper terrace at Sans Souci where several of Frederick's dogs were buried and where he planned graves for himself and his horse. He was buried in the Garrison Church at Potsdam.

the matter, whereupon he confessed. He was sent to a regiment in a remote part of Prussia.

Once out of bed, Frederick dressed fully, in boots and hat. He did not possess slippers, and even when he was ill or had gout he always wore boots. He would not allow them to be blacked, so they turned a curious reddish colour and differed from those of other men in having no spurs. While his hair was being curled he composed on a spinet the music he would play that evening on his flute. He practised the flute at least four times a day and said that many political ideas came to him while doing so. Then his post arrived, baskets full of letters. With his vast knowledge of coats of arms, he examined the seals; letters from people who bored him went into the fire unopened. Letters from friends and especially from Voltaire were his greatest joy, and he answered them himself. The rest he arranged in three baskets: granted, refused, and those about which he would consult some minister. While he had his breakfast a secretary came for the letters, and reduced each to one sentence, whereupon Frederick, in one sentence, gave the gist of the answer. If the writer was a woman he would add, 'Please answer civilly'. Three secretaries had to write all these letters in their own hand and have them ready for signing at 4 p.m.

The secretary having gone, Frederick's first A.D.C., a general officer, arrived and took away orders. He left with enough work to keep him hard at it all day. At 10 a.m. the King either went out and directed military exercises or wrote letters to his friends. In fine weather he would walk in his garden with a book, followed by two or three Italian greyhounds. These dogs were his constant companions and his favourite, who slept in his bed, was called his 'Mme de Pompadour'. If they took against somebody he would assume that the person was ill disposed towards him. It was a great sin to tread on their toes accidentally. He always had his favourite with him out riding, carrying her under his coat. Once, during the wars, when he was reconnoitring alone (a habit which his generals detested but could never break) he hid under a bridge while a company of Austrians rode over it; he was terrified that his horse would neigh or that his dog would bark and give him away; the two creatures hardly breathed. They are both buried on the terrace at Sans Souci.

At noon he dined in the company of writers, wits and soldiers; his Brunswick brothers-in-law were generally there. The food was excellent and at this time of day he was in good spirits, chatting away sometimes until 3 p.m., although, if the weather was fine, he would bolt his food in order to go out. He was susceptible to weather and passionately loved the sun. After the pudding the chef came with a block of paper and Frederick ordered the next day's dinner. The meat in Prussia was poor but he was fond of cheeses and *pâtés* and of a sort of caviar that Algarotti used to send him — all his food was highly spiced. He drank an immense amount of coffee, and champagne, into which he put water. His twelve cooks were of all nationalities including English; the two chefs, Joyard and Noël, came from Lyons and Périgord. He paid them so much for each dish thus saving himself the trouble of house books. Wood for the cooking, butter and game were free but the chefs paid for the wine and coffee. He was so fond of fruit, hitherto unknown in Brandenburg, that

LEFT: *One of Frederick's flute compositions. Some of his music is still played and has been recorded. Quantz only played with the King if a work was scored for two flutes.*
RIGHT: *Johann Sebastian Bach; painting by E. G. Haussmann. When Bach sent his* Musikalisches Opfer *to Frederick he said that the presentation would not be as well judged as so excellent a theme demanded owing to lack of time, and he set himself to work out the theme more perfectly.*

speculators built glasshouses in order to supply him with it at enormous prices. It laid the foundation of a new industry; but finally he grew his own at Sans Souci.

In the afternoon he did administrative work or sometimes went for a walk for his health. People were not fond of going with him as he amused himself at their expense. General von Schwerin, for instance, well over seventy, who had always ridden and never walked in his life, could hardly keep up with him and became extremely crusty; Frederick only laughed. One day when they had been further than usual, and the General was fit to drop, they were met by a sedan-chair. Frederick put Schwerin into it but then flew round it asking questions through first one window and then the other so that Schwerin was even more exhausted than if he had been on foot. He lost his temper, and for a while was no longer invited for the walks. He was very peppery. Frederick loved him because he was not only an invaluable officer but also an intellectual and a man of the world, knowing perfect French and Italian as well as Latin; since early childhood Schwerin had made him laugh more than anybody; he allowed him every licence but never could resist teasing him.

154

Supper was at 10 p.m. and afterwards there was a concert held in the round room—two violins, a viola, a 'cello and one of Silbermann's pianos. The King and Quantz played flutes; the other instruments accompanied them. Frederick seems to have been a good flautist, rather erratic in timing, so that it was not easy to accompany him; Karl Philipp Emanuel Bach, who had been in his service as cembalist since Rheinsberg days, was said to have been *littéralement torturé* by him. Dr Burney went to one of these evening concerts and says:

> he played the solo flute parts with great precision, his *embouchure* was clear and even, his finger [*sic*] brilliant and his taste pure and simple. I was much pleased and surprised with the neatness of his execution in the *allegros* as well as by his expression and feeling in the *adagios*; in short his performance surpassed in many particulars anything I had ever heard among the dilettanti or even professors. His *cadenzas* were good, but long and studied. Quantz beat time with his hand and cried out 'Bravo!' to his royal pupil now and then at the end of solo passages.

But Quantz also used to cough if Frederick played a wrong note—on one occasion he coughed so much that the King said crossly, 'What are we to do about Quantz's cold?' Highly strung, nervous in everything, Frederick would often tremble violently when about to perform. He composed a great deal of music, some of which is played to this day. After the Battle of Hohenfriedberg he composed the well-known march of that name.

One evening, soon after he had moved into Sans Souci, he was playing the flute when d'Argens handed him the list of passengers who had been set down from the daily coach. Frederick read it: 'Gentlemen, old Bach has arrived!' It was Johann Sebastian, whom the King had never met. A carriage was sent for the old man and he was told to come at once without changing into his cantor's robe. The King made much of him; the concert was abandoned and the two men went to try out Frederick's new Silbermann pianofortes, Bach extemporizing on them to the King's admiration. He asked the King to give him a subject. Frederick sat down and played one and asked for a fugue in six parts. His theme,

very modern with its descending chromatics, presented Bach with a difficult problem. He worked out several little canons, of a sad and haunting beauty, rather in the spirit of Beethoven's last quartets, and sent the fugue to Frederick as a *Musikalisches Opfer* dedicated to 'a sovereign admired in music as in all other sciences of war and peace'. Frederick ordained, at this time, that the children in the schools should have singing lessons three days a week.

The Marquis d'Argens was engaged in one of those interminable eighteenth-century lawsuits. It took him to Paris. Frederick told him to get actors, wits and artists to amuse them all

LEFT: *Marianne Cochois, later Marquise d'Argens; painting by Antoine Pesne.*
RIGHT: *Barbara Campanini, known as La Barbarina; painting by Antoine Pesne.*

at Potsdam. He wanted one or two good painters, an actor for such parts as Sganarelle, some actresses who must be pretty, and at least one agreeable man of letters. The mission was not easy. Among the artists, Frederick's first choice, Van Loo, refused to go to Berlin—d'Argens said they might be able to get Natoire or Pierre, the pupil of LeMoyne but nobody of any parts would move, so great the inclination of French people for Paris. 'Everybody is mad about intellect and wit—business men as well as dukes like it to be known that they entertain scholars.' Another difficulty: good writers are so often impossible in company; some have despicable natures and have even been in prison. As for actors, d'Argens had to go as far as Marseilles before finding some reasonably good ones. Here he also found a dancer whom, if H.M. did not care for her, d'Argens would keep to see him through the winter. However, soon after his return to Berlin, he married Mlle Cochois, an actress of whom he said that she was a learned man of letters, an enlightened artiste and a kindly wife, and of whom Frederick said, 'She is a delicious woman, witty, learned and talented'. They were very happy.

Frederick had already got the famous dancer Barbarina whom he had practically kid-napped from Venice and the arms of her Scotch lover, James Mackenzie. Mackenzie was the brother of Lord Bute, who was to be Frederick's implacable enemy in years to come, some think for reasons not unconnected with this episode. La Barbarina was paid more than a Cabinet Minister, and soon had a nice little nest-egg in the English funds; but she was too attractive to men to stay long at the opera. The King himself was thought to have had skirmishes with her (her limbs were those of a boy); she had an affair with Algarotti during which Frederick said that the Italian showed a sordid cupidity; finally she caused a scandal by marrying young Cocceji, the son of Frederick's Chancellor. The Cocceji family were so furious that Frederick had to banish the couple to Silesia. There she found a nobleman whom she preferred to her husband, managed to get a divorce, married him, had a large family and was heard of no more.

Algarotti reappeared at Berlin. Frederick sent him a note summoning him to Potsdam:

> Your brilliant imagination, your genius and your gifts are passports to any civilized country. It is now six years since you dived out of my sight and I've only had secondhand news of you; all the same I am delighted that you have surfaced at last. Are you often going to dive like this? To what extent have we got pretensions as regards your person? You will answer all these questions when I see you.

The answers seem to have been satisfactory and the Venetian was decorated with the new order *Pour le Mérite*, which was exclusively for Prussian subjects. His title of Count had been given him by Frederick. But Algarotti was a restless creature. He began to feel ill at Berlin. Frederick sent him to take the waters at Eger; it was very dull there and he asked for leave to go and stay with Prince Lobkowitz at Sagan—the doctor thought the journey would be good for him. Short leave was granted. But the weather changed; he sweated and suffocated during meals, and the doctor thought the journey to Berlin would not be good for him. All these fevers and feeblenesses, Frederick said, could only mean that Algarotti was in love. He told him to answer this letter in person, which he did. Frederick, who was a great believer in exercise, advised him to go out riding. Algarotti hated riding; he said it would be tiresome if, in order to activate the blood, he were to break a few vertebrae in his neck.

A new secretary, Claude Étienne Darget in some ways took the place of Jordan; like Jordan he was a good, almost saintly man, and devoted to the King. He had been attached to Valory and had shown courage and loyalty during the Silesian war when Hungarians broke into the house where he and Valory were billeted, bent on kidnapping His Excellency. Darget calmly pretended to be the ambassador and they took him away—it was a brave act on his part as these irregulars were highly so in their behaviour, and almost anything might have happened to him—luckily they did him no harm. Darget, like many of Frederick's associates, was a hypochondriac. D'Argens was another; Voltaire and Algarotti used poor health, real or imaginary, to further various designs. The King himself, who was never really well, seldom out of pain, hardly mentioned the fact; in no way did it interfere either with his work or with his amusements. Rothenburg, dying now, in agony, from his wound, was utterly stoical.

The moans and groans of healthy people exasperated the King or made him laugh. 'One does as one wishes with the body—when the soul says quick march it obeys.' His intellectual friends, his *beaux esprits*, were incapable of saying 'quick march!' and he was very much inclined to tease them. He ends a note to Darget: 'Good-bye—I wish you a good job in the privy, abundant urination and those agreeable movements of nature which reassure you as to your virility.' To d'Argens, prolific in new illnesses, 'As I'm clearly never going to see you again in this world I'll give you a rendezvous in the valley of Jehoshaphat and there hand over to you the pictures in Sans Souci which you have coveted for so long.' 'One is entitled to like being ill but overeating is incompatible with health, nor is total rest good for the body.' D'Argens played up to Frederick's teasing and enjoyed it until, years later, Frederick went too far. The illness of Rothenburg was deeply distressing to the King. He loved him and he prized him because, like Schwerin in the older generation, he was not only an excellent soldier but also able to shine in any company. The same could not be said of the other young general, Winterfeldt, with whom the King shared his military secrets. He could be very funny in his own way but he had no French and used to beg the King to give him a regiment and let him leave the court where he felt bored and out of it. But Frederick could not do without him. Winterfeldt had a beautiful wife, whom he had met while on a mission to St Petersburg. She was the stepdaughter of Marshal Münnich. He had smuggled her out of Russia and she had been obliged to leave all her jewels and possessions behind.

In 1748 peace was signed at Aix-la-Chapelle; it almost amounted to a *status quo ante*. Louis XV gave up his huge acquisitions in the Netherlands thinking that, if he kept them, war would soon break out again. He said he went to the conference table as a king and not a tradesman. He did, however, take Parma as an establishment for his daughter and her husband, the Infante Philip of Spain. (They founded the family of Bourbon-Parma.) The chief beneficiary of this cruel war was the King of Prussia who had started it eight years ago: he was now seen to hold the balance between France and Austria.

Soon afterwards Maurice de Saxe stayed a few days with Frederick, whom he fascinated, and who picked his brains shamelessly. He said he ought to have a school for generals. He apologized for keeping him up so late, having only thought selfishly of his own longing to learn from him. Saxe was desperately ill and a few months later he died, aged fifty-four, saying that his life had been a beautiful dream. His book on warfare, *Mes Rêveries*, was always by Frederick's bed.

The King now acquired two new Keith brothers, very different from the wretched fellows who had helped with his escape. There was an amazing quantity of Scotch and Irish Jacobites in all European armies; as they were splendid fighters, many aristocrats rose to the highest rank. Even humble fellows often got on very well. General the Hon. James Keith led Russian troops to victory against the Turks and was then empowered to treat with the Sultan's envoy. They exchanged many a formal salutation, after which Keith was astounded to hear, from under the turban and over the beard: 'Unco happy . . . sae far frae hame.' The envoy had been the bell-ringer at Keith's village in Scotland. James Keith, more and more aware of the uncertainties of serving in Russia, where at any moment you might suffer a dreadful fate such as having your tongue cut out, got away with some difficulty and offered his sword to Frederick. The two men liked each other at once, and Frederick was so delighted to have him and, knowing that other courts would welcome such a first-class officer, so keen to keep him, that he gave him a Field Marshal's baton and cast about for

Lord Keith, tenth Earl Marischal of Scotland; painting after Placide Constanzi.

ways of making him happy. When Keith mentioned the fact that his adored elder brother was living at Treviso in extreme poverty Frederick immediately invited him to Berlin.

Lord Keith, born about 1690, was hereditary Earl Marischal of Scotland and had owned vast estates there. His family was Jacobite on both sides, and his mother, daughter of the titular Duke of Perth, wrote a famous ballad called *Lady Keith's Lament*: 'And I'll be Lady Keith again when the King comes o'er the water.' Her sons both took part in the 1715 Rising but Lord Keith's orderly soul was outraged by the confusion of that campaign. After the Battle of Sherriffmuir his groom was murdered and his baggage stolen by a fellow officer, the young Laird of Bohaldy, with a party of MacGregors. The battle itself was a mess. 'And we ran and they ran and they ran and we ran and we ran but they ran awa', man.' Lord Keith, though always faithful to 'James III', partly for the sake of his adorable mother, Mary of Modena, lost his ardour for the cause and if there was one thing he could not abide thereafter it was Jacobites. Nevertheless, from a sense of duty, he took part in Alberoni's rising (1719), and when it failed he escaped from Scotland by the skin of his teeth. His land was confiscated by George I and he was condemned to death in his absence. But King George could not take away his title of Earl Marischal, and to the end of his days he subscribed himself 'Maréchal d'Écosse'—the foreigners among whom he lived called him 'Milord Maréchal'. He settled at Valencia, whose climate he loved and which was his base for many years. He travelled incessantly and was at home in the courts of Spain, France and Russia—there were few important or interesting people in Europe whom he did not know. He kept in touch with his King, now living in Rome, but could never endure Charles Edward: the aberrant behaviour of the Bonnie Prince repelled him; he saw no future for him. He felt that he had done enough for the cause, which had cost him everything except his life, and he took no part in the '45.

Milord Maréchal was always accompanied by what he called his menagerie: 'a little horde of Tartars with whom I get on very well'. They were Ermetulla the Turkish lady, Stepan the Tibetan, Ibraham the Kalmuck, and Mocha the Nigger. Ermetulla was the daughter of a janissary. A little girl at the Battle of Ochakov (1737), she ran beside the horse of James Keith, hanging upon his stirrup. He took charge of her and gave her to his brother. When she was grown up Milord Maréchal thought he would like to sleep with her, but she said, 'I am your property but I have always loved you as a father and would prefer to go on doing so'. And thus it was. Her contemporaries all agree that Ermetulla was a tremendous bore. Stepan was related to the Grand Lama of Tibet and Lord Keith called him 'my chaplain' or 'my illegitimate son'; the two black boys were 'my bastards'.

As soon as Frederick saw Milord Maréchal he conceived the warmest feelings for him, and until his death thirty years later Keith was an intimate friend of the King's. 'I have a sad and Calvinistic phiz', he said of himself and no doubt this was a change from the phizzes of Algarotti and Co. Part of the charm that the Keith brothers had for Frederick was that they were honest-to-God gentlemen who could be treated as equals without

ABOVE: *Gilded snuff-box set with diamonds with a miniature of the King. The box was given by Frederick to the Old Dessauer after the Battle of Kesselsdorf in 1745.*
BELOW: *Snuff-box set with diamonds. The enamel paintings are by J. G. G. Krüger.*

OVERLEAF: *Sans Souci from the south front. The terraced greenhouses, which Frederick himself sketched for Knobelsdorff, were to protect the vines he hoped to grow.*

becoming uppish and could be counted on not to have hurt feelings or to suffer ill-concealed agonies of jealousy. Lord Keith was extremely well-read and had a dry and pawky wit; he shone at the supper parties and everybody liked him. He and his brother lived in Berlin but did not share a house — James Keith had a beautiful Swedish mistress, an orphan, whom, like Ermetulla, he had picked up at the wars. He had her educated and when she was old enough they lived together and produced several children. Probably she did not take to the little horde of Tartars. Frederick made a good allowance to Lord Keith, who now was more at his ease than at any time since leaving Scotland. He was also given the Order of the Black Eagle which he wore in preference to the Garter. The English looked upon the friendship with no good eye and Legge, a stop-gap minister at Berlin, went so far as to complain of Frederick's reception of the brothers, both under sentence of death in London. The King observed that it would not occur to him to choose King George's friends for him. Valory, having taken a long leave, was replaced as French minister at Berlin by Lord Tyrconnel, another Jacobite.

Frederick's feelings for the various English ministers accredited to him were seldom indifferent — he loved or he hated them. Gidikins (Guy Dickens) had become an old family friend; Hotham was greatly liked; Robinson was regarded as a joke and was so regarded in London; Hyndford was loathed; Villiers (later Lord Clarendon), who had negotiated the Peace of Dresden, was loved. The most hated of all was the one who now appeared at Berlin, Sir Charles Hanbury Williams. He was only there three weeks before going off on a visit to Poland. Heads of State never care for foreign ambassadors who leave their post to intrigue in neighbouring countries; the Kings of Prussia were particularly ticklish about Poland on account of the situation of East Prussia. As the Kings of Poland were elected, there was always uncertainty about the succession; Augustus III was not old but he did not seem a good life; and the day he died anything might happen. This preoccupied Frederick — one wondered what the English minister might be up to. He was, in fact, trying to find out what the Prussians and the French were up to. He distributed a few bribes among highly placed officials and came away with a portrait of Augustus III framed in diamonds.

Hanbury Williams was an odious man, a busybody and a gossip with a violent temper. But he was very funny and has left, chiefly in letters to Henry Fox, a hilarious picture of life at Berlin — yes, at Berlin, not at Potsdam since Frederick took such an intense dislike to him that he was invited to none but official functions. After his first reception, which was short but civil, the two men never exchanged a word. Horace Walpole wrote to Mann: 'Sir Charles Williams is to teach the King of Prussia to fetch and carry.' He had no chance to administer this lesson. He frequented the two Queens and went to anybody else who would invite him, but the dazzling centre of attraction at Sans Souci was closed to him and he spent much of his time supperless and alone. This was embittering to a man who was accustomed to be sought after for his wit, who had an exaggerated idea of the importance of ambassadors and who liked good company and rich living. His pen, when he wrote to

The music room at Sans Souci, with paintings by Pesne illustrating scenes from Ovid's Metamorphoses. The piano was made by G. Silbermann, almost certainly the first German to make a pianoforte. Frederick is known to have acquired at least three from him for Potsdam on one of which, though probably not this one, Dr Burney played.

Sir Charles Hanbury Williams; painting by J. G. Eccardt.

London, was dipped in sparkling vinegar. Nobody could turn a better phrase. He called Frederick's friends 'the he-muses', and said, 'No female is allowed to approach this court. Males wash the linen, nurse the children, make and unmake the beds.'

Hanbury Williams describes dining with the Queen Mother, saying that after every dish of eatables a dish of non-eatables was handed round. He likes Frederick's wife:

> It is a melancholy sight to see this Queen. She is a good woman and must have been extremely handsome. It is impossible to hate her and although his unnatural tastes won't allow him to live with her, common humanity ought to teach him to permit her to enjoy her separate state in comfort. Instead of this he never misses an opportunity of mortifying this inoffensive and oppressed Queen. The Queen Mother assists her dearly loved son in this by never showing her common civility.

However, a few days later the Queen Mother gave a banquet for her daughter-in-law's birthday. Hanbury Williams often got things wrong. He said that Ermetulla was Lord Keith's mistress, which nobody who knew them ever thought. He said: 'The thing his Prussian Majesty has in the greatest abhorrence is matrimony. No man, however great a favourite, must think of it—if he does he is certain not to be preferred.' But Frederick had encouraged Keyserling, the greatest favourite of all, to marry; Maupertuis married the daughter of a minister at Berlin; d'Argens and the greatly cherished Winterfeldt were also happily married. One would like to know of a single case proving Hanbury Williams's point.

Of Wilhelmine the Minister wrote:

> There is a little Bitch Royal for you. She is an atheist and talks about fate and destiny and makes a joke of a future state. She speaks of dying as of going to dinner . . . she thinks all time lost that is not spent with books or with such people she has heard other people say are learned. She passes her whole time between conversing with her brother's *beaux esprits*, writing volumes and being read to, for as she has weak eyes she cannot read herself. . . .

> Now for a little about the compleatest tyrant that God ever sent for a scourge to an offending people. I had rather be a post horse with Sir J. Hind-Cotton on my back than his First Minister, his brother or his wife. He has abolished all distinctions. There is nothing here but an absolute Prince and a People all equally miserable, all equally trembling before him and all equally detesting his iron government. There is not so much distance between a curate and a bishop as there is between the King of Prussia and his immediate successor the Prince of Prussia, who dares not go out of Berlin one mile without his tyrant's leave nor miss supping every night with his Mamma. Another of his brothers is at this moment sent to banishment in a country town and a third [Prince Henry, no doubt] is in frequent danger of being put in irons for daring in conversation sometimes to have an opinion of his own. It is known that Princess Amalie has a mind to be married to the Duke of Deux Ponts. But he, Nero, told her that she must never marry. And his reason is that she is to be Abbess of Quedlinburg which is worth about £5,000 a year. He will have her spend that money in Berlin. Besides that he does not care to pay her her fortune which is quite £20,000.

> He makes a great rout with his Mother; but people who know him well say he does not love her and that the duty he has accustomed himself to pay her makes Berlin disagreeable to him and

Lord Keith's Turkish girl, Ermetulla; painting by an unknown artist.

therefore it is that he resides at Potsdam. . . . She is an old gossip with all the tittle-tattle of that sort of people. . . .

Berlin is a very fine and large town but thinly inhabited. It is big enough to contain 300,000 souls and yet without the garrison there is not above 80,000 inhabitants. And among these there is not one at whose house you can dine or sup without a formal invitation; and that is a thing that very seldom happens. The one place that is open is the courts of the two Queens.

But Hanbury Williams found them pretty dull. The only amusing house, that of the Jacobite Lady Tyrconnel, was closed to him. One of the few people he liked in Berlin was the Prince of Prussia, who had 'great modesty and sweetness and has not that contemptuous insolence with which his Prussian Majesty speaks to everyone. The Prince likes every woman better than his wife, the Queen's sister, which is sad as they are two such amiable princesses.' He never once heard German spoken at Berlin.

Can we doubt that if Sir Charles had been favoured with Nero's friendship he would have written differently? He made no headway in Prussia, and left after a stay of only eight months. He is to a great extent responsible for Frederick's unpopularity in England to this day.

Gold snuff-box by Daniel Baudesson of Berlin. The miniature inside the lid is of Frederick.

CHAPTER FOURTEEN

The Poet

After the end of the Second Silesian War the letters between Frederick and Voltaire were more frequent and more enthusiastic than ever before—Frederick asking Voltaire to live with him and be his love; Voltaire hanging back, but less and less convincingly. The offer tempted him, but he had promised Mme du Châtelet never to leave her. Although she now had a new lover, as well as a husband with whom she was on comfortable terms, the habit and affection of twenty-odd years kept Voltaire at her side. For some time now they had lived with ex-King Stanislas at Lunéville. Voltaire's life had a secret complication: he was enamoured of his sister's daughter Mme Denis, a fact successfully concealed from history until, in 1957, Mr Theodore Besterman discovered and published their love-letters. Mr Besterman, who knows Voltaire better than anybody, says he loved her 'sincerely, tenderly, passionately, blindly'. But it is obvious from the available evidence, that Mme Denis cared not for her uncle, but only for his fame and his money. She kept his Paris house for him and their friends thought he looked upon her as a daughter.

In 1749 Mme du Châtelet died giving birth to a baby by her new lover. Voltaire was almost unhinged by this death; the whole tenor of his life was upset; his anchor had gone. He could no longer bear Lunéville, although Stanislas begged him to stay there and was un-failingly kind to him. He had got a room and a job at Versailles, but they gave him little satisfaction since the one king he longed to please never threw him a word. Although Louis XV knew that Voltaire was his most distinguished subject he happened to loathe him; he gave him all the favours and appointments which were his due and avoided his company like the plague. Voltaire also had a house in Paris which he shared with Mme Denis, but he was not happy there. She was extremely promiscuous; he must have known it and must have minded—indeed it may have contributed to his highly nervous state at this time. He was continually upset by the behaviour of certain failed writers who, maddened by jealousy, were doing their best to destroy him and his work. No real man of letters joined these despicable hyenas (Jean-Jacques Rousseau had only just appeared on the horizon) and one wonders why Voltaire paid any attention to them. No doubt he would have snapped his fingers at them if Louis XV had asked him to his supper parties, but the King's neglect ate into his soul, tortured him and made him touchy.

Frederick and Voltaire in the study at Sans Souci; engraving by P. C. Baquoy after N. A. Monsiau.

About a year after the death of Mme du Châtelet, Voltaire decided to go and live at Berlin. He wrote to all his friends giving the reasons for taking such a step. He said he was persecuted in France, but as examples of this persecution he was obliged to hark back to the reception of *Le Mondain*, many years before, and to the black deeds of the late Bishop of Mirepoix. Even he could hardly pretend that he was being persecuted in 1750, unless by an occasional cross look from Louis XV. He also complained, as old people do, of deteriorating standards in France, of taste having gone downhill; there was no place for him in the brash new world. Each friend in turn was told that only he and Mme Denis made life in Paris tolerable for Voltaire, who was therefore leaving France in order to enjoy the protection of a king, the company of a philosopher and the charm of a delightful man. Mme Denis would have a house in Berlin and, he hoped, spend several months there every year. Voltaire's contemporaries were puzzled. Lord Chesterfield wrote to a French correspondent: 'Do explain the motives of this emigration. Academician, Historiographer of France, Gentleman-in-Ordinary to the King and rich into the bargain. . . .'

Frederick, like a Victorian lady of the manor engaging a neighbour's butler, told his minister at Versailles to ask Louis XV if there would be any objection to his having Voltaire. The answer was none whatever, but it was doubted whether His Prussian Majesty would find Voltaire's character very comfortable in the long run. Louis XV continued the poet's pension but not his appointment as Historiographer. Frederick wrote very lovingly to Voltaire saying he would do his best to make him happy and Voltaire said he was now assured of eternal tranquillity.

At first all went well. Voltaire had beautiful rooms at Sans Souci next door to Frederick's; Frederick wandered in and out at all hours, chatting, joking and bringing his *Histoire de Brandebourg* to be criticized. Voltaire thought the King had been too hard on his grandfather, Frederick I, whom Voltaire rather liked because of the beautiful architecture he had left. When Frederick held his ground, Voltaire said, 'Oh well, he's your grandfather, not mine.' The other he-muses, though envious, were under control; Frederick disciplined them as if they were soldiers and all pretended to be delighted at the arrival of the master wit of the world. Only Maupertuis sulked. Conversation at the supper parties was dazzling; Voltaire, Frederick and the Marquis d'Argens did most of the talking; the others listened and laughed and applauded. All those brilliant words which, said Voltaire, nourished the soul have vanished into air but we have an echo of them in the letters of Voltaire and Frederick, since these were men who wrote as they spoke.

Too soon Voltaire began to get on the King's nerves. For one thing, he talked so stupidly about warfare. He pretended that the subject bored him to death—very well, but then he would come back to it. He made idiotic remarks: 'the bullet speeds, the powder flames', instead of the other way round. He supposed that when Frederick was fighting he was in a rage? Certainly not—that is the moment when you must have 'Marlborough's cold head' (*sic*). Then his behaviour over Countess Bentinck was tactless in the extreme. She was an

The room that Voltaire is thought to have occupied at Sans Souci. Frederick changed the decoration which is by J. C. von Hoppenhaupt. Originally the panelled walls had paintings by F. W. Höder. The carved wood, picture-frames and furniture were silvered, and the upholstery and silk hangings were yellow.

old friend of Voltaire's, now in Prussia for a lawsuit against her husband. Frederick suspected that she was having an affair with the newly married Prince Henry, which might have accounted for his indifference to his bride. Voltaire bombarded the King with requests on her behalf and then urged her to buy a house in Potsdam where she could entertain the wits.

Voltaire arrived at Berlin in July; in November the gilt was wearing thin. One evening at supper they were all teasing him about Mme Denis—his letters were full of her and so no doubt was his conversation. It all began in quite a good-natured way, Frederick saying, 'Do admit, Voltaire, that your niece is rather absurd.' 'But she is witty and well informed.' 'Perhaps that makes her more absurd.' Then Baculard d'Arnaud, a young protégé of Voltaire's whom he had wished on Frederick, said annoyingly, 'So true!' Now Voltaire could take it from the King but this was too much and he flew into a rage. Declaiming like an actor: 'Sire, my niece whom I love and esteem is being attacked in my presence—as for you, little d'Arnaud, abortion from Parnassus, you to whom I gave the first inkling of what is poetry, you whom my niece took in and protected in your poverty—away with you and your base ingratitude!' D'Arnaud replied, 'Your absurd niece was good to me, I don't deny it, but in return I had to sleep with her.' Frederick noticed that Voltaire, who generally had a ready reply, was suddenly turned to stone; he looked so desperate and the King felt so sorry for him that he broke up the party there and then. Furthermore, at Voltaire's request, he sent d'Arnaud back to Paris. Of course none of them knew the real reason for Voltaire's distress.

'My dear child,' he wrote to Mme Denis, 'the weather is turning cold.'

Three days later he sent for Abraham Hirschel, a diamond merchant, to meet him at Sans Souci on urgent business. The glass was going down.

Voltaire was a rich man, but not from his writings. His books were nearly always pirated; his plays brought in money but he generously distributed it among the actors. He was interested in high finance, and by clever transactions had greatly increased the fortune which he had inherited from his father. He now heard of an investment which seemed profitable indeed. Under the Treaty of Dresden, Prussian holders of Saxon bonds had to be paid in gold by the Saxon Treasury. As these bonds were only worth a fraction of their nominal value this naturally led to abuses and to very bad feeling at Dresden; Frederick soon forbade his subjects to speculate in them. Voltaire knew it, but the smell of lucre was strong; he gave Abraham Hirschel a sum of money, part of which was in the form of a letter on a Paris bank, and sent him to Dresden to buy the bonds, at a thirty-five per cent discount; he was then to smuggle them out and sell them for gold in Berlin. Hirschel left some diamonds with Voltaire as a security. Frederick heard of this transaction, but refused to believe what he took to be spiteful gossip.

The sum involved, not translatable into modern money, was a large one; as soon as Hirschel had left for Dresden Voltaire began to worry, and he was in a pitiable state of

The marble room at Sans Souci, which was used as a formal dining-room. It was designed by Knobelsdorff on the lines of the interior of the Pantheon at Rome.

anguish when weeks went by with no numbers of bonds, only an occasional vague and unsatisfactory letter. He consulted financiers in Berlin who said they only hoped everything was tied up so that Hirschel could not cheat; they hinted at dire dishonesty. So Voltaire told his Paris banker not to honour his bill and this brought Hirschel hot-foot from Dresden. There were awful scenes and almost every day the affair took some new turn which fascinated not only the Berliners but, soon, the whole of Europe. Voltaire went for the Jew, tried to strangle him and dragged a ring off his finger: Hirschel's honest old father began to die of a broken heart; Hirschel accused Voltaire of having substituted sham stones for the diamonds he had left with him.

Frederick was naturally displeased; he refused to keep Voltaire at Sans Souci and lodged him at the palace in Berlin: 'Brother Voltaire is here in penitence', he told Wilhelmine. Voltaire went no more to the two Queens, was ill, wretched and lonely. Finally he brought a lawsuit against Hirschel. He seems to have imagined that Frederick and his Chancellor Cocceji would arrange for him to win it, but they were proud of their new law reforms by which litigation in Prussia had been made speedy and cheap and justice put above reproach; they would not have dreamed of interfering with its course. Before the reforms such a case would have dragged on for years, but now it only took two months. Voltaire and Hirschel both lied like troopers. Facts very damaging to Voltaire and annoying to Frederick came out.

Voltaire and his niece, Mme Denis; crayon drawing by C. N. Cochin the Younger.

Hirschel had been several times to Sans Souci where he and Voltaire had plotted almost within earshot of the King. When Hirschel had told him of the risks involved, Voltaire let it be understood that Frederick had no objection to the arrangement and he even hinted that if it succeeded Hirschel might become court jeweller. Each man declared that the other had tempted him. The judges struggled to understand what had really happened, but a great deal of the matter remains obscure to this day.

Frederick to Wilhelmine, 22 January 1751:

You ask about Voltaire's lawsuit with a Jew. It's the story of a knave cheating a scamp—unpardonable for a man with Voltaire's gifts to make such use of them. The case is now being tried and in a few days we shall know which is the greater scoundrel. Voltaire assaulted the Jew; he was rude to M. de Cocceji—in short he has behaved like a madman. When the case is over I shall wash his head and see if, at the age of fifty-six one can't induce him to be, if not more sensible, at any rate less crooked.

2 February 1751:

Voltaire's case is not yet over though I think he'll dodge his way out of it. It won't affect his talent but his character will be more despised than ever. I'll see him again when it's all over but in the long run I'd rather live with Maupertuis. He is dependable and easier company than the poet, who lays down the law.

Wilhelmine to Frederick, 6 February 1751:

I've had a very funny letter from Voltaire describing his adventures with the Israelite. I wouldn't swear that he won't now become a Christian from rage and vexation.

Baron von Pöllnitz to Wilhelmine, Potsdam, 13 February 1751:

Y.R.H. asks me for news of our wits. The head of the band is still exiled from the court of Augustus but better treated than Ovid was at the height of his favour. He is lodged in the palace at Berlin where he has food, carriages and all expenses paid. His salary is 5,000 *écus* and he is allowed to plead against Israel and give rise to all sorts of jokes. The satirists practise their verve on him and he commits a new folly every day. He went to see the Chancellor [Cocceji] and told him that the new code of law is full of absurdities, especially as regards letters of credit. The Chancellor thanked him warmly and said he would look into it, but not until Voltaire's case was over. . . . To go back to the poet, one begins to see the Jew was in the wrong. . . .

Pöllnitz adds that Algarotti is back at Potsdam, rather distracted, but he will soon find his feet. M. de Maupertuis is in the ascendant, the Marquis d'Argens is at Menton and will return when the snows have melted and M. Darget is still sad from the death of his wife, greatly attached to the King and to his duties and talks of hanging himself during his hours off.

At last the court delivered its verdict. Voltaire was to have his money back, and if Hirschel could prove that the diamonds were not the ones he left with Voltaire he could bring a new action. (He never did.) He was fined a nominal sum for contempt of court. Voltaire had won a technical victory which he blew up into a triumph.

He wrote to the King, a long letter of which this is the gist: he had never bought a single Saxon bond; most people had, but Voltaire found out that the speculation was wrong and refused to touch it. Why is everybody against an unfortunate foreigner, an invalid and a solitary who is only here to be with the King? He did his best not to bring a lawsuit but had he not done so he would have lost a huge sum of money which he needs to maintain his Paris house. He has won the case on every point. He can only endure the torments of his illness by the thought that he does not displease the great man for whose sake alone he lives and feels and thinks. He begs His Majesty to take pity on his distress.

Five days later the King replied:

I was happy to receive you here; I admired your wit, your talents, your learning; I suppose I thought that a man of your age, tired of fencing with other authors and of exposure to storms, came here to find a haven. You prevented me from engaging Fréron [to write a news letter from Paris]. D'Arnaud behaved badly but a generous man would have forgiven him—he had done nothing to me but I sent him away on your account. You went to the Russian minister to talk about things which were not your business and led him to suppose that I had commissioned you to do so. You have been meddling in the affairs of Mme de Bentinck who is nothing to do with you. You have had a disgusting mix-up with the Jew, making a frightful stink in the town. The matter of the bonds is well known in Saxony whence I have had grievous complaints. Until you came here I had peace in my house. I must warn you that if you have a mania for intrigue

The town palace at Potsdam; engraving by A. Krüger after F. Meyer. The palace was demolished after the Second World War.

and cabals you have come to the wrong place. I like easy-going, quiet people whose conduct is not that of tragedians. If you will resolve to live like a philosopher I shall be happy to see you, but if you must burn with the flames of passion, bearing grudges to right and to left, it gives me no pleasure to have you here and you may as well stay in Berlin.

After this they made it up. Voltaire wrote and apologized; Frederick answered in a friendly tone: he hoped that in future Voltaire would quarrel neither with the Old nor the New Testament—it was not suitable that wretched little crooks should be named in the same breath as he. But their friendship had cooled. Voltaire was given a pretty house near Sans Souci and also rooms in the Potsdam town palace. Here he finished his *Siècle de Louis XIV*, one of his most remarkable works and unequalled in the enormous literature on the Sun King. He said he would never have finished it in Paris. The *Siècle* was published in Berlin at Christmas 1751 and at the same time Frederick's *Art de la Guerre* in six volumes appeared, read for him and corrected by Voltaire. When he was cross with Voltaire the King used to say that he put up with him because he helped with his writing, and he is supposed to have remarked to somebody, who repeated it to Voltaire, that when you have squeezed an orange you can throw away the rind. Whether he really did say it or not, Voltaire was cut to the quick; he retorted that he got all the King's dirty linen to wash. Maupertuis told this to Frederick.

Frederick began to tease Voltaire at the supper parties; all the art with which as a little boy he had maddened his father was now employed in maddening the poet. He hardly looked in his direction; he laughed at the jokes of the other wits and ignored his—he singled out Maupertuis for exaggeratedly deep and undivided attention. It is odd that Voltaire, himself such an accomplished tease, should not have been able to counter Frederick's naughtiness or to rise above it. But he minded, passionately. His Paris friends worried about him: they could see in his letters that he was miserable. The charming d'Argental, his greatest friend, begged him to come home, saying very sensibly that in Paris he could avoid people who tormented him, whereas in Potsdam he had to live cheek by jowl with them. Unfortunately, those friends of Frederick's who might have smoothed things over happened to be away: Milord Maréchal (Lord Keith) was now Prussian minister to Versailles (to the fury of Uncle George, who, with Tyrconnel as French minister at Berlin, was beginning to suspect some Jacobite plot between the two countries); Valory, greatly regretted, was dividing his time between his estates and Versailles; d'Argens too was in France. Darget was a help, although he was only a much-loved secretary and had not the weight of the others, but he, distracted by the loss of his wife and real or imaginary ill health, soon went back to Paris. He lived there for many years as deputy governor of the École Militaire; he and Frederick corresponded to the end of his life and he never had anything but good to say of the King.

It may be some excuse for Frederick's unkindness to Voltaire to remember that at this time he had three bereavements and was very sad. His little dog Biche died. She had been a beloved companion for years—he used to write letters from her to Wilhelmine's Folichon. Frederick said he was ashamed to be so much affected by this loss but he confessed that his philosophy was deranged by it. The Old Dessauer died, broken-hearted at the death of his old wife, the apothecary's daughter; that was in the nature of things. The death that utterly shattered Frederick was that of Rothenburg. 'Oh my dear sister,' he wrote to Wilhelmine, 'with your tender heart have pity on the situation in which I find myself. I have lost the Prince of Anhalt-Dessau and yesterday Rothenburg expired in my arms. . . . I can think of nothing but the loss of one with whom I have spent twelve years in perfect friendship.' And —after she had written—' I must confess to you that I am disgusted with the stupid part I play and that the world seems very dull. You ask how he died? Alas, dearest sister, he died in my arms, heroically firm and indifferent. Sometimes he exclaimed in his agony, "O God, have pity on me!" But there was no superstition or weakening at the end. He held out his hand to me, saying, "Adieu, Sire, I must leave you and there will be no return." My condi-tion the first days was frightful. I am calmer now but I am left with a deep melancholy which I shan't be able to root out yet awhile. . . . I see the only happy people on earth are those who love nobody.'

The situation between Frederick and Voltaire could not have lasted indefinitely; when Voltaire and Maupertuis fell out over the scientist Koenig things came to a head. Koenig, some years before, was supposed to have behaved treacherously to Mme du Châtelet and at that time Maupertuis took his part against Voltaire and his mistress. Now Koenig was in trouble with the Berlin Academy and its President Maupertuis for publishing what they thought was a forged letter from Leibniz; so of course Voltaire took his part, to annoy Maupertuis. It was quite unnecessary for him to enter into this quarrel: he really was a maddening guest. The King never fully understood what it was all about, but naturally felt inclined to stand by his own Academy and wrote an anonymous *Letter from a Berlin Academician to a Paris Academician* in which he referred to 'an impostor in our Academy, retailer of lies and slanders'. There was no open breach, things went on as before, but the atmosphere was wretched.

Voltaire boiled and boiled and then boiled over; he gave vent to years of poisonous feelings for Maupertuis in *Le Diatribe du Docteur Akakia*, a pamphlet making fun of the President's scientific notions. Some of these were very absurd—he wanted to bring up a group of children in silence, thinking that they would then speak the original human language and so one would know if it had been Greek or Hebrew. But others are common-place in the twentieth century. Maupertuis thought one could learn more about the nature of the soul by the study of dreams. He wanted to have different doctors for different diseases. He thought it would be possible, eventually, to go to the moon. If such ideas are really those of a President, said Voltaire, he must be President of Bedlam.

Le Diatribe du Docteur Akakia was more amusing to Voltaire's contemporaries than it is to us. He read it out to Frederick; they had the happiest evening together for months and Frederick laughed till he cried. He said it must never be published, so together they sadly pushed the manuscript into the fire. But of course *Akakia* was already in the presses and soon 30,000 copies were circulating in Paris, Berlin and Dresden. Maupertuis was stricken; he fell gravely ill and Frederick visited him with much publicity. Voltaire fled from the King's wrath, not, this time, to a royal palace but to furnished lodgings in Berlin where he in his turn fell, or so he said, gravely ill. On Christmas Eve, 1752, the public executioner burnt *Akakia* in the street under Voltaire's window. A week later Voltaire returned his Chamberlain's Key and the Cross of the order *Pour le Mérite* to the King with a pathetic letter—'You have been my idol'—in which he made it plain that he intended to leave Berlin as soon as the weather permitted. But the same day Frederick sent Fredersdorf to call on Voltaire and to give him back his insignia. They talked for a long time and Fredersdorf advised him to do nothing in a hurry but to write again to the King. Voltaire is so hard to understand. He seemed really wounded in a sincere love for Frederick; he seemed touched to the heart by what Fredersdorf said; and all the time he was writing bitter sarcasms about *le Salomon du Nord* to Mme Denis. Frederick sent him quinine for his illness, with a charming letter, full of intimate jokes, saying that he was forgiven. He invited him to Potsdam, but Voltaire said he was too ill to move. The truth is that he would already have left Berlin and shaken its dust from his feet, but money had reared its ugly head again. He had invested a fairly large sum in Prussia and could not bear to go until he had found some way of removing it. For several weeks most of his letters, very brisk and practical, were to business people; his wounded soul and broken heart were reserved for a few friends, and the wild recriminations against Frederick for his niece. He gave out that he could not leave Prussia because the King would not give permission; however, as soon as he asked for it Frederick replied: 'You can leave my service when you wish; only before you go please send me the contract of your engagement, the Key, the Cross and the volume of poetry I lent you.'

Again the whole of Europe was fascinated by Voltaire's goings-on, and the French minister in Berlin was told on no account to become involved, as Louis XV had no desire to be dragged into the affair.

Voltaire left Berlin on 26 March 1753. Frederick, for the first and last time in his life, allowed rage to take the upper hand. He wrote such terrible letters about his departed guest that two of his correspondents, Wilhelmine and Milord Maréchal, were obliged to tell him that he went too far. Wilhelmine knew from experience her brother's dreadful talent for teasing; Lord Keith was one of those on whom he never exercised it; but they both loved Frederick tenderly and both felt that in getting rid of Voltaire he was cutting off his nose to spite his face: he had lost so many friends through death and Voltaire would not be easy to replace. Lord Keith wrote to Mme Denis, as a true friend both of hers and her uncle's, suggesting that it was bad policy to quarrel with kings. In which countries could Voltaire now take refuge? He would be in danger anywhere under the rule of the Inquisition; the Turks and other Moslems were furious about his play, *Mahomet*; he was a bit old to go and settle in China. There remained France, but one word from Frederick, and the French King would send him packing. Milord Maréchal was a close friend of Louis XV and knew what he was talking about. Countess Bentinck wrote Voltaire a long, loving, scolding letter, saying, among many sensible things, that as his printed works were fulsome in praise of Frederick, the whole business made him look foolish.

One might imagine that the episode was now closed. Not at all, the worst was yet to come. Voltaire went to Leipzig on business and then stayed for a month with the Duke and Duchess of Saxe-Gotha. The Duchess was an adorable person, later to be a great friend and correspondent of Frederick's—the Saxe-Gothas were ancestors of the Prince Consort. When Voltaire left Gotha he made for Frankfurt on his way to Strasbourg where he was to meet Mme Denis.

It will be remembered that Frederick said to Voltaire, 'Go when you like, but when you do, send back your Chamberlain's Key, the Cross of *Pour le Mérite* [an order for Prussians only], your contract and the book of poetry I lent you.' Now Mme Denis had the contract and Milord Maréchal had been trying for weeks to get it from her, but she had made many specious excuses and had now left Paris for Strasbourg. Voltaire had taken the other things with him. Frederick wanted the Key and the Cross because he could not bear to think of Voltaire parading about in them, but above all he wanted his *Œuvre de Poésie*. It was not a manuscript but a book, secretly printed in a tiny edition, full of satires against Frederick's fellow rulers, and Voltaire in his present mood might easily have used it to do him mischief. Frederick himself now left Berlin for manœuvres in Silesia; he gave strict orders to Fredersdorf and to his Resident at Frankfurt, Baron von Freytag, to get back the *Œuvre* by all means in their power.

When Voltaire arrived at Frankfurt Freytag immediately called on him. He had got the Cross and the Key and handed them over, but the *Œuvre* was among his other books in a packing case at Hamburg—Freytag put him on parole not to leave his hotel, Der Goldene Loewe, until he could produce it. Mme Denis hurried to join her uncle; the people at Der Goldene Loewe were in no doubt as to their relationship and Freytag refers to her as 'the so-called niece'. She later told Voltaire that she had become pregnant by him at this time and had, or said she had, a miscarriage some months later. She now busied herself with the burgomaster, pointing out that Frankfurt was a free city where Frederick had no right to detain or arrest people. But these free cities were defenceless, and a prince with a large army at his disposal could really do as he liked within their walls.

In due course the *Œuvre* arrived and was given to Freytag; Voltaire naturally thought he

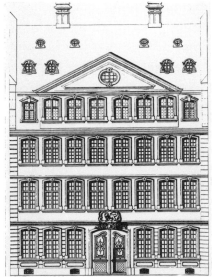

Der Goldene Loewe (The Golden Lion Inn), Frankfurt; engraving by Wicker.

would be allowed to continue his journey. But Freytag, a tremendous ass, was not quite clear about his orders; he said he must have confirmation from Berlin first. Frederick, back from his manœuvres, immediately sent word to let Voltaire go but meanwhile Voltaire had decided to escape. He and his Italian secretary Collini made off in a hackney-cab, leaving Mme Denis to follow with the luggage. Freytag, however, had a look-out who warned him at once. He commandeered the nearest carriage, caught up with Voltaire at the city gate, got into the cab with him and ordered it to go back to the hotel. Voltaire had his head out of the window, screaming all the way and telling people in the street that he had paid 1,000 *thalers* for his freedom to the King, who was now double-crossing him. When the cab stopped at the hotel he dashed out of it, pursued by Freytag. 'Kindly allow me to vomit!' He fell heaving into the gutter and tried to make himself sick by putting his hand down his throat. Collini, alarmed, lent over him: '*Mon Dieu*, are you ill?' '*Fingo*' (I pretend). A huge crowd gathered to see the fun. Der Goldene Loewe refused to take back Voltaire and his party on account of their incredible meanness, so they were all hurried off to the more modest Bockhorn. Voltaire was guarded by soldiers; Mme Denis, pretending to be frightened, gave Freytag's secretary Dorn a golden *louis* to sit in her room all night. Their great complaint, which they wrote to everybody they could think of, including Louis XV, was the expense of two hotel bills—their boxes had been left at Der Goldene Loewe and so they were still paying there. Had they but known it Freytag was keeping a strict account of everything, the cab, the soldiers and so on, and eventually took the sum from Voltaire's luggage. By every post Freytag was getting letters from Frederick saying he had never had orders to arrest Mme Denis—let them go, let them go—but the fool still hesitated because Frederick did not know that Voltaire had broken his parole. He did remove the guard. Voltaire and Mme Denis were beside themselves. They beat up a little boy Freytag had sent with a letter and Voltaire pointed a loaded pistol at Dorn. Freytag wanted to bring proceedings for these acts of violence but Frederick's orders had become too insistent to be ignored any longer and on 7 July 1753 uncle and niece took themselves off.

Frederick has been much scolded for this episode, though he was really more to blame for keeping Voltaire after the business with Hirschel had shown the impossibility of living with him, for teasing him cruelly, making him unhappy and driving him into an open quarrel with Maupertuis. What happened at Frankfurt was a muddle due to the ineptitude of Freytag. Besides, why did Voltaire take away the Key, the Cross, and the book when he had expressly been asked not to? Certainly not by mistake.

Voltaire always said '*qui plume a, guerre a*' (he who has a pen has war); he now declared war on Frederick with his pen. His account of the Frankfurt episode lost nothing in the telling: he and his niece were dragged to prison on foot through muddy streets. Mme Denis had to sleep behind a curtain of bayonets instead of a bed curtain, being raped from time to time by Dorn who sat carousing by her bed. They were told that their prison would cost 128 *écus* a day. They were robbed of everything they possessed. Then Dorn came pretending to bring back their money—he saw a pistol which was put out to be mended and said that Voltaire had tried to kill him. And a great deal more.

Milord Maréchal heard these awful tales in Paris and shuddered, though he admitted that they caused a good deal of merriment. He did what he could to put about the true version and was believed by many people: this sort of thing had happened too often to Voltaire. A typical well-to-do bourgeois of Paris, Barbier, wrote in his journal: 'This man is one of the geniuses of the age, very rich on his own account by his savings and the way he has cheated Paris booksellers; he was greatly honoured at the French court where far too much indulgence is shown to brilliant people; he now hardly knows where to go and finish his days and is despised all over the world.'

Voltaire's tales of horror having aroused more laughter than indignation, he manufactured a weapon with which to destroy the King in the eyes of posterity: *Mémoires pour Servir à la Vie de M. de Voltaire*. They are almost entirely concerned with Frederick and are a brilliant mixture of truth and falsehood, written in Voltaire's best manner—light, mocking, readable. He put them by, to be published after his own death. Those historians who are inimical to Frederick or who cannot be bothered to verify Voltaire's pronouncements have ever accepted them without question. All facets of the King's nature are invoked and belittled. Here are a few of the accusations; the present writer feels obliged to answer them.

'Frederick considered himself a literary genius.' But he was for ever saying the contrary and saying it to Voltaire: 'I love good, but I write bad verse'; 'the rough accents of my Teutonic muse disguised in French'; 'Only those who are nurtured in Paris can write elegant French.'

'Frederick was a homosexual who, owing to an injury in youth, was incapable of the manly role.' Frederick's sex life remains rather mysterious. If he was anything at all he was homosexual, but after Keyserling and Rothenburg, there was no favourite and there was never anything in the nature of a minion. The general impression one gets after reading his works and letters is of somebody less interested in sex than in friendship. Most of his entourage were happily married. The fact that he disliked the company of women means nothing—homosexuals generally delight in it. Probably Voltaire was right when he says all happened with handsome young officers—*allez-oop!*—as a matter of routine. But nobody who studies the life of Voltaire can doubt that he had homosexual tendencies and one wonders whether his feelings for the King were not exacerbated by unrequited passion?

Voltaire lays great stress on the King's miserliness. It certainly does not appear in his dealings with real friends, though when he thought that people were abusing his confidence over money he could become very tough indeed. In an often-quoted aside Voltaire says that Frederick used to watch the flogging of deserters—nobody else ever said so, and it is unlikely from all we know of him. He finally accuses the King of being a bad friend and this has stuck more than the other calumnies. An examination of the facts shows that nothing could be more untrue. He was unlucky in that the solid buttresses of his affections, as well as the volatile *beaux esprits*, all died long before he did, leaving him to a lonely old age. (Voltaire had better luck: his friends seem to have been immortal and at least two schoolmates survived him.) But few people have had more loved, loving and constant friends than Frederick the Great.

It is a pity that these two extraordinary men ever met. Their correspondence, brilliantly amusing, is full of affection for each other as well as of high-minded philosophy. Buried in the 107 volumes of Voltaire's letters, it might well be published by itself one day. But there was something about their physical contact which made the sparks fly and, as a result, the reputation of both of them has suffered.

CHAPTER FIFTEEN

The Reversal of Alliances

Life at Potsdam now became calmer if less brilliant. Frederick was worried about Wilhelmine. Her health was not good—she had the family illness. In 1753 the palace at Bayreuth burnt down, so quickly that Wilhelmine saved only her dog and her jewels. She begged Frederick to send a flute to her husband, which he did, with some music and six silk shirts. While the palace was being rebuilt, Wilhelmine and the Margrave went, via Montpellier, to Italy. Frederick, who so longed all his life to see those places, was fascinated by her accounts of them. He told her there was a tiresome rumour that she and her husband had turned Catholic; he advised her to put in a little abracadabra in the Protestant chapel of a certain Marseilles merchant and send a report to the papers. She picked laurel leaves for her brother at the tomb of Virgil. With her great love of history she enjoyed every minute of the journey, although the effort was evidently great. She was often miserably unwell, but was intent on seeing everything: her Roman diary is like that of a conscientious modern tourist. The journey did not, as had been hoped, improve her health, and she returned to her new palace as delicate as ever.

In May 1754 the Comte de Gisors, Belle-Isle's son of twenty-two, went to Berlin. Belle-Isle, racked with sciatica and unable to sit on a horse, never had another active command after the retreat from Prague but became Minister of War; his ambitions were centred on his only child who was a prodigy of charm, intelligence and virtue. Frederick received Gisors with open arms. He had always liked Belle-Isle and probably had guilty feelings about the way he had treated him; he could make amends by being kind to his boy and soon became fond of him for his own sake. He had him to dinner every day of his visit and talked only to him, mainly disserting on the art of warfare. He scolded him for going to bed too late and getting up too early, and told another Frenchman, who told Belle-Isle, that Gisors had a great future. Presently he left Berlin for Vienna and Frederick made him promise to go back for the manœuvres in Silesia. The Emperor and Empress also liked Gisors, and took him to their manœuvres at Kolin near Prague. He stayed a fortnight and then joined Frederick at Breslau. Frederick could not wait to hear all about Kolin. 'What were the troops like? How many men to a battalion? Above all, what about the artillery?' Gisors replied that there was talk of increasing the light artillery although General von Neipperg was against it.

ABOVE LEFT: *Frederick II of Prussia; painting by J. H. C. Francke.*
ABOVE RIGHT: *George II of England; painting by T. Worlidge.*
BELOW LEFT: *Maria Theresa of Austria; painting by J. É. Liotard.*
BELOW RIGHT: *Louis XV of France; painting by C. A. van Loo.*

'He only said that to you, *mon cher*', said Frederick, and told Gisors to inform his father at once: otherwise the French would find themselves at a disadvantage when facing the Austrians. It never occurred to him that a day might come when the French would no longer face the Austrians. Then he began to ask about the Empress. 'Does she caress the troops? Does she talk to the officers?' Gisors said she was affable, but he never saw her address a soldier. 'And the Emperor?' 'Most courteous—seems to see the mistakes but leaves everything to Marshal Browne.' 'Would you say it is the Empress who wears the breeches? Isn't the Emperor rather like a jolly innkeeper who lets his wife run the establish⁄

The Duc de Nivernais; engraving by James McArdell after Allan Ramsay.

ment?' Gisors lowered his eyes and said that the Empress was most attentive to her husband. At dinner the interrogation continued, Gisors rather embarrassed by the presence of Count Schaffgotsch, who had property in Bohemia and Silesia and felt more Austrian than Prussian. Frederick, by threatening to confiscate his land, was forcing him to put two of his four sons into the Prussian army; after dinner all four were lined up for the King to make his choice. The eldest looked stupid and the youngest ill, so he took the two middle ones. When Schaffgotsch was alone with Gisors he embraced him for having spoken so well of the Empress. Members of this family, one of whom was a bishop, were always a nuisance to Frederick. Later that day the King had a look at Browne's orders, which Gisors had brought. He said they were too complicated. 'Simplicity is all, in warfare.' He then came back to the Empress, saying she was more like a man than a woman. Gisors said that if she were backed up by good politicians one felt there was nothing she could not do, but her financial situation was bad. Frederick said he thought the English would not be able to support her and her bankrupt allies the Saxons much longer and that therefore if war should come 'we' (he and the French) would have nothing to fear. Frederick said good-bye to Gisors and sent him off with Field Marshal von Schwerin to look at Mollwitz before leaving for Poland and the northern capitals. He only had another four years to live and Frederick never saw him again—he always said he could forgive the French anything for having produced Gisors.

Clouds seemed to be gathering in Europe. Maria Theresa openly longed for revenge. The Empress Elizabeth of Russia, secure internally and no longer troubled with a Swedish war, was known to be inimical to Frederick, who might interfere with her designs on Poland. France and England were fighting an undeclared war, and it was essential to Prussia to be allied to one or the other. The King was flirting with England but, unsuspected by him, the French were flirting with Austria.

The next Frenchman to arrive at Berlin was the Duc de Nivernais, Gisors's father-in-law; he was sent by Louis XV to find out Frederick's intentions as to renewing the Franco-Prussian alliance. There had been a good deal of unsatisfactory correspondence on the subject between Berlin and Versailles and the silly old French Foreign Minister, Rouillé, had considerably annoyed Frederick by advising him to invade Hanover and seize George II's treasury. Louis XV was furious with Rouillé, but the harm had been done and Frederick said the French ministers seemed to have lost their wits. He never guessed that the French were even now putting the finishing touches to a treaty with Maria Theresa, the famous *Renversement des Alliances*. Although Nivernais was the great friend of Mme de Pompadour, whose cherished scheme this was, it is probable that he knew nothing of the *Renversement*, which was against all his political principles. He arrived in Berlin on 1 January 1756 and was immediately informed, to his surprise and dismay, that Frederick and George II had just signed the Treaty of Westminster by which Frederick guaranteed the neutrality of

Hanover and the English his possession of Silesia. He told Nivernais that it was a purely defensive German[1] arrangement against the Russians and that he wished to renew his treaty with France as soon as possible. Nivernais passed on all this to Versailles.

The negotiations took time, and meanwhile Frederick delighted in the company of Nivernais, a soldier (he had been with Belle-Isle in Prague), a member of the Académie française and a man of the world. He was a Mancini and had the brains and charm of that famous family. Frederick wrote and told Maupertuis that if Nivernais were his subject he would not send him on foreign missions, but keep him always at his side. It was sad to have met only to lose him again so soon. He impressed the King by talking Greek to d'Argens, Frederick trying to follow with a dictionary. No foreign nobleman since Maurice de Saxe had been so well received by the King: he was the only ambassador who ever stayed at Sans Souci. He was allowed to dine with the King's brothers, which was against the rules for diplomats, and they too did all they could to please him. Prince Henry, having heard that the Duke did not care for large dinners and having asked forty people to meet him, divided them up into tables of eight. Frederick spoke much of Gisors, and amused Nivernais by asking if his marriage had been consummated.

Nivernais wrote an account of life at Potsdam. Musical himself, he enjoys the concerts and says the King plays very well but that his own compositions are poor. His old music master Quantz doesn't mind what he says to him and is rather severe—he coughs every time he hears a mistake and this exasperates the King. Supper is more amusing than dinner, with Frederick displaying his lively wit—brilliant, teasing and aggressive; he never turns it against Nivernais. He has a most beautiful speaking voice. He is very particular that the Queen be respectfully treated but he hardly ever sees her. However, Prince Henry is not allowed to follow this example with his wife, much as he would like to do so. Nivernais does not name the company at Sans Souci, but it must have been down to the scrapings of the barrel, with d'Argens the only amusing person there. Though Milord Maréchal had left Versailles, Frederick had sent him to govern his principality of Neuchâtel. Maupertuis had been like a bear with a sore head ever since *Akakia* and was now in his native Saint-Malo. Algarotti too was at home, in Italy, writing lively letters to Frederick and sending him seeds for his garden. Nivernais gave a pen-portrait of Frederick to his brother-in-law Maurepas:

Impetuous, vain, presumptuous, scornful, restless, but also attentive, kind and easy to get on with. A friend of truth and reason. He prefers great ideas to others—likes glory and reputation but cares not a rap what his people think of him. . . . He knows himself very well but the funny thing is that he is modest about what is good in him and boastful about his shortcomings. Well aware of his faults, but more anxious to conceal than to correct them. Beautiful speaking voice. . . . I think that, both as a matter of principle and character, he is against war. He'll never allow himself to be attacked, as much from vanity as from prudence—he will find out what his enemies are

---

[1] The word Germany in its modern sense, that is, excluding the Habsburg hereditary lands, was first used in the Treaty of Westminster.

The dining-room in the rebuilt palace of Bayreuth. Frederick gave it to his sister Wilhelmine as a present.

planning and attack them suddenly before they are quite ready. Woe to them if they are not strong, and woe to him if a well-organized league should force him into a sustained effort of great length.

Nivernais strongly advised his government to renew the treaty with Frederick. He said that if they did so they would find that the Treaty of Westminster had little importance, but that if they refused Frederick would be thrown into the English camp. The advice was not heeded. Nivernais was recalled and the Marquis de Valory sent back to Berlin. Frederick told the Duke that Valory, old friend as he was, could never replace him. All the same, when he saw Valory he hugged and kissed him, saying that Nivernais must forgive two old comrades who had hardly expected to meet again. Like the Duke, Valory, who knew Frederick so well, thought he was playing a straightforward game this time; that the Treaty of Westminster was against the Russians and that Frederick ought to be allowed to renew his treaty with France. They both blamed the incompetent French minister who had replaced Tyrconnel and each said that if the other had been at Berlin the Treaty of Westminster would never have been signed. But the initiative had already been taken by Louis XV. When Maria Theresa's Ambassador to Versailles, Kaunitz, suggested a Franco-Austrian alliance the French King realized that, once he got used to it, this astonishing idea suited him very well. Frederick had twice proved a treacherous ally and had twice made a separate peace; Louis XV disliked and distrusted him. He preferred the noble Roman Catholic matron to the mocking Voltairean sodomite whose disobliging remarks about his person, his mode of life, his mistress and his army had not failed to be repeated to him. The diplomatic tables were now turned on Frederick with a vengeance.

Frederick wrote to Milord Maréchal, of Maria Theresa: 'She appoints fasts and prayers; the *venerabile* has been exposed at Vienna—doubtless God will now think twice before attacking Austria.' But in his *Histoire de la Guerre de Sept Ans* an unwilling admiration of his lifelong enemy is apparent.

> She succeeded in putting an order and economy in her country's finances which her ancestors had never achieved and her revenues exceeded those of her father even when he had owned Naples, Parma, Silesia and Serbia. She insisted on improved discipline in the army and supervised it herself; she had a particular talent for bestowing favours and for rewarding the officers in such a way that they were filled with enthusiasm. She established a military academy in Vienna and found clever professors of warfare, so that the army reached an excellence it had never known under her ancestors. This woman's achievements were those of a great man.

Maria Theresa had not wasted time after the Treaty of Aix-la-Chapelle. She had the feminine capacity for getting things done; and she had also found a first-class minister with whom she could work. Count (later Prince) von Kaunitz, having prepared the ground, as Ambassador to Louis XV, for the *Renversement des Alliances*, became Maria Theresa's Chancellor. They formed a strong team (Frederick used to say there were only two statesmen in Europe, Kaunitz and Pitt). The Empress was soon dominated by him; he treated her in a most cavalier fashion. If she spoke out of turn at a Cabinet meeting he would leave

The countryside in Saxon 'Switzerland'.

Prince von Kaunitz; painting by J. Steiner.

the room; when she ventured a remark on his immoral private life he said he was there to speak of her affairs, not his. She loved fresh air, he dreaded it; and all windows had to be shut when he was there. The Emperor disliked both him and his pro-French policy—indeed the *Renversement* was almost equally unpopular in Vienna and in Paris—but there was nothing to be done when the Empress and her Chancellor had made up their minds. Kaunitz's guiding idea was to re-establish the Austrian domination of Germany, which had weakened under Charles VI and was now threatened by the rising power of Prussia. As Maria Theresa was obsessed by her despair at the loss of Silesia, he had no difficulty in per-suading her that the treaties by which she had given it up counted for nothing.

194

William Pitt the Elder, first Earl of Chatham; painting by the studio of R. Brompton.

On 17 May 1756 the Treaty of Versailles between Louis XV and Maria Theresa was signed. France was to help Austria to retake Silesia, and in return would receive various towns in the Low Countries and the Rhineland. To begin with the Empress had every reason to congratulate herself on her new ally. In the early months of 1756 the French had beaten the English wherever they met them. They massed in Normandy as though to invade; the English were so short of troops that they begged Holland for the loan of 6,000 men; but the Dutch were themselves frightened of the French and refused. England was going through one of her periodical phases of government by mediocrity and not until the following December did the pressure of public opinion force George II to send for Pitt, a man he dreaded worse than defeat. After that the foreign policy was stabilized, summed up by the new Prime Minister: 'We shall win America on the continent of Europe'—in other words, keep the Europeans fighting among themselves for as long as possible. This was to be done by subsidizing Frederick and giving him some Hanoverian troops. As soon as it became obvious that France and Austria were going to fall upon tiny Prussia, there was the usual rush of jackals to break up the quarry. The Empress Elizabeth joined the coalition and was to receive East Prussia. Like Louis XV she hated Frederick, whose bawdy jokes about her and her lovers were repeated all over Europe. Sweden, whose Queen, Ulrica, was Frederick's sister but whose Senate was paid by France, put in for Pomerania. The Empresses Maria Theresa and Elizabeth made no secret of intense military preparations and it became evident that Prussia, with a population of five millions, would soon be obliged to fight countries whose joint populations were about a hundred millions.

Even the intrepid Frederick began to feel anxious. In July he learnt that the attack had been put off until the following spring when Austrian preparations would be complete. He summoned a meeting of his three most trusted generals, Schwerin and Retzaw, of his father's generation, and Winterfeldt, his own contemporary and his chief confidant in military affairs. He set forth all he knew about the intentions of the French King and the two Empresses, and asked for advice. The old men said, 'Remain on the defensive!' Then Winterfeldt produced proof that Augustus III was going to join forces with the Austrians, who had promised him Magdeburg in the event of victory. Now Berlin was only thirty miles from the Saxon frontier—with Saxony in enemy hands it would be impossible to defend the homeland, Brandenburg. The old generals said Frederick should attack and Winterfeldt said, 'If we have to wait until every little prince in the Empire does us the justice to admit that we are not the aggressors we shall lose the war.' Prince Henry, who was entirely opposed to the war since it brought a rupture with his beloved France, blamed Winterfeldt for this preventive policy, but Frederick had already made up his mind to attack. The English, who had lost Minorca and were anxious for the Prussians to make a diversion in Europe, sent a message to the effect that nobody could blame H.M. if he forestalled his enemies.

Sir Andrew Mitchell was now at Berlin as English Minister. None had ever been so much liked and he became one of Frederick's greatest friends. Sir Andrew was a heart-broken Scotch widower, the last sort of person one would expect to be charmed by the wayward and fantastic King, of whom he said, 'Such a mixture of delicate honour and caprice never dwelt in one breast.' For the next seven years they were hardly separated; Frederick took him to the wars as he used to take Valory, and behaved better to him. We never hear of his teasing Mitchell. At the Minister's suggestion Frederick sent a note to Maria Theresa asking to be told whether the massing of troops on his frontiers portended war. He begged that the reply might be straightforward and not as from an oracle. It came on 26 August and was utterly evasive. Two days later, calling God as his witness that, had he wanted this war, he would have attacked in the spring of 1756 with the advantage of surprise, Frederick sent an ultimatum to Augustus III demanding his neutrality and marched on Dresden.

To his wife: 'Madame, a rush of business has prevented me from writing until now; this letter is to take my leave of you, wishing you health and contentment during the troubled times ahead. I am, etc . . .'

He did not see her again for seven years.

A set of entrée dishes with the Prussian coat of arms, from a service made in China for Frederick, about 1750.

An episode in the Seven Years' War; painting by J. B. Le Paon.

CHAPTER SIXTEEN

The Seven Years' War

When Frederick crossed the Saxon border he heard that Augustus, his Minister Count von Brühl and his army had taken themselves off to the mountains near Pirna, a few miles south-east of Dresden on the road to Prague. The position was on a curiously formed peak like a sugar-loaf, which made a formidable redoubt, and although the Saxons only numbered 18,000 they would have been difficult to dislodge. Winterfeldt, who went there to see if Augustus could not be induced to resume neutrality, thought an assault was feasible (and so, later, did Napoleon, who blamed Frederick for not having tried it), but Frederick did not want to fight the Saxons. In the back of his mind there was always a hope that one day he would possess their beautiful land; so, instead of finishing them off and plunging straight into an unprepared Austria, he wasted precious time starving out the Saxon army. Augustus was allowed food for his own table; in despair at having left his art collection he collapsed into a dressing-gown or Polish robe, bombarded Maria Theresa with demands to be rescued and proclaimed to all Europe that his intentions had been pure.

In Dresden Frederick set about procuring the documents which proved that Augustus's intentions, so far from being pure, had been to join with Maria Theresa in attacking Prussia. The palace guards were replaced by Prussians who prepared to break into the archives. The Queen in person arrived and stood before the door but she was pushed aside, whether roughly or not was a matter of opinion; the door was burst open and several packing-cases labelled to Warsaw were removed. The documents were duly there and Frederick published them. But the proceeding was unwise: his enemies said the publication was a forgery; and he had infuriated crowned heads everywhere by his treatment of the Queen. She, 'small, dark, ugly beyond painting and malicious beyond expression' (Hanbury Williams), was particularly well-connected—daughter of the Emperor Joseph, sister-in-law of the Emperor Charles VII, first cousin of Maria Theresa, mother of the Queen of Spain and of the Dauphine of France. When Marie Josèphe, the Dauphine, was told how her mother had been treated she rushed unannounced into her father-in-law's room, an unheard-of proceeding, and implored him to help her parents. The result was that Louis XV, who loved Marie Josèphe, sent an army, known as *La Dauphine*, of 100,000 men to Germany instead of the 24,000 he had promised. Furthermore, Frederick could hardly now keep the title,

to which he always aspired, of the champion of German princes against the Emperor.

Maria Theresa ordered Browne, her marshal of Irish descent, to go and save Augustus and his army. Frederick marched to meet him and defeated him at Lobositz, about half-way between Prague and Dresden, with light casualties on both sides. Frederick saw that the Austrian fire-power had greatly improved in the eleven years since he had last fought against them and that their army had up-to-date equipment. In spite of Lobositz, Browne nearly rescued the Saxons; he himself led a small force to the mountains in a dashing and clever attempt to do so. He failed because the Saxons made no effort to co-operate. So Augustus was obliged to sign a treaty with Frederick. He and Brühl were allowed to go to Warsaw; the Saxon officers were put on parole, which most of them broke, never again to fight against Frederick; and the men, with eighty big guns, were taken into the Prussian army—it is hardly surprising that they proved to be its most unsatisfactory element.

Saxony was now administered and its revenues collected by Prussians. Frederick bled it white during the years to come, though not whiter than Brühl had on behalf of his master. Augustus III spent even more wildly on pictures, diamonds and baubles of every kind than his father; also Poland, far from bringing in revenue, cost a great deal of money. Hanbury Williams, who had been minister at Dresden some years before, said that Saxony writhed under taxation. Frederick at least was ashamed of himself. In 1760 he wrote to Algarotti, who knew Saxony well: 'I spared that beautiful country as far as possible but now it is utterly devastated. Miserable madmen that we are: with only a moment to live we make that moment as harsh as we can; amusing ourselves with the destruction of the masterpieces of industry and of time, we leave an odious memory of our ravages and the calamities which they cause.' The Saxons have never forgiven Frederick for the harm he did them. Dresden suffered as much damage from Prussian bombardments as during the great British air raid in 1945 — the difference is that in the eighteenth century a town could be rebuilt as beautiful as ever; now it cannot.

Frederick had not foreseen that it would take so long to reduce Augustus; it was now too late in the year to continue the campaign; so the surprise, which had been the reason for attacking first, no longer worked. But he had a solid base for his operations. He took Prince Henry to Berlin for two days to say good-bye to their mother, and then spent the winter in Dresden. Here he carried on a sort of guerrilla warfare with the Queen of Poland. She gave him Correggio's *La Notte* from Augustus's collection on hearing that he had sat gazing at it for half an hour (he must have given it back, as it still hangs at Dresden); but sausages and barrels of wine for her kitchen were found to be full of spying messages and instructions from Poland; and she was very successful in stirring up Frederick's Saxon troops against him. He called her 'the Fairy Carabosse' and heartily disliked her.

Many people thought that, since Frederick's treaty with Augustus had taken away Maria Theresa's excuse for fighting, a peaceful solution would now be found. However, as Voltaire remarked, wars generally go on for no better reason than that they have begun. He was fascinated, indeed obsessed, by this one. 'If Frederick continues to be lucky and glorious my old liking for him will be justified. If he is beaten I shall be avenged.' One is left in no doubt that Voltaire wished for the second alternative. He sent a model of an armoured vehicle he had invented to the Duc de Richelieu saying he hoped that it would serve to kill many Prussians; at the same time he wrote to Wilhelmine, 'My heart has always loved him, my spirit has always admired him—madame, madame, the King of Prussia is a great man.' All through the war he was wildly on Frederick's side in letters to the King's

The Battle of Lobositz, 1 October 1756; engraving by P. P. Benazech.

supporters and wildly against him when writing to Paris. How did he explain such contradictions to himself and how, knowing that his letters were kept and treasured, did he have the face to be so inconsistent? He was maddened by the problem of news which, at Geneva where he now lived, arrived late and was far from reliable. It came in various round-about ways and when a battle was reported there was often doubt, at first, as to who had won it. The Duchess of Saxe-Gotha and Wilhelmine were Voltaire's correspondents nearest the scene of action, since he and Frederick were still on non-writing terms. The Duchess had not yet met Frederick but she had already fallen under the spell and her letters are full of funny stories about him. Luckily for us, letter-writing was an occupation of the age. Frederick himself was never without his pen and his brother Henry shared the habit: after fighting or marching all day they would spend half the night describing its events.

In April 1757 Frederick, who knew that Maria Theresa's French and Russian allies were massing huge armies against him, decided to try and knock out the Austrians before the others were ready to take the field. The Austrian generals were quite sure that he would remain on the defensive and when a spy employed by the Queen of Poland told them his plans down to the last detail they thought them too crazy to be true and paid no attention. So to begin with Frederick had everything his own way: he found the Austrians weak and unready and he captured six large magazines in Bohemia whose supplies were more than useful to him. Then he advanced on Prague. The Austrian army was holding the heights of Žižkaberg outside the city, with Charles of Lorraine and Browne in command. They were on bad terms as Prince Charles had refused to let Browne make a sortie to prevent Schwerin's army from joining Frederick's. Frederick was beginning to know Prince Charles's methods and had taken a gamble which came off. So Schwerin arrived at midnight, 5 May, his troops very tired from forced marches. The next morning Frederick was unwell; he had been sick all night and could hardly get up on to his horse. Schwerin wanted to put the battle off for twenty-four hours, to rest his men, but Frederick thought that another Austrian army under Daun was on its way and insisted on fighting at once. He, Winterfeldt and Schwerin galloped off in different directions to see where it would be possible to attack; a place was found; Schwerin's regiment launched the assault.

The battle was extremely tough. Winterfeldt was wounded in the neck and lay uncon-scious. When he came to (blood was pouring over him as though from a tap), he found that his men were retreating and the Austrians not as yet pursuing. He shouted threats, entreaties and insults at the men but could not rally them. Schwerin appeared and gave up his second horse so that Winterfeldt could go and find a surgeon; then the old fellow seized a standard, rallied the men and led them forward—he fell, shot dead; another officer took the flag—he and yet another were killed. Both Prussians and Austrians fought heroically—the Austrian Grenadiers who survived the day had double pay thereafter. Browne's foot was shot off. When after twelve hours of fighting Prince Charles realized that the battle was lost, he had a sort of fit and became unconscious; his army streamed into Prague

La Notte; *painting by Correggio.*

The bombardment of Prague, 29–30 May 1757; engraving by P. P. Benazech.

bearing him and Browne. The victory cost Frederick dear. He lost between 12,000 and 18,000 killed or wounded and, what was very serious at this early stage of the war, 400 officers. He grieved over the loss of Schwerin 'who was worth 10,000 men'; he and Prince Henry, who had greatly distinguished himself by plunging waist-deep into a bog and storming a battery, sat together at sundown and wept for their old friend.

Thirty thousand fresh troops under James Keith were brought up and Frederick laid siege to the strongly fortified city of Prague where he knew there were enough provisions for eight weeks. He tried to take the town by all possible means and failed; after a month he decided to go and attack Marshal Daun whose presence at Kolin, about forty miles away, was making Frederick's position far from comfortable. He was much blamed afterwards, especially by his brothers, for taking this step against all advice, and he explained his reasons at some length in the *Histoire de la Guerre de Sept Ans*. They were partly political and partly strategic. He was always afraid that Uncle George the Elector of Hanover would take a different line from Uncle George the King of England and that, if the French looked like invading Hanover, the Elector, who loved that country more than anything, would declare it neutral. So Frederick wanted to be free to attack the French at once. If his gamble at Kolin had succeeded he might well have been able to end the war there and then—Austria's allies seemed to be cooling off—but if he left Daun in possession of Kolin the Battle of Prague would have been fought in vain.

On 18 June, a day which, he said, was always unlucky to him (such a fateful day it seems to be, having seen the downfall of Napoleon and the appearance of General de Gaulle), Frederick attacked Marshal Daun. He was greatly outnumbered—60,000 Austrians against 34,000 Prussians; Daun, on the heights of Kolin, was in an excellent strategic position;

and the Prussians were tired by a long march through fields of high, ripe wheat. Frederick had to let them rest for three hours before beginning the battle, which he did at 2 p.m. He said to his brothers, 'Do what you can—I shall not spare myself.' For a long time all went well with the Prussians and one by one Daun's positions were taken; but then two officers in two different parts of the battle disobeyed or misunderstood Frederick's orders, throwing out his plans and causing confusion. Daun took advantage of this new situation and soon the Prussians were in disarray. Frederick made desperate efforts to restore order. He shouted, in his curious Frenchified German: '*Aber mein Herren Generals, wollen Sie nicht attackieren? Allons, ganze Cavalerie, marche, marche.*' (But, Generals, aren't you going to attack? Come on the whole of the cavalry, quick march.) He tried to lead his Cuirassiers into action but they melted away; not until Colonel Grant, his A.D.C., asked if he intended to take the batteries by himself did he realize that the two of them were alone. He retreated, got hold of another battalion—'Dogs, would you live forever?'—but was forced to concede that a single battalion, however brave, cannot win a battle. The Austrians with their superiority of numbers made havoc of the exhausted and disorganized Prussians; only at 9 p.m. did all fighting stop. Frederick did not wait to think of his losses, which were shattering (another 400 officers, at least 13,000 men, 43 pieces of artillery and 22 standards); as soon as it was certain that there was no hope he galloped away. 'Phaeton has fallen', Prince Henry wrote to their sister Amelia, 'Phaeton has saved his own skin.' Henry and the Prince of Prussia, with loud and bitter sobs, blamed Frederick for what they thought was the downfall of their House.

Phaeton, meanwhile, accompanied by his A.D.C.s, had gone to save not his skin but his army outside Prague. When he reached it, after having made dispositions for his defeated regiments, he had been thirty-six hours in the saddle. Even so he had found time to write to Milord Maréchal on 18 June 1757:

Fortune has turned her back on me. I ought to have expected it: she is a woman and I am not gallant. Henry performed marvels. . . . What do you say to this league against the Marquis de Brandebourg? The Great Elector would be surprised to see his great-grandson fighting the Russians, the Austrians, nearly all Germany and 100,000 Frenchmen. There is little glory in defeating me.

In Prague the dying Browne implored Prince Charles to make a sortie and prevent the Prussian retreat, but he was too dilatory and too half-hearted; Frederick's rearguard easily dealt with him. As for Daun, instead of following up his victory he seemed to fear that the King would come back. By the time the two Austrian armies joined forces the Prussians had made themselves scarce.

So, at the very beginning of the war Frederick was practically knocked out and thereafter there was no time, during the next seven years, when he and his generals thought that they could prevail. The only emotion he showed after Kolin was when he saw what remained of his favourite regiment, the Lifeguards (infantry). He had known every man of it by name

LEFT: *Augustus William, Prince of Prussia; engraving by J. C. Sysang.*
RIGHT: *The Prince de Soubise; painting by an unknown artist.*

since the old days at Ruppin; hardly any were left alive. The now useless death of Schwerin, Colonel von der Goltz and so many brave men at Prague was a nagging sorrow and the future seemed black indeed.

Maria Theresa triumphed. To the end of her life 18 June was a feast and a holy day—whenever she felt depressed she remembered the Battle of Kolin. She went herself to tell the news to Daun's wife. Bounty was distributed to the army and the Order of Maria Theresa, for military merit, was struck. Now, she said, the King of Prussia will be destroyed and his lands divided. She herself would take Silesia and Glatz; the King of Poland Magdeburg and Halberstadt; the Elector Palatine Cleves, Mark and Ravensberg and the King of Sweden Prussian Pomerania.

Frederick still intended to go and fight the French. He encamped at Leitmeritz, putting the Prince of Prussia in charge of an army which was to remain in Bohemia and bar the way to Silesia. He gave him Winterfeldt to do the work and take the decisions. Now Schwerin, one of the oldest and most distinguished of German soldiers, had always acted in perfect harmony with Winterfeldt, had taken Frederick's orders from him and accepted the fact that the King confided in him alone, but the younger generals and particularly the King's brothers loathed him with a jealous loathing. Prince Henry said he was a bore and despised him for knowing no French, though he was obliged to admit that he had qualities in the field. Augustus William, in a particularly bloody-minded mood, talking loudly against his brother and writing indiscretions to Berlin, declared that he had no intention of

206

being put upon by Winterfeldt. The officers with the Prince said (which may well have been true) that Winterfeldt was not the same person since his wound.

When Daun and Prince Charles finally made up their minds to pursue the Prussians they went after Augustus William, thinking he would be easier game than Frederick. The Prince was nervous; he heard that the enemy force was immense and he kept on prudently retreating. Frederick, very angry, wrote every day trying to stiffen him, finally saying, 'If you go on like this you will find yourself in Berlin, and then what?' When he arrived in Saxony Frederick ordered him to shut himself and his army up in Zittau where there was a big magazine. Winterfeldt begged to be allowed to take a light force with which to go ahead and occupy Zittau, but the Prince would not listen to him nor follow the route which he had planned. He went by a devious way over mountains and lost all his baggage; when finally he arrived at Zittau Prince Charles had got there first and burnt it to the ground with fire-balls. Ten thousand particularly worthy and industrious citizens had perished in the flames and much horror at this deed was felt all over the Empire. The Prince of Prussia now had no provisions for his army nearer than Dresden; he left the way to Silesia wide open and made for Bautzen where he was told the King would join him. Winterfeldt went to Frederick to report on these doings.

Bad news was coming in from all sides. In a letter from his wife which she, by an extra-ordinary oversight, had sealed with red instead of black wax, Frederick learnt of the death of Sophia Dorothea. Unprepared for the shock, he was plunged into terrible grief, described

Glatz: an eighteenth-century engraving.

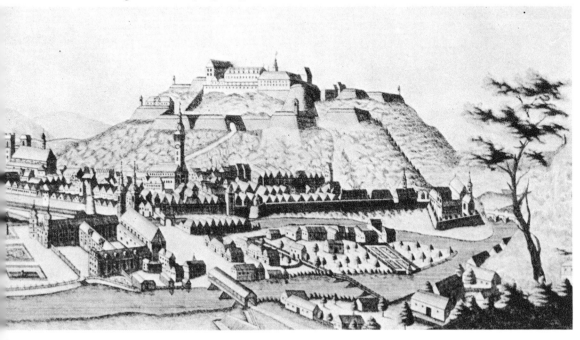

by Sir Andrew Mitchell, who was with him. He forgot how tedious the old Queen had become of late and only remembered the time when she had protected him against his father's rages and when she had seemed such a great and glamorous person. Coming on top of his other miseries, this death caused him to break down completely for two or three days. Sophia Dorothea left a wish not to be buried with her husband.

Frederick took his army to Bautzen, leaving Prince Henry at Leitmeritz with a small force to guard the magazine and a hospital full of wounded soldiers. The reliable Henry succeeded in this undertaking. On the road to Bautzen the King learnt that a Russian army had poured into East Prussia; that the Prince de Soubise, with French and Imperial troops, was advancing into Saxony and that Frederick's only ally, the Duke of Cumberland, with an Anglo-Hanoverian army, had been defeated by Maréchal d'Estrées and General de Chevert at Hastenbeck and was on the run.

Frederick and the Prince of Prussia met at 4 a.m., 29 July. As the King's party approached, Augustus William saluted and the King's retinue returned the salute, but Frederick did not. He dismounted and lay on the ground as though he were expecting somebody, with Winterfeldt and General von der Goltz sitting beside him. After a good long time the Prince and his generals were told they could approach. Goltz then read out a document to the effect that the King was displeased with H.R.H.; that he and his generals deserved a court martial which would certainly sentence them to death, but that H.M. cannot forget that the commanding officer is also his brother. The Prince demanded a court martial. The next day there was an exchange of letters, the King saying that Augustus William had done him more harm than the enemy, but that he loved him and always would. Augustus William hung about the camp for a few more days and then sent a message asking the King's permission to go to Dresden. 'He can go wherever he likes.' So he went home to Wusterhausen, blaming Winterfeldt for all his misfortunes, and made a centre for those who had real or imaginary grievances against the King.

During the next weeks Frederick tried in vain to bring the Austrians to battle, a trial for which they were not anxious. At last he decided to waste no more time. He left the greater part of his army, his best regiments and Winterfeldt under the command of his wife's cousin, the Duke of Brunswick-Bevern, with orders to defend Silesia and went off with a small force to try and clear Soubise out of Saxony. But Soubise played the same game as Daun, marched about here and there and refused to fight. Then Frederick heard that a contingent of Austrians was on its way to Berlin; he again divided his sadly diminished army and went, by a series of forced marches which killed many men from exhaustion, to save his capital. But he had been misinformed—there had only been a small raiding party at Berlin and it had gone away by the time he arrived there. Meanwhile, the Duke of Cumberland had signed a convention with the Duc de Richelieu at Kloster Zeven which engaged the Anglo-Hanoverian army to disband, leaving Richelieu free to besiege Magdeburg. There was one bonus. The Russians, having defeated a tiny but gallant Prussian contingent in

Pirna and its surrounding countryside; detail from a painting by Bernardo Bellotto.

East Prussia, were themselves defeated by their hopeless supply system and withdrew to their own country. Frederick decided that he would no longer try to defend East Prussia and he ordered his troops there to go to Stettin.

Surrounded and hugely outnumbered by French and Imperial armies, he thought there was little hope for him, and in his letters to Wilhelmine he hinted at suicide. Wilhelmine was beside herself with worry. She begged Voltaire, who by her good offices was again in correspondence with the King, to exert his influence and prevent so terrible a design, saying that she would never survive her brother. Voltaire and Prince Henry both told him that it was not the end of the world to give up some territory; many rulers had done so and been none the worse for it. Voltaire also remarked that the bigoted nations would vilify Frederick's memory if he committed such an unholy action. It seems probable that Frederick would have killed himself only if he had been captured by the enemy. Speaking of Mollwitz at about this time he said he had left the battlefield because he thought he might be taken prisoner; he had not yet got his 'little box' (of poison) which he always carried with him during the Seven Years' War. The idea of being taken alive haunted him and he left secret orders in Berlin that, if ever he were to fall into enemy hands, his brother was to assume power and above all to pay no attention to anything Frederick might say or write. He replied to Voltaire:

> Pour moi, menacé du naufrage
> Je dois, en affrontant l'orage,
> Penser, vivre et mourir en roi.

(In face of the storm and the threat of shipwreck I must think, live and die like a king.)

He had never read and written so much verse as during the months which followed Kolin. He hardly slept, and sat up all night with his books — his favourite reading at this time was Racine's *Athalie*, which he knew by heart. Much fun has been made of Frederick's poetry; his most ferocious critics are Voltaire, whose attitude to Frederick is never impartial, who uses the worst of his poetry as a weapon against him, but who also says that some of it was not at all bad; and such nineteenth-century writers as Lord Macaulay, hardly qualified to criticize eighteenth-century French verse. Light verse is one of the most difficult forms of expression — even Voltaire, who was a genius, did not always succeed with it — and anybody taking the trouble to read Frederick's must be rewarded by brilliant flashes here and there as well as an insight into the thoughts of a strange creature in an awful situation. As for his prose, when the *Histoire de la Guerre de Sept Ans* appeared, two years after his death, it was acclaimed in Paris as the work of a great French writer — Grimm said that there had been nothing comparable since Caesar's *Commentaries*. Sainte-Beuve puts him in the first rank of French writers and modern historians. His letters are certainly among the most entertaining ever written. No doubt Frederick would be recognized now as a writer had he written in German. The fact that his works are all in French has deprived him of German readers, while the French public never greatly cares for the writing of foreigners and is not

Eighteenth-century houses in Potsdam. Many exist but may be demolished in the new town planning.

much interested in German history. So the literary work of Frederick the Great has fallen into oblivion.

A little green isle in the deep, dark sea of misery was a visit to Gotha whose delightful Duchess, aged forty-seven, Frederick now met for the first time. He came to the château and had himself announced as the company was sitting down to dinner; embracing the Duke, he said he thought this was the least inconvenient way of arriving. The meeting was a pleasure to them all (the food, we know from Voltaire, would have been incomparable); Frederick and the Duchess practically fell in love—he certainly liked her better than any woman outside his own family. She was one of those who laugh and make fun of everything; she once told Frederick that a quarrel over some property with her brothers and sisters at Meiningen had ended in gales of laughter, which Frederick thought very unusual. Her Mistress of the Robes (of the Hearts, said Voltaire), Mme de Buchwald, was also a merry soul; indeed the court of Saxe-Gotha was most sunny, though for the moment the duchy was having a difficult time, with troops of every sort passing through it. Frederick said it would be worse for the Duke and Duchess if he left a force to defend them, and that, while he would always see to it that they were outside the battle area, they had better put up with temporary incursions. As a matter of fact, the Duchess was not averse from having French officers to supper occasionally—they could tell her the latest jokes and fashions from Paris. Once when she was enjoying such an evening Zieten and his Hussars put in an appearance. The guests, who thought the whole Prussian army was upon them, hurried off to rejoin their units and the party was ruined.

Frederick's pleasure in his new friend was cut short, for while he was at Gotha he heard that Winterfeldt had been killed during a small and unimportant action. The King was in no state to see anybody and had to leave without saying good-bye; nothing could have been more terrible for him than this death by which he lost his best and oldest friend and by very far his best general. The Duke of Brunswick-Bevern, now in sole charge of the army in Silesia, soon proved to be incompetent. Frederick seems to have had a premonition that Winterfeldt would be killed. When they parted, the General had asked for orders: Frederick was too much upset to give them and only said, 'Keep yourself safe, for me.'

At long last, on 5 November, Soubise gave battle at Rossbach near Leipzig, more or less forced to do so by his officers who were tired of marching about in a foreign land with much discomfort and no glory. His army, consisting of French and Imperial troops, was 41,000 strong against Frederick's 21,000. He seemed to be retreating as usual, and the Prussians had pitched their camp, when an officer came in with the news that the enemy was near at hand. Frederick gave orders; the tents collapsed all together as if somebody had pulled a string, and the army fell in. He had the advantage of surprise, since Soubise thought he was retreating; the careful reconnaissance of the land, without which he never fought a battle if he could help it, was also an element on his side. Whereas his plans were laid with minute precision Soubise seemed to have no plan at all; his infantry regiments milled to and fro getting in each other's way and hampering the cavalry. The battle, which began late in the afternoon, lasted only two hours; when darkness fell the French and Austrians were on the run, cluttering up all the roads in the neighbourhood—Soubise had given no orders in case of a retreat and it soon turned into a rout. Hundreds of prisoners were brought in to the Prussians by local peasants, including some of Frederick's own subjects from Neuchâtel. They were allowed by their charter to fight against him but even so he was rather put out. 'I see you know your charter very well!' He wrote, more in sorrow than in anger, to complain to Milord Maréchal about them. That night he slept in the nearest country house, the Schloss of Verbergen; he found it full of wounded French officers and had his bed put in a pantry so as not to disturb them.

The effect of Rossbach was prodigious. Voltaire said that German nationalism had been born on that day, thus changing the destiny of Germany. For the first time a German Protestant Prince was seen to inflict a humiliating defeat on Catholic Austria and France, eldest daughter of the Church. Frederick used to say that not even women cared any more about Calvin and Luther; he was forced to admit that he had been wrong. From now on simple folk regarded the war as a struggle for the Protestant religion, though Frederick, who regarded all religions as equally silly, could hardly see himself as a crusader. When his soldiers sang hymns before a battle he used to say, 'I don't like that—my buggers are frightened.'

George II now thought that Frederick was worth backing; he refused to ratify the Convention of Kloster Zeven and recalled Cumberland; he then asked Frederick to put Ferdinand of Brunswick in command of the Anglo-Hanoverians. Frederick did so, but not gladly. He was short of good generals, and his brother-in-law had distinguished himself wherever he had been in action. Duke Ferdinand kept the French busy in the west and they never troubled Frederick again. The English Parliament voted a million pounds for Prussia and though Frederick hoped he would not have to draw on it, this was a welcome sign that his stock was rising.

Having removed the French threat, he was at last free to go and see what was happening in Silesia, where the situation had deteriorated after the death of Winterfeldt. Frederick had told Brunswick-Bevern to keep the important town of Schweidnitz at all costs, but it had capitulated and Charles of Lorraine had collected much booty there. Then Brunswick-Bevern sheltered in Breslau, was obliged to evacuate his troops and was taken prisoner. Frederick thought he had given himself up and said if he had been in despair there was a more honourable way out. Maria Theresa magnanimously refused his ransom and sent him home. Frederick would neither answer his letters nor see him; he said he could go and govern Stettin, which he did; finally he distinguished himself there and was forgiven.

The Austrians were now in possession of Silesia and Frederick considered that unless he could drive them out immediately he could count that province lost to him for ever. He left James Keith with a small troop to keep an eye on the defeated French and took his army to

The castle at Lissa. Engraving by J. C. Richter.

the Oder by a series of forced marches (twenty-six kilometres a day). His soldiers were so much exhilarated by Rossbach that he had no desertions at all, whereas Brunswick-Bevern had lost thousands by desertion. When Frederick arrived in Silesia it seemed clear that he would have to fight Kolin all over again and, with a handful of exhausted men, attack an army twice the size of his in a strongly defended position. Charles of Lorraine and Marshal Daun had taken up winter quarters in a fortified camp at Leuthen.

On his way there Frederick picked up the remains of Brunswick-Bevern's army; the soldiers were discouraged and saddened by their recent defeats. With two days in which to pull them together, he did the thing which was so difficult for him. He turned the sun of his enormous eyes upon the men and spoke to them. They wept freely and called him Fritz; he exchanged coarse jokes with them; played upon such words as honour and patriotism; reminded each regiment of its glorious past; he issued wine to all ranks and did everything imaginable to raise their morale. Such an exhibition, as he felt it to be, had never been seen before nor would be again. The soldiers who had fought and won at Rossbach mingled with the others and told them to take heart. A French prisoner was brought in whom the King recognized as having once deserted from his army. 'What made you desert?' 'Oh, you know, the situation was so bad—' 'Tell you what,' said Frederick, 'come and fight today and if I lose we'll both desert tomorrow!'

On 5 December at sunrise, Frederick marched against the Austrians. He knew the country at Leuthen like the palm of his hand, having often held manœuvres there. Daun had only realized the day before, when the Prussians captured his bakeries, that they were upon him; he urged Prince Charles to remain on the defensive but Charles with a vast superiority of numbers thought that this was his opportunity to eliminate Frederick for ever. So he came out and faced him. Frederick advanced towards the Austrian right wing which was firmly entrenched in difficult terrain; Prince Charles sent reinforcements at the repeated request of the commander on the spot; but then Frederick led his army across the enemy's front. He was hidden from their sight by little hills; Prince Charles, on the church tower at Leuthen, failed to understand what he was doing and Daun thought he was retreating. The Imperial left was in an even stronger position than the right but it was held by Bavarian and Württemberger contingents who, owing to an old inimity for Austria, were far from reliable; when Frederick attacked many of them fled, as well as some Austrians. Now Daun had to bring his main force round to confront the Prussians; the manœuvre was too difficult— Frederick's army was probably the only one in the world which could have managed it in the time—and when the cavalry which had gone to bolster up the right finally arrived at the thick of the battle the ground was so covered with fugitives and their pursuers that it could not operate. The battle had begun at 1 p.m.; by 8 p.m. the Austrians were in full retreat; soon hundreds of prisoners were coming in and if Frederick had had two more hours of daylight he might have been able to knock out the enemy for ever.

Very late that night he arrived at the castle of Lissa, almost alone. He pushed open the front door and was startled to find the hall crowded with Austrian officers. He thought he had better put a good face on it and said, 'Good evening, gentlemen, would there be room for me here?' They could easily have captured him: they bowed deeply and took themselves off. Presently the countryside was filled with a tremendous sound: the Prussian army, accompanied by its regimental bands, was singing the Lutheran hymn *Nun danket alle Gott, mit Herzen, Mund und Händen* (Now thank we all our God, with hearts and hands and voices).

The mopping-up operations went on for another ten days. Thousands of Austrians fled into Breslau, where they soon capitulated; the remains of their army limped home, relentlessly pursued by Zieten who had had the honour of opening the battle and of fighting the last action in it. Prince Charles was relieved of his command and sent back to Brussels where, before the war, he and his dead wife had been governors of the Low Countries. He was a tragic figure, since all he cared for was soldiering and that was the end of it for him. The casualties at Leuthen were roughly: Prussians, 5,000 men; Austrians 300 officers, 21,000 soldiers, 134 guns, 59 standards; while at Breslau 13 generals, 680 officers and 18,000 soldiers were taken prisoner.

Maria Theresa was past tears. She said: 'In the end God will have pity on us and crush this monster.'

CHAPTER SEVENTEEN

Ma Soeur de Bayreuth

15 December 1757:

> Divine Marquis, now that you've been in bed for eight months and must be feeling rested, could
> you come and spend the winter with me in Silesia? I've got nobody to chat to and no resources.
> You would stay in my house in Breslau and see Bernini's mausoleum in the Cathedral. Of course
> bring Mme d'Argens if she likes.

Even the selfish d'Argens could hardly refuse such a request — he went with Mme d'Argens
and Frederick had rooms specially heated for them in all the inns on the road from Berlin.
Frederick himself was unwell, feeling the strain of eight particularly exhausting months. His
digestion was not functioning and he had become a skeleton — Voltaire heard rumours that
he was both ill and mad. He was filled with forebodings. 'If I have to face another year like
this one I only hope it will be my last.' He spent most of the time in his room; at night
he had terrible dreams. His father came to him with six soldiers who put him in irons. 'Why?'
he asked Wilhelmine. 'Because you don't love him enough.' Frederick woke up bathed in
sweat. Another time Frederick William and the Old Dessauer appeared to him. He asked
the Dessauer if he had done well. 'Yes.' 'I would rather have praise from you and my father
than all the world.'

For company at Breslau, as well as d'Argens, he had his unmarried sister Princess Amelia,
his youngest brother Ferdinand, Sir Andrew Mitchell and Captain Guichard who had
written a book on Greek and Roman warfare and whom Frederick always called Quintus
Icilius. One day the King, who was very apt to get foreign names wrong, said something
about a character in Guichard's book, the centurion Quintus Icilius. 'Quintus Caecilius',
Guichard corrected him. 'Oh indeed,' said the King, 'in that case you shall be Quintus
Icilius.' He sent for the Army List, crossed out Captain Guichard and substituted Major
Quintus Icilius. The name stuck and he was never called Guichard again. He began his
life with the King as a sort of court jester, and Frederick played so many horrid tricks on him
that at one time it seemed as if he might become a second Gundling. But he was a clever
man with a good deal of character and furthermore a first-class soldier; Frederick was soon
taking him seriously. He always teased him but in a friendly way, and they were on intimate
terms until Quintus Icilius died in 1775.

Wilhelmine; copy of a painting by Antoine Pesne.

Another new friend, who joined him at the beginning of 1758, was a Swiss, Henri de Catt. They had met two years before in Holland, where, anxious to see the picture galleries of various rich Dutchmen, Frederick had gone, in a round black wig, disguised as 'the King of Poland's first musician'. This character does not seem to have inspired much confidence in the collectors, and doors remained shut, but on his way to Utrecht in a ship he picked up Catt and they had an interesting philosophical discussion. The next day Catt learnt that this musician who was so well-informed, lively, pugnacious and sure of himself was the King of Prussia. Presently he got a letter from Potsdam saying that if he would like to renew acquaintance with the traveller who had made him so angry he would be very welcome. But Catt could not go; he was ill. 'One was kind enough to sympathize.' Now, having fallen out with his reader, Frederick remembered the young Swiss and engaged him. When he arrived the King said, 'Would you have recognized me?' 'Yes.' 'But how? I am so thin.' 'By your eyes.' He said he only asked for honesty and discretion—Eichel would see about Catt's salary. Catt was soon put in the picture.

D'Argens:

Our philosopher likes you very much—he makes up his mind about people once and for all. Don't get flustered or get involved with jokes and teasing, or seem too much interested when he talks about his family. Above all, don't criticize his writings. Never be familiar.

Mitchell:

The King likes you very much and I think you will like the post. You should talk chiefly about literature, philosophy, metaphysics and French poets, but let him do most of the talking. Only criticize his verse if he asks you to.

(Mitchell told Lord Holderness that, of all the authors he had met, the Philosopher of Sans Souci bore criticism the best.)

Frederick gave his own advice:

People will be after you the whole time to try and find out what I am saying. The A.D.C.s are all right but one is jealous, another bloody-minded and the third discontented and gloomy. If they make trouble you must tell me. Don't lend them money or gamble with them or go to their wild parties if you can help it. Mitchell is perfect.

He asked what impression he had made at their first meeting. Catt said he had thought he must be a French nobleman. Almost at once he was faced with a tricky situation. Frederick had been making unkind fun of Quintus Icilius and asked Catt what he thought of the absurd Major.

Catt said he seemed learned. 'Yes, but he has no *usage du monde*.' 'But Your Majesty, who loves letters, ought to be indulgent to behaviour which is not exactly that of high society.' Frederick went off at a tangent but no doubt felt the rebuke, as he always would when Catt scolded him. 'The greatest genius', he said, 'is useless without virtue and good character—it is but sounding brass and tinkling cymbals (you see, I know the Scriptures). The world has never seen a greater genius than Voltaire, but I have a sovereign contempt for him because he is not honest.' Then he showed Catt how to dance a minuet, saying he wished Daun and Prince Charles could see them now. Catt, who was a prig and had no sense of humour, felt sorry that the King should make such a fool of himself. But he came to love Frederick very much and his account of the next few years spent in his company throws a good deal of light on the nature of the King. When Catt became engaged to a girl in Berlin, Frederick told d'Argens that it seemed madness. D'Argens said he couldn't live without his wife. Then the King wrote love poems for Catt to give his fiancée, as though they were his own.

After two such smashing victories in the field, Frederick hoped that Mme de Pompadour, whom he affected to regard as all-powerful in France, and her great new friend Maria Theresa would be induced to make peace. One of his ways of teasing the Empress was by mocking at her alliance with the immoral Louis XV and his 'Sultana'; he composed and broadcast a letter purporting to be from Maria Theresa to Mme de Pompadour in which she called her 'cousin'; it was such a brilliant forgery that quite reputable historians, taking into account neither Maria Theresa's character nor the usage of those days, have quoted it as if it were genuine. But although she never wrote to Mme de Pompadour she sent her an escritoire mounted in real gold and kept in close touch with her through the ambassadors. So far from thinking of peace the two ladies urged each other to make greater efforts to crush the monster; in any case Louis XV would have thought it dishonourable to abandon his new ally after only one campaign. It became evident to Frederick that he would have to face another difficult year.

By March 1758 he had got his army up to strength again and on the 14th he and Field Marshal Keith left Breslau and went off to besiege Schweidnitz, the last strong place held by the Austrians in Silesia. During such sieges and indeed always while campaigning, Frederick moved about incessantly in the surrounding countryside, talking to the people, the gentry and the priests. When in Bohemia he would take a book of Czech phrases with him, though it was easier to ask questions than to understand the replies. Catt always went with him for company when the day's work was done. It took about five weeks for Schweid-nitz to fall and then he turned his attention to Olmütz in Moravia; when he had taken it he planned to march on Vienna. Daun had expected him to attack Bohemia and had spent the winter preparing to meet him there. The siege of Olmütz gave rise to anxiety in Vienna but Daun made no effort to relieve the town—he camped two days' march from it and waited. It did not fall as soon as Frederick had hoped; the siege dragged on and still Daun did nothing. On 16 June Frederick told Catt that the 18th was the day he always dreaded. He had dreamt that he saw his father with Wilhelmine and Augustus William, telling them to go on ahead. On the 18th a messenger from Berlin informed him that the Prince of Prussia had died. 'What of?' 'Of bitter grief' (*aus Gram*) was the reply. Frederick turned away. (But at the post-mortem the Prince was found to have a tumour on the brain.) Later Catt found

Stone sphinxes erected by Prince Henry in the garden at Rheinsberg. They are reputed to be Mme de Pompadour (left) and the Empress Maria Theresa.

the King in his tent bathed in tears, and they wept together, Frederick saying that he feared Catt had but a sad life with him. He told Wilhelmine that Augustus William had made things very difficult for him, but that it was probably more the fault of his entourage than his own. He added that if anything should happen to her he would have no desire to go on living. Prince Henry had always taken the side of Augustus William, who had cursed Winterfeldt almost with his dying breath; cold letters passed between him and the King, whose treatment of their brother had fed the hatred that Henry always half felt for him. The heir to the throne was Augustus William's eldest son, Frederick William, who became Prince of Prussia.

The King now suffered a severe military reverse. A convoy of 4,000 supply-wagons, on which he had counted, was wiped out by General Loudon and over 2,000 of Zieten's men guarding it were killed. Frederick's plans for 1758 collapsed and he had to rethink his campaign. He immediately raised the siege of Olmütz. It was typical of him that, from having been in black despair, his spirits rose as soon as he had taken this decision and anybody would have thought he had just won a battle. He had altered a few verses from Racine's *Athalie*, substituting the pious Empress for the impious queen:

> *Daigne, daigne, mon Dieu, sur Mathan et sur elle*
> *Répandre cet esprit d'imprudence et d'erreur*
> *De la chute des rois funestes l'avant-coureur*

(Deign, O God, to fill her and Mathan with that spirit of rashness and error which presages the downfall of disastrous kings) became *Daigne, daigne, mon Dieu, sur Kaunitz et sur elle*, and so on, and whenever he said *Daigne, daigne, mon Dieu* Catt knew that he was in a good mood.

He did so now and gave out that any officer who looked gloomy would be cashiered there and then; in a very short time he was on the march. The movement of a whole army, covering forty miles of a single road, gave Daun a superb opportunity to attack, but he was too cautious and Frederick settled unmolested into Königgrätz where he knew he would be safe. He took stock of the situation. The news from the west was good: Ferdinand of Brunswick had inflicted a severe defeat on the French at Krefeld, where the charming Gisors fell, and the English were now performing marvels against them in North America. But the Russians under Marshal Fermor had taken East Prussia and forced the citizens of Königsberg to swear fealty to the Empress Elizabeth. Frederick never forgave them and never again set foot there. Fermor was slowly but surely advancing towards the Oder, and such appalling tales of Russian atrocities were coming in that the whole of Europe trembled.

Frederick marched north and at the end of August he arrived at Küstrin where he met Fermor with about equal numbers. He could have reduced him and forced him to leave Brandenburg without fighting a battle; but as usual he was in a hurry: he wanted to get back to Silesia. Also, in spite of the warnings of James Keith, who was for ever telling Frederick that the Russians were incomparable soldiers, he thought they were a disorganized horde, good for terrorizing civilians but useless in the face of a highly trained army. He attacked Fermor at Zorndorf, near Küstrin; there was a particularly bloody engagement and although Frederick counted it as a victory it was an incomplete one—the Russians fought with obstinate heroism and refused to admit defeat, remained on the field and fought again the next day. The Prussians lost about 11,000 men and Fermor 20,000 but he was driven off only as far as Landsberg, where he remained and might have reorganized his army, had not the usual problems of supply sent him back to Russia. The Prussians were exhausted and demoralized, and certain regiments which had not fought too well were badly treated by Frederick to the end of his life. 'They ran away like tarts', he said. Another cause for worry was that the Swedes, under Count Hamilton, were doing better than usual in Pomerania where they were soon to be checked, however, by mutinies.

Henri de Catt had been told to stay behind in Saxony but he had doggedly followed the King. When he caught up with him Frederick's entourage strongly advised him to go away again: 'He is in a frightful temper and you are not supposed to be of this journey.' Catt calmly went in to the King, who was touchingly pleased to see him but said there were no carriages and he would have to ride, which he did. He joined in the Battle of Zorndorf on his nag; he was told that half-way through the King had asked if anybody had seen him and if he was all right. For the next few days he and Frederick stayed at Tamsel, the house of Frederick's old love Mme de Wreech. The Russians had been there and left it in an appalling state; a dead woman, horribly mutilated, lay by the front door and the contents of the house had been smashed or burnt. Mme de Wreech had fled to Berlin; Frederick sent her a little money and received in return a flood of begging letters. He answered every one in his own hand but said he could do no more for her: 'We are all in the same case'. He was so hard

The siege of Schweidnitz, 1758; engraving after P. P. Benazech.

pushed now that he was reluctantly obliged to draw the first £200,000 on his loan from the English.

Altogether things looked bad for Frederick. He turned south to meet Prince Henry whom he had left to defend Saxony. Henry was thirty-two and beginning to show that he was a remarkable soldier. He had done wonderfully well with the small force at his disposal, and Dresden, which had been threatened by Daun, was safe; they dined together there and the King said that nothing so cheerful had happened to him for months. Henry was quite friendly again and the brothers united by a new worry—Wilhelmine was desperately ill. 'Remember', Frederick wrote to Henry, 'that I was born and brought up with my sister Bayreuth, that these first attachments are indissoluble, that the tenderness between us has never changed and that though we have separate bodies we have but one soul.' His letters to her at this time are heart-rending—they beg and implore her not to desert him: 'My life without you would be unbearable and that is the truth.' Dead tired, Wilhelmine could no longer write herself; her sad little letters are dictated: 'I live and die content if I know that you are happy.'

The Austrians were everywhere in Silesia, living off the country and besieging Neisse and Kosel. Frederick wanted to relieve Neisse but Daun was hanging about near Dresden, encamped in a strong place, and refusing an engagement as usual. Frederick used to say Daun must have been born on a mountain—he had but to see one to rush up it and stay there. For about a month there was nothing to be done but wait and watch—very bad for Frederick's nerves. At last he decided to be off, followed by the Austrian army. He could

The siege of Olmütz, 1758; engraving.

see it from a village called Hochkirch on a hill surrounded by forest. There he camped. His generals told him he had chosen a poor position. They might have saved their breath: he never listened to them and never in his life called a council of war. The favoured Field Marshal Keith arrived the next day and spoke out: 'If the Austrians let us stay here, they deserve to be hanged.' Frederick only laughed and said he hoped they were more frightened of him than of the gallows. Daun had never attacked him yet and the King had begun to think he never would do so.

But as the church clock at Hochkirch struck five on 14 October 1758, the Imperial troops fell upon the Prussians and began to massacre them in their tents. It was pitch-dark, until the Austrians lit up the scene by setting fire to the village, and the utmost confusion reigned. James Keith, Frederick's brother-in-law Francis of Brunswick, five other generals and more than a quarter of the army were killed; 101 guns and most of the tents were captured. Frederick, disdaining to sound the retreat, extricated his remaining troops almost single-handed, re-formed them in perfect order and killed some 6,000 Austrians, who also lost at least 2,000 deserters in the woods. Then, while Daun was trying to decide on his next move, Frederick had got between him and Silesia. Daun made for Dresden—Frederick was again too quick for him. He had once more mitigated the effects of a defeat by his extraordinary presence of mind, courage and energy.

The Austrians celebrated Hochkirch as a total victory and Pope Clement XIII blessed a sword and a hat and sent them to Daun, a reward which the early Popes bestowed on generals who had defeated the Infidel. (His predecessor Benedict XIV, who had just died,

General von Loudon; painting by J. Steiner.

would not have made such a fool of himself.) For Frederick there was above all the sorrow of losing Keith. But all sorrows and all defeats were as nothing to him now; he was brought to the very depths by the bitterest grief of his whole life. On the day of Hochkirch, Wilhelmine died. The news arrived as he was finishing a letter to Prince Henry—'*grand Dieu, ma sœur de Bayreuth!*' Between marches and renewed attempts to bring the Austrians to battle before the winter he would shut himself up in the dark, keeping Catt always with him. Prince Henry came and was a comfort; but he, Ferdinand and Amelia were so much younger that they seemed to belong to a different family—they had not shared the strains and stresses of Frederick's childhood and could not take the place of Wilhelmine. Besides he must have known that Henry's love for him was uneasy. After the death of his sister, the King changed very much; he lost a great deal of his buoyancy and never cared for society again. 'I, who used to be as frisky as a young horse bounding in a field, have become as slow as old Nestor, greying, eaten with grief, riddled with infirmities, just about fit to be thrown to the dogs.' He told Mme de Camas that like all old people he no longer ate any supper— only a cup of chocolate. 'You will hardly know me, my hair is grey, my teeth are falling out, my face is wrinkled like the furbelow of a skirt, my back bent like a bow and my outlook as sad as that of a Trappist monk.'

In November, after long freezing days in the saddle, Frederick fell ill with a high fever and red patches on his hands and face. Catt begged him to continue the march in a carriage. 'In a carriage! What an idea! I'm not an old lady, you know, and then what would my army say if it saw *le Monsieur* taking it easy in a carriage? What an example for my officers! — they would start pampering themselves for the least little thing.' General von Zastrow then came to see how the King was and also urged him to drive. 'You take me for an old whore', said Frederick. At daybreak on a freezing morning he was up on his horse again, saying he had never felt so cold in his life; very ill that night with such an appalling headache that he could not attend to business; much better the next day and back on his horse, and thereafter cured. These attacks became more and more frequent; he always treated them in the same way unless he was so helpless with rheumatism or gout that he had to be carried. He had no faith whatever in physicians — 'the impotent witnesses of our sufferings' — and Catt used to bore him by saying and repeating how odd it was that he had no doctor.

He stayed at Dresden for three weeks that winter, and never went out of doors. The Queen of Poland had died, killed, it was said, by his evil treatment of her, so he lived in the palace and enjoyed the pictures, spending sometimes five hours on end in the gallery. He had

Porcelain soldiers from a set presented by Frederick to the Tsarevich Peter of Russia and made by J. J. Kändler of Meissen, 1740–45.

begun to write his *Histoire de la Guerre de Sept Ans* and the *Épître* to his sister. He thought and spoke of her continually—grief, he said, rode with him wherever he was. Catt, himself religious, thought that the King instinctively believed in a future life and had to force himself not to do so. 'Perhaps I shall see her again, and my brother and my mother whom I loved so much, and all the great men of antiquity I have so much admired—and if we don't believe in Providence how can anything be explained?' But when the full force of his sorrow was abated he relapsed into his old ways, making naughty jokes about religion to Catt, who took them calmly saying, 'One day you will believe—it will happen all of a sudden.' In December he went into winter quarters at Breslau. He was still the master of Saxony and Silesia in spite of Daun's holy hat and sword. Frederick called him the 'blessed one' and said if he had had a *toque bénite* he would have won the war by now—God seemed to have heard his prayer: *Daigne, daigne, mon Dieu, sur Kaunitz et sur elle* . . .

*A ribbon commemorating Frederick's
victory at the Battle of Leuthen.*

Prince Henry of Prussia; painting by Anton Graff.

CHAPTER EIGHTEEN

The Great Frederick

The year 1759 must have been the worst that Frederick ever knew. He was ill, he was sad, he said himself that he was tired of life and that were it not for honour he would have committed suicide long ago. Almost all the people he had loved were dead, as well as his marvellous veterans. His army now consisted of green recruits whom he got where he could; some of his officers were only fifteen years old. Like Mme de Maintenon and the Duke of Wellington, he said he hoped they would frighten the enemy as much as they frightened him. These less disciplined soldiers were much rougher with the civilians than their predecessors had been, and Frederick and Prince Henry, both more humane and sensitive than formerly, expended themselves in trying to make them behave. The peasants suffered horribly in this war. Much of their produce was stolen as a matter of course and their crops were trampled; worst of all, their houses were burnt to make bivouac fires. They never failed to assemble heaps of logs for the purpose but after an exhausting day the soldiers found it easier to set fire to a house and sit round that—it burnt quicker, gave out more heat and lasted longer. Of course they were absolutely forbidden to do this; and Frederick reckoned that his soldiers had not burnt more than 1,000 houses, whereas the Russians had burnt 15,000. The Prussians were not cruel for the sake of cruelty—the Austrians and especially the Hungarians were far worse. They had a wicked habit of slitting up the peasants' beds and scattering the feathers, which had taken years to collect, so that the owners were left without the only comfortable thing they had in life. Even the Austrians were appalled by the behaviour of their allies the Russians: they committed every atrocity under the sun and raped everybody, including the Burgomaster of Beuthen, whose wife said she really thought they might stick to women.

Frederick began to be very hard on his generals, almost unbearably sarcastic. 'Attack, as I do', was his perpetual cry. Easier said than done: the only generals he now had capable of carrying out a difficult enterprise on their own were Ferdinand of Brunswick, tied down on the French front, and Prince Henry, of whom Frederick used to say, 'He is the only one of us who has never made a mistake.' Henry did not return the compliment. His temperament and talents were defensive and he affected to regard his brother as a mad gambler who might at any moment lose all by some ill-considered action. He said that Frederick's victories had

Frederick; painting by J. G. Ziesenis.

nothing to do with his generalship but were due to the perfection of their father's army. (But Napoleon said it was not the army that defended Prussia for seven years against the three European powers, it was Frederick the Great.) Among the higher ranks at Henry's H.Q. it was the fashion to decry Frederick and all his works, although Catt, who spent some weeks there, said the younger serving officers worshipped him.

In France the Duc de Choiseul who was now at the head of affairs pursued the war with more energy than his predecessor, Cardinal de Bernis; born a Lorrainer, his loyalties were divided between France and the Empire, and nobody was more faithful than he to the new alliance. The separate peace which Frederick had hoped to make with the French King was now out of the question; on the contrary a new and more binding treaty was signed by Louis XV and Maria Theresa. The English were proving half-hearted allies. They paid the promised money: that was all. Frederick asked for ships to be sent to the Baltic, but they were busy elsewhere. He became rather cold to Mitchell, who was seen one day by Prussian generals going off to his own tent at the King's dinner-time, sadly remarking 'no fleet, no dinner'. They told Frederick, who laughed very much and sent for him. At the Porte, where Frederick was hoping to stir up the Sultan to open another front with the Austrians, the English Ambassador did everything in his power to undermine this policy.

The campaign started late. The Russians under a new general, Soltikoff, were rolling back towards Brandenburg while Frederick, as usual, was trying to come to grips with Daun. It was not until August that Daun sent a force under the excellent General Loudon, who had served ten years in the Russian army and spoke the language, to join Soltikoff; once more Frederick left Prince Henry to play the watch-dog and hastened north-east. There was a heat-wave; the men were sometimes short of food and generally short of water; they hated such marches worse than a battle—the last, over the burning, shifty, sandy soil of Brandenburg was a nightmare. The King had not slept for a week. He was too late to stop Loudon from joining forces with the Russians at Frankfurt-on-Oder. The Allies were not on happy terms. Although Loudon had the cavalry which the Russians needed, Soltikoff covered him with insults and reproaches because he had not brought food. The Russian commissariat was as usual disorganized, and although the soldiers had stolen everything in sight they were still half starved. Soltikoff had been on the point of going home again when the Austrians appeared.

Frederick had 50,000 men against 68,000 of the Allies. At the beginning of the war that would have meant nothing; now he doubted if they could win a pitched battle. However, an Austrian corps under General Haddik was advancing on Berlin, obliging Frederick to attack the Russians—he said a soul in purgatory was not in a worse situation than he.

One can hardly bear to read about the Battle of Kunersdorf, 12 August 1759. All the circumstances were against the King. His soldiers had been up for two nights with hardly anything to eat, moving the heavy artillery. The terrain, unfamiliar to him, favoured the enemy. Loudon was a better general than any of Frederick's. The courage of the Russians was equal to their barbarism, as he had already noted. Nevertheless, the battle started well for the Prussians who, fighting like fresh troops, overcame the Russian left and took seventy guns. Frederick sent word to his wife in Berlin that the day was won. After three more heroic attacks which dislodged the Russians from their prepared positions, Frederick's generals told him that the men were done for and urged him to disengage; after the fourth attack they implored him to do so, but only one more hillock, surmounted by a battery, remained to be taken in order for the victory to be total. It was not in Frederick's nature to stop at such a moment. When he was about two hundred yards from the crest Loudon arrived there with his Grenadiers and repulsed the Prussians. Frederick ordered the artillery

Sir Andrew Mitchell; painting by an unknown artist.

to advance but the guns stuck in the sandy soil. Then the King himself led the cavalry up the hill: 'Boys, don't leave me, don't desert me.' They did not, but it was murder. His best remaining cavalrymen were almost wiped out, all for nothing. Loudon counter-attacked; the Prussian infantry, which had now been under fire for fifteen hours, still held firm, but then he returned to the charge with fresh troops who carried all before them. Half Frederick's army lay dead and dying on the field. He himself did everything he could to be killed—two horses were shot under him, his clothes were torn and a snuff-box in his pocket was pulverized. 'Won't some damned bullet finish me?' But he was unhurt and a few devoted Hussars dragged him from the battlefield. He seemed like a sleep-walker and very soon fell under a haystack where hours later he and his escort were found, all snoring.

Everybody supposed that the Allies would now occupy Berlin and seize the whole of Brandenburg. Frederick placed himself, with six depleted battalions, in a country house at Fürstenwalde between the enemy and the capital and here he shut himself up for two days, giving out that he was gravely ill. He handed over his command to General von Finck, made his officers swear allegiance to his heir, the Prince of Prussia, and appointed Prince Henry as Commander-in-Chief of the army. He sent word that the Queen must take his archives, go to Potsdam or Brandenburg and there await events; he even found time to write to d'Argens in Berlin with the same instructions. Obviously he was contemplating suicide; what prevented him may well have been a brave, sensible letter from d'Argens, who said that he would not budge as long as the King was alive and well, but that indescribable horrors would befall his subjects if anything should happen to him. Caesar, Turenne and Condé had all been in a similar case—Frederick must take a long view, and in the end things would turn his way. If he died now he would be blamed everlastingly for the ruin of his country. Two days later Frederick replied, saying that the enemy seemed to be retreating to Frankfurt-on-Oder and he would love to see d'Argens—would he come and bring Frederick's cook, Noël, with him? But on the same day he sent another note; 'Daun is marching on Berlin—I forbid you to come; leave my unhappy country at once. The troops are utterly discouraged; I shall give them *eau-de-vie* and hope to die sword in hand.'

But days went by and the enemy did nothing to follow up the victory. 'They applaud their success', Frederick said, 'and bless their good luck instead of giving the *coup de grâce*.' His spirits began to rise. At the Allied headquarters a furious quarrel was going on, the Russians saying that the Austrians had left them to bear the worst of the fight and threatening to go home unless they were immediately given money and ammunition; but Maria Theresa was short of both. The Allies finally made for Silesia. Frederick, pulling himself and the remains of his army together, managed to bar the way; soon the Russians were going home for the winter. Daun besieged Dresden whose tiny garrison soon surrendered; then he shut himself up there. In Vienna, where the news of Frederick's final knock-out had been expected hourly, the disappointment was intense; Daun's stocks were so low that his wife dared not leave her house.

Frederick spent the winter at Freiberg in Saxony and busied himself vainly making overtures for peace to all the allies of Maria Theresa. He scraped together a new army of 100,000 men, composed, he admitted, of untrained Saxon peasants, deserters from the enemy and every sort of riff-raff. He said it was more for show than anything else. He was in a mood of black despair. 'My soul is anxious, agitated, overwhelmed.' As always he turned for comfort to books and the post-bag. 'Do write', he said to his friends. D'Argens's letters were full of encouragement. He had heard from Paris that the French had lost Quebec and were more utterly ruined than during the blackest days of Louis XIV. They would surely be unable to give the Empress money to pay her barbarians and there would be peace in the spring. Frederick asked him to go to Sans Souci and have a look at the garden. 'I feel so old, so ill, so utterly discouraged.' He was writing regularly to Voltaire now and this caused some anxiety to Mitchell:

for I believe the court of France make use of the artful pen of Voltaire to draw secrets from the King of Prussia, and when that Prince writes as a wit to a wit he is capable of great indiscretions. But what surprises me still more is that whenever Voltaire's name is mentioned, his Prussian Majesty never fails to give him the epithets he may deserve which are 'the worst heart and greatest rascal now living'—yet with all this he continues to correspond with him. Such, in this Prince, is the lust of praise from a great and elegant writer; in which, however, he will at last be the dupe: for, by what I hear of Voltaire's character, he may dissemble but never can or will forgive the King of Prussia for what has passed between them.

The English did not want Frederick to make peace with Versailles until the French were willing to give up all pretensions to 'the land of the cod and the beaver' (Canada). Though he launched a few tentative overtures to be passed on to Choiseul by Voltaire, he always said he would not make peace without the consent of the English and he certainly divulged no secrets. The correspondence at this time still consisted mostly of Voltaire scolding away about the occurrences at Frankfurt, with Frederick good-naturedly putting his own side of the affair. But he got tired of Mme Denis and her alleged sufferings: 'Let me hear no more of this niece who bores me and who has not, like her uncle, got the qualities of her faults. People still speak of Molière's cook, but nobody will remember Voltaire's niece.'

Qualified observers thought it improbable that Frederick and his army could survive the campaign of 1760 and he himself would not have betted very much on it. He had a shock when a Prussian force under General von Finck, which he had sent in pursuit of the enemy near Maxen, laid down its arms without firing a shot. Prince Henry and his set said it was Frederick's fault for giving Finck an impossible task, but many people saw it as the beginning of Prussian demoralization. 'The whole *boutique* is going to the devil', Frederick said. Daun, from the vantage-point of Dresden, was determined to conquer Saxony; the Russian tidal wave was again pounding towards Berlin and Loudon was waiting to join another Russian army in Silesia with only Prince Henry and an army well under strength to prevent him. Frederick tried in vain to retake Dresden and, in a desperate mood now, his

The Kreuzkirche, Dresden; etching by Bernardo Bellotto. The tower collapsed during the rebuilding of the church after the Prussian bombardment, 1760.

back to the wall, he subjected the town to a cruel bombardment which shocked the civilized world. In vain. Then he heard that Glatz had fallen to Loudon. He said he would be crushed either that month or the next and it mattered not which. 'God is on the side of the big battalions.' Sir Andrew Mitchell burnt his papers; the end seemed near.

Frederick was so ill from gout and haemorrhoids that he had to be carried about 'like a sacred relic', but he was on the move the whole summer. As always with him there were moments of jollity. He passed through Meissen where the workmen at the china factory were very fond of him—they came out and serenaded him with their band. He designed a dinner service for d'Argens, with four dozen of everything, and sent presents to Mme de Camas, Fouqué and other old friends. Prince Henry was still gallantly harrying the huge Russian army in the east of Silesia. As usual they were disorganized; the wretched soldiers used even to go to the Prussian camp to beg a little bread. Their atrocities were so appalling that Frederick wrote to Loudon about them, but the depopulation of a country which paid taxes to him suited the Austrians and they made no attempt to control their ally.

In August Breslau was besieged by Loudon; Soltikoff, who was to meet him there, was already on his way. Frederick's commander Tauentzien had only 4,000 men and was encumbered by 9,000 Austrian prisoners; the town was difficult to defend. Loudon sent a message to say better surrender before the barbarians arrive. When this bore no fruit he sent another: if Tauentzien persisted in his obstinacy Loudon would be obliged to put the whole population to the sword, not even sparing the child in its mother's womb. Tauentzien replied that he was not pregnant. He thought that all these threats probably meant that Loudon was short of ammunition. Training his own guns on the Austrian camp he scored a direct hit on Loudon's sitting-room, and had the great satisfaction the next morning of seeing that the enemy had vanished. Henry, having marched ninety miles in three days, was upon him, preventing a junction with the hungry Russians. When Tauentzien died thirty years later he was buried on the ramparts of Breslau.

On 1 August Frederick, knowing nothing of all this, left Meissen to try and relieve Breslau. He was preceded and followed by Daun and his colleague Lacy, so that the Austrians and Prussians looked from afar like one huge army. The whole enterprise seemed hopeless enough at the beginning; when he arrived at Liegnitz to find that Daun, Lacy, Loudon and Soltikoff were waiting for him with their armies it looked desperate. His generals told Mitchell that they only had provisions for four days. Frederick's camp was in the country outside Liegnitz. On 13 August a drunken Irishman who, with some grudge against the Austrians, had deserted from them, reeled up to the King's tent and insisted on an audience. It took some time to sober him enough to make him coherent—they gave him gallons of tea and several enemas—but what he wanted to tell the King was that Daun was going to attack him that night. So Frederick quietly moved his soldiers from the camp, leaving peasants to keep the fires burning and a few drummers to make the usual noises, and slept, with the men, in open fields beneath a beautiful starry sky. At daybreak the whole Austrian army under Daun and Loudon launched an attack on the camp he had just left. Loudon was supposed to capture the supply-wagons while Daun was massacring the main army. But he found nobody to massacre; Frederick fell on Loudon's flank, put 6,000 men out of action and took 4,000 prisoners. When Daun tried to go to Loudon's rescue he was foiled by Zieten and was unable to form in order of battle. Then he realized the extent of Loudon's defeat and abandoned the field.

Frederick survived this battle by a miracle—enemy soldiers shot at him point-blank, his horse was killed and his clothes were torn. The men spent the night clearing the battle-field, assembling the prisoners, putting the wounded into wagons and packing up the booty. Early next morning, in a heat-wave, they were on the march—everybody, even the King and his generals, on foot, so that the slightly wounded could ride. With his handful of exhausted men Frederick put himself between the vast Russian and Austrian armies, and they dared not attack him. The Russians retreated across the Oder, Soltikoff in the usual rage against Daun, and Prince Henry sent his troops to join his brother's army.

Henry himself retired to Glogau and sulked for several months. He had differed from Frederick over strategy and thought himself ill-used. He had played a brilliant part in the

Frederick writing dispatches in a church after the Battle of Torgau; painting by C. B. Rode.

campaign with the slender means at his disposal (as Frederick was the first to recognize); now with their two armies joined he would be under his brother's command: it was more than he could endure. Not until the following April did he appear at Frederick's H.Q., when he was again given a separate command and told to stand on the defensive in Saxony. As usual when Henry tried to pick a quarrel Frederick behaved as if nothing had happened. He wrote lovingly to his brother the whole winter and, in May, wrote to Princess Amelia: 'Henry performs the impossible. I must say I truly love him. He has wit and ability, both very rare. I depend upon him.'

In October 1760, 30,000 Russians at the gates of Berlin were repulsed, according to d'Argens who was there, by the citizens and two old, wounded generals in a battle that went on for five days. Finally, the city had to capitulate and was occupied by Russian and Austrian troops. Greatly to everybody's surprise the Russians, especially the Cossacks, behaved in a perfectly civilized way, while the Austrians committed every crime and horror under the sun. Things would have been even worse had not a worthy republican, the Dutch minister Vanderelst, made strong representations to the Allied generals. D'Argens said it would be impossible to praise the people too much; he always stressed in his letters how splendid the Berliners were—their one thought was for the King. He reassured Frederick about his houses: no damage at Sans Souci or the Potsdam town palace, where Prince Esterhazy was quartered and had taken away no more than a pen, as a souvenir of the Great King. But Charlottenburg was sacked and many pictures stolen, though mercifully not the *Enseigne de Gersaint*. Cardinal de Polignac's antiques were smashed but it would be quite easy to mend them again. (Frederick heard that all this damage as well as a filthy mess in the palace had been the work of Saxons.) The Austrians were levying enormous contributions, but the city fathers, particularly the rich and honourable Gotzkowski, seemed to have found a way of paying them. As soon as the enemy thought that Frederick was marching towards Berlin they left the town. Frederick, in the middle of all these anxieties, told d'Argens to go and see Gotzkowski's pictures which he had heard were very fine. What were they? Answer: a superb collection, including a Titian and a Raphael he had smuggled out of Rome. Gotzkowski owned a china factory which Frederick bought from him after the war.

On 3 November Frederick, with 44,000 men, defeated Daun with 50,000 at Torgau near Dresden. The battle might easily have been a second Kolin, for Daun was, as usual, holding a first-class defensive position whence, only a year before, he had tried in vain to evict a tiny force under Prince Henry. Before the battle Frederick sent word to the men that he was about to lead them in a desperate enterprise and they promised that they would do their best. His gamble succeeded and the Austrians were driven out of Saxony, except for Dresden, which they held until the end of the war. Guns were fired in London for Torgau and with it and Liegnitz Frederick recovered his reputation, though he said himself that these battles hardly altered his case, which, after all his campaigns and all his victories, seemed hopeless. His western front was causing him anxiety: the French, having pulled themselves together, had done well that summer against Ferdinand of Brunswick. The King thought that 1761 must bring the end: 'Everything seems as black as if I were at the bottom of the tomb.'

Maupertuis died. D'Argens said his ghost had appeared to him and that he had besought it to go off and tease Arouet de Voltaire and suck his blood. Frederick wrote to the Duchess of Saxe-Gotha: 'I have lost all my friends and old acquaintances—philosophy can't cure that.' His letters to her show him at his best: they are simple and modest, with no showing off. Sometimes they are almost love-letters, and she has to rebuke him. He said the luckiest thing that ever happened to him was the hazard which led him to her court. '*Madame ma Cousine*, you rule over my soul.' He was still under canvas when the snows came. Then he wrote and begged M. and Mme d'Argens to meet him at Leipzig for the winter—it was an age since he had had anybody to talk to. D'Argens said, 'Of course, on a stretcher if necessary', but he must go home again in March—he was always ill about the middle of that month when the humours rushed to his bowels. He knew the King's indifference to health but H.M. would admit that a glorious death on the battlefield is very different from being carried off by diarrhoea.

The King had a pleasant winter in the Apel House, Leipzig, with d'Argens, Mitchell and Quintus Icilius for company. Mitchell, who had learnt German and was interested in it, encouraged him to meet the professors at the university and there was much conversation about this language and its future, in which Frederick did not believe. He read a great deal and decided that *Candide* was the only novel one could read over and over again.

D'Argens's first-hand account of the looting and smashing and filthy goings-on in Charlottenburg by Saxon soldiers rankled with Frederick. He wrote to Augustus III in Poland about it but had no reply. So he decided to retaliate by emptying Augustus's favourite shooting-lodge, Hubertusburg, and selling the contents in aid of his own field hospitals. He sent for General Saldern, who had distinguished himself by packing up the battlefield at Liegnitz in record time, and ordered him to take a detachment and pack up at Hubertusburg. Saldern, very much embarrassed, asked to be excused. The King explained that the only way to make the great ones of this earth realize when they had behaved badly was to pull their hair. Saldern said he could not do it. The King furiously left the room and Saldern left the army (though after the war he returned and Frederick regarded him as his best infantry general). So Quintus Icilius was sent to do the job; the King never let him hear the end of it, chaffing him mercilessly about the huge amount he was supposed to have embezzled during the operation.

Back at Berlin, d'Argens rushes to Sans Souci where the gallery is finished—absolutely wonderful—the prettiest thing outside Rome. He wants to tell Frederick that Catt is perfect and he must never have any doubts on that subject. What would Louis XIV say if he knew that Pondicherry had fallen, taxes were higher than at any time in his reign and 150,000

LEFT: *Hubertusburg.*
RIGHT: *The picture gallery at Sans Souci.*

men were dead in Germany—all to increase the power of Austria and engineered by a whore from the rue Saint-Denis (Mme de Pompadour) and a bad poet from the seminary of Saint-Sulpice (Cardinal de Bernis)?

The day of great pitched battles seemed to be over; Frederick's army and treasury were too much depleted for him to take the offensive. For much of 1761 he was shut up at Bunzelwitz, near Schweidnitz. Though nobody dared to attack him, he was powerless to prevent the fall of Schweidnitz or the Austrians from settling for the winter in Silesia and Saxony. In the north the Allies had taken the port of Kolberg and Pomerania lay at their mercy. All these places were now paying taxes and supplying recruits to the enemy instead of to Frederick. The death of his Uncle George had been another blow. Frederick had not cared for him but he said he was an honourable man who would never abandon an ally. The new King was English through and through and took little account of his German possessions; the colonial war with France was won and George III wanted peace. He was under the in-fluence of Lord Bute and Pitt left the Cabinet. Bute invited Frederick to contribute to a settlement by giving up some territory; when he refused to do so his English subsidies were cut off. He wrote to the Duchess: 'Messieurs the English have betrayed me. It has given poor M. Mitchell a stroke.' The Duchess suggested that she should write to George III's mother, who was the Duke of Saxe-Gotha's sister. But Frederick said no, it would do no good and might cause a family coldness. He was furious with Bute for saying that England would always sacrifice her allies when it was in the national interest to do so, having for-gotten, no doubt, that he himself used to sing that very song.

In the *Histoire de la Guerre de Sept Ans* Frederick described his situation at the end of 1761, when he was wintering in Breslau, as follows. Among the King's generals, Duke Ferdinand of Brunswick (in the Rhineland) was the only one to finish the campaign without losses. The Prussians had done badly wherever they fought. Prince Henry had lost the Saxon mountains and so little territory remained to him that he could hardly feed his troops. The enemy (in Saxony) held all the strong places and one could expect the worst very soon. But, bad as was the plight of H.R.H., it was nothing to the King's. The loss of Schweidnitz resulted in that of the mountains and half of Silesia. The King now held only Glogau, Breslau, Neisse and Kosel; he controlled both banks of the Oder, but the Russians had laid waste to the countryside and there was no food left. The army had to defend itself against the Austrians on one side and the Russians on the other; communications with Berlin were precarious. But the most desperate loss was that of Kolberg. Nothing could now prevent the Russians from taking Stettin, Berlin and Brandenburg in the spring. The King had 30,000 men in Silesia, Prince Henry hardly more, and the troops which had fought the Russians in Pomerania were ruined. Most of the duchies and principalities were occupied or destroyed—one did not know where to turn for recruits or horses or goods, where to find food or how to get munitions.

The King's only hope now was that the Turks might come into the war against Austria; but if they made no move at the opening of the next campaign he thought he would commit suicide. 'Having sacrificed my youth to my father and my maturity to the State, I believe I have the right to dispose of my old age.'

Mitchell had written to Lord Bute: 'I cannot conceal from your Lordship that I am in the greatest anxiety of mind about the King of Prussia.'

The Empress Catherine II of Russia; painting by Vigilius Erichsen.

On 5 January 1762 Frederick, having received one of d'Argens's ever-hopeful letters, answered, 'I have often told you the age of miracles is over.' Had he but known it, the miracle which was to save him was happening that very day: the death of the Empress Elizabeth of Russia. She was fifty-three and for years had been in poor health. At the beginning of the war Frederick had rather counted on her dying soon—in which case it seemed certain that the Russian front would collapse. Latterly he had not given this possibility a thought. '*Morta la bestia, morto il veneno,*' he said on hearing the news. It had been slow in coming. A fortnight after the death the Danish envoy in Berlin heard it and maddened people by saying an important crowned head had died but refusing to say which; and everybody else had to wait three more days. The immediate results were dramatic. Elizabeth's nephew and successor was mad and his folly was the saving of Frederick, for one of its manifestations was an hysterical idolatry of the King of Prussia. The very day he came to the throne Peter III ordered his troops in Germany to change sides and put themselves under Frederick's command, while East Prussia and the other Russian conquests were handed back to him. The Swedes, whose participation in the war had always been half-hearted, took the opportunity of getting out of it and gave up Pomerania. Frederick once more had the revenues of these places.

To d'Argens: 'The Messalina of the North is dead and we are rid of the people whom the Hyperboreans vomited over us.' So d'Argens and Berlin are no longer in danger. But then what if the new Emperor should die? Not very likely—he is young and they are not living in the age of the Medicis. It seems the Queen of Hungary spends her time weeping and praying but as for Frederick, a sweet tranquillity possesses his soul. Charlottenburg must immediately be restored, d'Argens to be in charge.

Too soon the world realized that Russia *was* in the age of the Medicis: Peter III was strangled by order of his wife, a Princess of Anhalt-Zerbst who used to play as a child with Prince Henry. The following year, she murdered Frederick's nephew, the deposed Ivan VI, after which Catherine the Great never had another rival to deal with, and ruled the Russias until her death in 1796. Frederick said the Russian prisoners in Prussia were divided over the succession, about half favouring Ivan, so no doubt she had acted prudently. She reversed nearly all her late husband's policies but by great good luck for Frederick she found letters from him urging Peter to behave better to her, and so, although she put an end to the Russo-Prussian alliance, she did not recommence the war. Frederick managed to persuade the Russian general to stay on a few days after he had been ordered to go home and help with a skirmish against Daun, after which the troops went off, all the officers begging for copies of Frederick's *Poésies Diverses*. 'Probably the only place in the world where I shall pass for a good French poet will be in Russia.'

France was ruined and longed for peace; it was realized at Versailles that the Austrians would never now get back Silesia, the condition upon which France was to receive the Austrian Netherlands. Her war effort ground to a halt. So to all intents and purposes

An allegorical representation of the Peace of Hubertusburg; engraving by J. D. Schleuen.

Frederick and Maria Theresa were left to face each other alone. The only major engagement that summer was fought by Prince Henry who won a decisive victory over the Prince de Stolberg, his best action and the last of the war. Frederick said, 'You alone have the glory of breaking down Austrian obstinacy.'

The French and English signed a treaty at Fontainebleau (3 November 1762) which was very dreadful for France. As Pitt had planned, Frederick had won Canada and India for England on the battlefields of Germany. Louis XV and Frederick had never declared war, so they had no peace to negotiate; the French simply evacuated those of Frederick's Rhineland possessions which they were occupying. Austria, Prussia and Saxony agreed to peace terms which were signed at Hubertusburg, 15 February 1763, and which amounted to a *status quo ante bellum*. It seemed mysterious at the time that Frederick, who was really beaten to his knees, should have got away with such huge rewards as Upper and Lower Silesia and Glatz; and many rumours were rife in the chancelleries as to the reason of the Austrian collapse. Some said that the Emperor refused to lend his wife any more money to carry on the war—certainly both he and Archduke Joseph were against it, while Daun doubted the wisdom of going on with it. Probably Maria Theresa thought that, in spite of the punish﹄ment the Prussians had received, she could never hope to conquer them by herself.

The Duchess wrote to Voltaire on 31 December 1762:

Perhaps you don't know that for twenty﹄four hours we had the honour to possess under our roof the Great Frederick . . . His spirit is unchanged, grand, brilliant and fascinating. I can never express his courtesy and goodness to us. But I found him terribly aged.

*A porcelain teapot of about 1762
made in the Berlin factory under Gotzkowski.*

ABOVE: *Porcelain figures made at the Berlin factory under Gotzkowski's management. (Left) Water, 23·5 cm high; (centre) Air, 23·5 cm; (right) Earth, 22·5 cm.*
BELOW: *Porcelain figures made at the Berlin factory under royal management. (Left) A youth with a vegetable, 10·9 cm high; (centre) a* vivandière, *11·5 cm; (right) a boy with striped breeches, 11·6 cm. All the figures except Water bear the sceptre mark of the factory.*

CHAPTER NINETEEN

Man is made to work

Now that peace had come at last Frederick's life was as much in ruins as his country. His physical sufferings were always severe and often atrocious; his high spirits had almost gone and he had even lost his fierceness. Fouqué begged him to be angry sometimes as it was good for his health, but his anger took the form of a calm and deadly sarcasm. At fifty-one he was an old man. But he still had energy and he devoted it to the good of his country, according to his lights. He wrote to the Duchess on the very day he signed the Treaty of Hubertusburg: 'This peace brings enormous labour with it—but man is made to work.' In his memoirs he paints an appalling picture of the misery to which his country was reduced: 'Nobody who has not seen it with his own eyes can have any idea of it.' He must have dreaded his return to Berlin because he put it off for as long as he could; he travelled about the ravaged province of Silesia and only arrived in the capital six weeks after signing the peace. He said he found nothing there but empty walls and the memory of those he had loved. His faithful Berliners had made him a triumphal coach and awaited him with flags and flowers; he could not face them and slipped through dark, unlighted, side streets to arrive unperceived at the palace. The Queen gave a small family dinner for him, to which Mitchell and Vanderelst the Dutch minister were also invited. But the next morning he did get into the coach, with Ferdinand of Brunswick, and they received a rapturous welcome. Then he began his work. The deputations which came to congratulate him were told to cut out the thanks-giving and let him know what they needed to put agriculture on its feet again. His first step was to distribute 35,000 army horses, free, to the peasants.

Frederick has been blamed for never delegating the burdens of administration and for seeing to everything himself. There is nothing so unbearable, says Lord Macaulay, as to be governed by a busybody. Later in the reign, after the recovery of Prussia, this criticism probably becomes valid, but in 1763 it was the King's own unsleeping labours and the simple, imaginative steps he took that were needed. No detail ever escaped his eagle eye and he regarded nothing as being out of his province. For instance, during the Battle of Kunersdorf he had noticed various mistakes in the cultivation of the farmland there; now he spoke about them and reforms were made.

Prussia was the only belligerent Continental country to be solvent after the war. Frederick

Frederick's desk and clock in his study-bedroom at Sans Souci. The desk, mahogany with bronze fittings, with its matching chest of drawers surmounted by a clock, was probably acquired from Caffieri's workshop in Paris in 1746. The room was decorated by F. W. von Erdmannsdorff, 1786.

The Brandenburg Gate, Berlin, in 1764; etching by Daniel Chodowiecki.

had kept enough cash in hand to pay for two more campaigns and this money was now used to restore the country's economy. Many towns had had to pay enormous indemnities to the enemy; Berlin was repaid out of the treasury, but everywhere else the bourgeoisie was left to carry the burden—Frederick had decided to give priority to the nobles and the peasants, in other words the army and agriculture. The bourgeoisie was divorced from both. He reckoned that a ninth of the population had perished (120 generals had been killed), so he encouraged immigrants, to work on the land, by all the means in his power. They were mostly of German or Polish stock, although there were Greeks and other Mediterraneans. He had an agency in Venice. He thought that mixed races produced intelligent people. Like Queen Victoria he was tired of looking into blue eyes and wanted to bring in strong dark blood—he even thought of building a mosque to encourage Turks. By the end of his reign one-sixth of his subjects were born foreigners. Work was put in hand to improve the sandy soil of Brandenburg. Wherever a bush or a tree would grow, one was planted; wherever a farm could exist, one was built. The State controlled everything—it found markets for the farm produce in good years and helped the peasants through the bad ones— and the State was Frederick himself. He did what he could to help the peasants who, all over Europe, were a downtrodden class. He prevented the enclosure of their land (which was happening elsewhere in the Empire) and allowed the peasants on the huge royal estates to hold hereditary farms. But in those days it was regarded as a sad but inescapable fact that the prosperity of a State depended on an underpaid and overworked peasantry. As they were so wretched they were naturally not very clever. Frederick's simple agrarian reforms, such as the rotation of crops and improvement of the livestock by selective breeding, were

248

hampered by the conservatism of the countrymen. All his authority was needed to overcome it and he was driven nearly mad by the stupidity and wastefulness he saw and by the failure to carry out, or even to understand, his orders. The richer Silesians were more virtuous and less dense than the Prussians; he loved them more and more. He spent at least two months at Breslau every year, for the army manœuvres. At the end of his life he said that in the forty years he had governed Silesia he had only signed one death-warrant there.

The Duchess wrote to Voltaire, 'Frederick is working night and day for the good of his people, by whom he is adored.' But it almost seemed as if he were trying to get rid of this adoration: he was amazingly harsh, almost cruel, in his conduct of affairs. His army reforms were not softened by any human touch: he never once praised or congratulated his men after the war. His first action was to dismiss all the young bourgeois officers whom he had been

Frederick inspecting plans for mining galleries; painting by J. C. Frisch.

Claude Adrien Helvétius; engraving by A. de Saint-Aubin after C. A. van Loo.

obliged to employ during the last campaigns and whose mates had died for him in hundreds.
He preferred foreign officers with the requisite number of quarterings to native Prussians
without them. He had no superstitious idea that the nobility provided better human material
than any other class; he simply thought that, given their outlook and the organization of
society, they were in their proper place as commanders. The ideal officer was a large land-
owner leading the tenants with whom he had been brought up. Yet such men could count
on no special treatment. Quintus Icilius begged him to do something for those officers who
had ruined themselves by paying and feeding the men out of their own pockets. 'Your
officers have stolen like ravens', was the reply; 'I'm damned if I'll give them a penny.' Those
generals who had been taken prisoner, including the beloved Fouqué, were put in the cells
on their return to await court martial. Fouqué, who, the King said, had fought like a
Roman before he was captured, got off, but General von Finck was sentenced to a year in
Spandau. Frederick placed young civilian inspectors, responsible to himself, over the
colonels who had hitherto been all-powerful in their own domain. The last insult was that
he now paid each regiment according to what he considered had been its performance in the
wars. With so few veterans left the new soldiers had to be trained from the very beginning;
it was seven years before the King was satisfied with them, although in 1764 he wrote to
Fouqué to say that his army was rising like a phoenix from its ashes. In spite of everything
Frederick was popular in the army to the end of his life; he amused the men with his oddity
and many were the stories they told about 'Old Fritz'. Besides, they were proud of him and
proud to be led by such a hero.

He was determined to turn Prussia into an industrial country but his ideas were old-

Two plates from the Japanese dinner-service made for Frederick in the Berlin porcelain factory.

fashioned, based on those of Colbert, and rigidly protectionist. The Prussian recovery could have been more startling than it was had he gone about its organization in a more modern way. His adviser was the French philosopher Helvétius, whom he persuaded to leave his English exile and go to Berlin. Helvétius made him change the Prussian system of tax collecting for the French, and Frederick bitterly hurt the feelings of the bourgeoisie by importing French tax-gatherers to put it into effect. He had got it into his head not only that the Prussian methods were hopeless but that the officials were dishonest; he put a Frenchman, M. de Launay, over them. The Prussians execrated him for his influence at court and his enormous salary. Mitchell wrote:

> The directors of the new excise, mostly recommended by Helvétius, are all French of low condition and totally ignorant of the language, manners and customs of the country. Three of them are bankrupts, of whom M. de Candi was one. He, however, had a dispute with Launay and was shot by him. The new projects of the excise give the utmost dissatisfaction to the subjects and have alienated their affection for their sovereign to a degree hardly to be described.

Only ten per cent of the tax-gatherers were French but the idea of them infuriated the Prussians. However, adverse public opinion never prevented Frederick from getting his own way.

His most famous industrial venture was the Berlin china factory, into which he put his heart and soul. Some of his friends at Meissen consented to leave Saxony during the war and take their secret process to Berlin (another bad mark for him with the Saxons) and they were soon turning out porcelain of a rare quality. Frederick sent the first piece of china made there to the Duchess (10 January 1763): 'If my homage is found unworthy of the goddess it can be broken, thrown away and forgotten. Your friendship is my most precious possession.' Like the French kings with their Sèvres he bullied people into buying Berlin; he always used it at his own table and sent presents of it to his friends at home and abroad. But most European princes now made their own porcelain, and the Berlin never sold as well as he had hoped. Other industries also disappointed him. He had stolen a lot of sheep from the Saxons, partly for the stock and partly to create an artificial shortage of wool; but even so his own wool trade stagnated. Silk did well, owing to the bright and beautiful colours on which he insisted, cotton developed fast and linen was a good export. Mining in Silesia, rich in minerals, was nothing much until, in the seventies, Frederick acquired a remarkable Saxon, von Heinitz (who educated Humboldt), and appointed him Minister for Mines. Some of the Prussian goods were of poor quality; others, like clocks made in Berlin by his Swiss subjects from Neuchâtel, were too expensive. When he asked why his paper was so bad he was told there were not enough good rags for making it. He said he knew why—he was for ever seeing housemaids lighting the fires with rags; this practice must be forbidden at once. There was not much of a market for manufactured goods inside Prussia, as the peasants were too poor to buy them, nor, with his old-fashioned economy, could Frederick's exports compete with the great trading cities like Hamburg and Leipzig. To sum up, it may be said that in spite of the practical difficulties—soil, climate and so on— agriculture flourished while industry lagged behind. A financial crisis in 1766, general to most of the Empire, was a setback. When that was over, Prussia by degrees recovered from the war.

Frederick, who interfered in most things, left his judges alone (except, as we shall see, on one famous occasion). His law reforms were a source of great satisfaction to him. The death sentence had to be ratified by him, and never was, except in cases of murder. When a father and daughter were once sentenced to death for incest Frederick asked how they could be certain that he was her father, and let them off. He never executed women who had killed their babies. At a time when in England and most European countries people were executed for stealing Frederick only signed between eight and twelve death-warrants a year.

To the end of his days the King expected the Austrians to force another war on him and as soon as the Seven Years' War was over he began to cast about for allies. The Bourbons and Habsburgs seemed irrevocably bound together by a series of marriages. The English had no goodwill left for him, quite the contrary: having themselves behaved badly, they very naturally hated him. His reputation in England was that of an aggressor and a tyrant, 'from whose vices History averts her eyes and which even Satire blushes to name' (Lord Macaulay). Besides, as Mitchell observed, the English would never care for a Prince who said, 'The butcher kills for the necessities of man but he does not enjoy killing; the sports-man kills for pleasure and should therefore be classed below the butcher.' For some time England had been treating him as a potential enemy rather than an ally, and in 1762

Frederick's envoy to Russia was shown a report from Prince Galitzin, in London, of a conversation with Lord Bute: he advised Peter III not to make peace with Frederick, since to do so might delay a general settlement. Frederick hated the English Prime Minister so much that one of his own horses, named Lord Bute, was put to the plough and other humiliating work. There remained Catherine the Great. Frederick signed a treaty with her and took immense pains to be on good terms with her, but he could hardly look upon such an ambitious and powerful woman as a reliable ally, even apart from the fact that, having seen the Russians at work, he was disinclined ever to call them into western Europe again. Although this treaty, after various ups and downs, proved durable and became a corner-

Frederick with two of his greyhounds.
A nineteenth-century bronze by Johann Gottfried Schadow.

stone of Prussian policy, Frederick thought it was his duty to make his country powerful enough to be independent of all alliances, and the rest of his life was given up to this objective.

Frederick, probably owing to his illness, was now becoming decidedly eccentric and his habits of economy touched on miserliness. His uniform was patched and his boots were fit to be thrown away. His one suit of plain clothes was never renewed. His Italian greyhounds, fearfully spoilt, made messes everywhere and tore the silk of his curtains and chairs to ribbons; Sans Souci began to look like a rich man's house inhabited by a tramp. But he was still generous to old friends. Fouqué, who lived in the country, wrote to say that presents of money were unnecessary though he loved the coffee, the china and the ear-trumpet he had just received.

In view of all his public thrift and private parsimony Frederick's new building venture caused a good deal of surprise and annoyed the bourgeoisie considerably. The moment the war was over he put in hand an enormous palace, the Neues Palais, in the park of Sans Souci, and decorated it regardless of cost. He never lived in it but went there from time to time with visiting sovereigns or house parties of young people. Some thought he built it to show the world he was far from ruined; others that the palace was intended to be a shop front for Prussian goods. Perhaps the truth was that Frederick, whose life for the past seven years had been so hard and had now become so bleak, thought that fate owed him a little pleasure. The palace was built in three years; it is impressive and contains some very beautiful interior decoration. Bearing a closed crown on the roof are the naked figures of the Empress, the Tsarina and Mme de Pompadour.

The Empresses, Maria Theresa and Catherine,
and Mme de Pompadour on the top of the cupola
at the Neues Palais.

The Neues Palais. It was built between 1763 and 1769 by J. C. Büring. All the
servants' quarters and the kitchens are in a separate building.

OVERLEAF: *The Marble Hall in the Neues Palais. The stucco work is by J. B.*
Pedrozzi; the floor by J. M. Kambly.

CHAPTER TWENTY

The Uncle of Germany

Frederick wrote constantly to the Duchess and told her all his news. M. d'Alembert has arrived at Potsdam (June 1763), even better in real life than in his books—natural, frank and peaceful by nature and very gay and witty. Frederick wants him to oblige the public by writing two works: an amplification of his *Éléments de Philosophie et de Géometrie* and an account of all the discoveries in physics since Bacon. If an old lady (the Empress Elizabeth) had not spat some blood and died, all the glimmerings of good sense and reason that illuminate Germany would have been smothered in triumphant superstition. But Frederick, who has much cause for rejoicing, finds nothing to console him for the fact that, now the war is over, he never sees his divine Duchess face to face. He is thinking of ways and means by which he can do so. He is sorry to hear that the Duke is not well, and he noticed, when last at Gotha, that he did not look like a good life—she had better make up her mind to an approaching separation. Now Frederick is expecting a crowd of nephews and great-nephews and -nieces—he'll soon be the Uncle of Germany, as Mlle de Sonsfeld used to be Everybody's Aunt. When one can't be a grandfather one falls back on being a great-uncle and making the young giggle with one's senile ramblings—it's the fifth act of the play and one ends by being booed. (He told Prince Henry that he really ought to give a ball for the children but there seemed not to be enough people to ask—perhaps he should advertise for guests in the *Intelligenzblatt*.) There are many bankrupts at Amsterdam and Hamburg among financiers who made huge fortunes out of the war—how odd to think that the princes who ought to have been ruined by it are quite solvent. Things always happen differently from what one expects. Why are we born? Why this idiotic childhood? Why do we bother to educate the young? Why are we for ever eating, drinking, sleeping, pulling down, amassing and dissipating? It seems rather puerile when one thinks that death passes a sponge over all that has been.

Frederick had sympathy for young people and was one of those who remember in old age what it is like to be young. Mme de Camas, in charge of the Queen's household, wrote to him of a maid-of-honour who was in the family way and must be disgraced. He replied, 'Somebody takes a poor girl in a moment of tenderness, says a lot of pretty things to her and gives her a child. Is it so dreadful? I'm bound to say I prefer a nature which is too loving to

259

One of the reception rooms in the Neues Palais, with hunting decorations. The desk is by the brothers Spindler.

LEFT: *Jean Le Rond d'Alembert; painting by Maurice Quentin de La Tour.*
RIGHT: *Maria Antonia of Bavaria, Electress of Saxony; painting by Anton Raphael Mengs.*

these dragons of chastity. You must get the poor girl away from the court without a scandal and preserve her reputation if you can.' Mme de Camas was not pleased, but she had to obey.

He often had his house full of nephews and nieces and was touchingly anxious to amuse them, once getting the great actor Lekain to come all the way from Paris on their account. He would urge them to go and visit Voltaire, saying that nothing was so useful to society as *belles-lettres*—a comfort and a consolation all through life and in the end the only pleasure left to somebody lucky enough to have cultivated a taste for them in youth. These young guests never knew for how long they were expected to stay; when the King was tired of them he would say, 'I'm so sorry to hear you have got to leave tomorrow—ah well, pleasant moments cannot last for ever.'

Unfortunately the heir, Frederick William, was a disappointment. When he was quite young, during the war, Frederick had been fond of him and proud of his looks—he was a blond giant—but too soon he became fat, self-indulgent and stupid. When Frederick sent him to visit foreign courts he did more harm than good, and was ignored or treated as a joke. He was married to his first cousin twice over, Elizabeth of Brunswick who, beautiful and high-spirited, refused to accept his infidelities in the usual meek way of princesses, and having had one daughter (the future Duchess of York) began to take lovers herself. This led to such tremendous quarrels that all hope of an heir disappeared. The King's brothers, saying they refused to see their heritage bestowed upon a bastard, made him consent to a divorce—reluctantly, as he was fond of Elizabeth. He was always good to her. She went to live at Stettin where she survived until 1840 and made a centre for visitors to that town; she seems to have been unfailingly cheerful. Frederick William married again and became a family man *par excellence*, with two wives, two mistresses, countless concubines and a horde of children, all of whom he brought up himself. He really had time for nothing but filling cradles and rocking them.

As much as Frederick despised Frederick William he loved his younger brother, a second Prince Henry, who was beautiful, good and studious, with the judgment of a grown-up man. He called him his child: 'He has stolen my heart.' But in 1767 death once more took away a creature to whom the King was attached; the young man caught smallpox. Frederick's letter telling Prince Henry that their nephew was no more is stained with tears. 'Grief is eating into me—I know that everything comes to an end but this, my dear brother, does not diminish one's sadness.' It is probable that, had the smallpox taken the elder brother, Frederick would have worked with Henry and given him responsibility as he never did with Frederick William—not that the history of Prussia would have been different, since nothing could have stopped the French Revolution from sweeping the board; but Frederick's old age might have been happier.

That same year he lost the Duchess. He paid her a visit in the spring—in October she was dead. She was in a way replaced, as a much-liked female correspondent of the King's, by the Electress Maria Antonia of Saxony. Augustus III, Augustus's eldest son and Count Brühl all died within weeks of each other, soon after the end of the Seven Years' War; the new Elector was a little boy of thirteen. His forty-year-old mother, Maria Antonia, became Regent. She was the daughter of the Emperor Charles VII, but had more spirit than he and more looks than her mother. She first wrote to send Frederick an opera she had composed; she asked him to do what he could to see that her son should be elected to the Polish throne. Frederick told her right out that it was impossible; the Empress Catherine wanted a puppet of her own in Poland so there was nothing to be done. But the friendship blossomed. The Electress paid a nine-day visit to Potsdam and said she had never had such an amusing time in her life and thereafter she and the King wrote to each other regularly.

A nephew Frederick thoroughly disliked was the son of Ulrica, King Gustavus of Sweden, who was murdered at a masked ball in 1792. Nor was Frederika, the only child of Wilhelmine, anything but a worry to him. When she was sixteen and he twenty she had married a Prince of Württemberg. Frederick said at the time that they were too young and too much in love to be happy for long, and when the Prince began to take mistresses he said Frederika must make up her mind that their relationship would never be the same again— her best plan would be to turn her husband into her dearest friend. Wilhelmine had success-fully done that very thing, but perhaps Frederika had not the character to do so; in any case the marriage was unhappy, childless and ended in divorce.

Although Frederick was so loving to his wife's brothers and sisters, whom he counted as his own, and to their children, and although, in his old age, he had less objection than formerly to the company of women, he remained as cold as ever to the Queen. When he dined at her house, which he did several times a year, he never spoke to her; he merely bowed and took his place at the table, opposite her. About fifteen years before his death he astounded the company by going up to her and asking after her health; they seem never to have exchanged another word.

Prince Henry also got rid of his childless wife after the war, giving her a wing of his Berlin palace to live in and forbidding her to go to Rheinsberg. He was probably a homosexual— after an early age he had no women in his life. We hear of him dancing as a slave girl in the market, not that that means much, since people in those days loved dressing up as the opposite sex: that most manly of men, Frederick's father, would dance with the Old Dessauer. As the years went by, Frederick and Prince Henry grew ever more intimate, though Henry was still eaten up with his jealousy of the King and said dreadful things about him to all and sundry, even foreign visitors to Rheinsberg. When Frederick's *Histoire de Mon Temps* appeared, two years after his death, Henry poured out his malice in marginal notes to it; Frederick's homage to his father calls forth the observation that 'these are the only true words in the whole book'. In 1791 he put up a memorial at Rheinsberg to Augustus William and those officers who had distinguished themselves in the Silesian wars. Winter‐feldt was not among them and, even more extraordinary, nor was Frederick. All the same the King was his lodestar, and he for his part noticed, or pretended to notice, nothing. His letters to Henry are written on an even tone of brotherly love. He wrote to him nearly every day, telling him all the State secrets and all that went on at Potsdam, the illnesses and deaths of his dogs and his own dreadful ills. These letters generally began '*Mon très cher frère*',

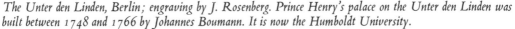

The Unter den Linden, Berlin; engraving by J. Rosenberg. Prince Henry's palace on the Unter den Linden was built between 1748 and 1766 by Johannes Boumann. It is now the Humboldt University.

LEFT: *Jean-Jacques Rousseau; painting by Allan Ramsay.*
RIGHT: *Prince Henry; painting by Anna Dorothea Therbusch.*

occasionally '*Mon cher cœur*', or, if Henry had overstepped the mark with tiresome complaints, '*Monseigneur*'. Henry was always called Henri by his brothers and sisters, as Frederick was Fédéric, Amelia Amélie and Ulrica Ulrique. But there are a very few letters to Henry from the King in German, and these begin '*An meinen Bruder Henrych*'. He built a palace for him in the Unter den Linden, Berlin, and rewarded him for his services in the war by giving him the property of their childless cousin, the Margrave Charles of Brandenburg, who had died in 1762. Henry was now a rich man.

The only intimate friend from old times whom the King found at Berlin on his return was d'Argens. Frederick owed him a great deal for his unfailingly optimistic and spirited letters during the war, and was truly very fond of him, but he no longer found him easy to live with. They were both ill, their nervous systems not up to much. Frederick made his usual mistake of seeing d'Argens all the time, and began to overdo the teasing. This note shows what it must have been like: 'I promise to laugh at your jokes; to say that the *place* at Aix is the most beautiful in all Europe; that you've got the best laundress in the kingdom and the best valet of all the wise men. . . .' In 1765 d'Argens went home to Provence for a year and their letters were most loving. But when he came back the teasing was just the same and in 1768 he again asked permission to go home. He wrote pathetically from Dijon saying that nobody could have more admiration, attachment or respect for the King than he. He lived in gilded rooms at Potsdam but only left them in terror and hardly ever returned to them without having his heart wounded by some harsh joke. After that, silence, until, in July 1769, the King wrote to say that he hoped for him in September. He did not return then, and died in February 1771, a sad ending to a friendship of nearly thirty years. Frederick wrote three long, kind letters in his own hand to the Marquise—if there was anything at all he could do for her she only had to say the word. By her replies we can see that she bore him no grudge. He put up a monument to d'Argens in the Minims' church at Aix-en-Provence.

Lord Keith, accompanied by his little horde of Tartars, had been Governor of Neuchâtel since 1754. He had disliked it from the day of his arrival—the climate was so bad that one had to be indoors for eight months of every year and there was nobody to chat to; a book such as Montesquieu's *L'Esprit des Lois* aroused no excitement in that deadly place. A pastor who, evoking the love of God, had suggested that He would be unlikely to punish anybody for ever, was being persecuted by his colleagues; the population was engaged in desperate disputes about whether punishment after death was eternal or not. Frederick said surely those who longed for eternal punishment could have it without wishing it on others. As to punishment here on earth, he learnt to his horror that the 'question' and the stool of repentance, long ago abolished in Prussia, were still used in Neuchâtel. There was no theatre or opera and that, he said, accounted for the bigotry—men need a spectacle and, if there is nothing better, will make do with the Sacred Scaramouche. Milord Maréchal very nobly put up with the gloom of Neuchâtel in order not to add to the King's burdens.

The Empire, showing Prussian and Austrian territories, in 1786.
Prussia dark tint, Austria light tint.

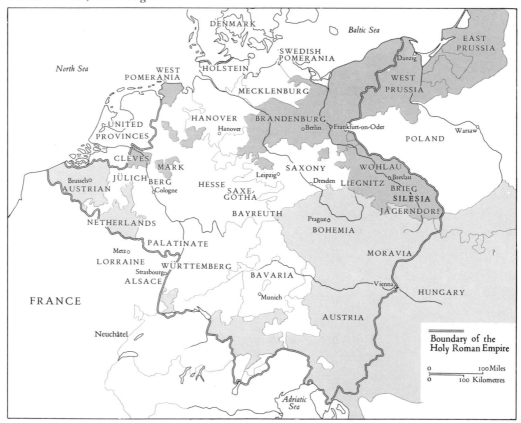

A view of Potsdam in 1772; painting by J. F. Meyer.

In 1759 Frederick had asked his new ally George II to forgive Lord Keith and reverse his attainder, and an Act of Parliament was passed to that effect. Meanwhile, the Milord had gone to Spain on a secret mission to see if Charles III would use his good offices to call off the French, who were fighting Prussia without having declared war. Unfortunately Charles III was the son-in-law of Augustus III so there was nothing to be done there, but Milord resumed his friendship with the whole Royal family, the grandees and Wall, the Irish-born Minister for Foreign Affairs. He thus got wind of a secret family pact between the French and the Spanish Bourbons. He sent a report to Pitt who would have immediately declared war on Spain had he not been overridden by his colleagues in the Cabinet and forced to resign. In the event no harm was done to the Spaniards, while Lord Keith had greatly furthered his own interests in England. However, when his mischief became known to Wall he had to get out of Spain quickly, and it was to London that he fled.

He was well received by the King, took the oath of allegiance and went back to Neuchâtel. The British Government soon did more for him. His confiscated lands, like those of other Jacobites, had been bought by the York Building Society, now in liquidation; in 1763 the estates of the Earls of Panmuir, Southesk and Pitcairn and those of the Earl Marischal were put up to public auction in Edinburgh. The owners all went to the sale, nobody bid against them and each retrieved his own lands for a song, amid loud cheering. It seemed as if Lord Keith had come home for good. But he had hardly settled into Keith Hall before he caught a fearful cold; he was soon complaining loudly of the climate and the neighbours—even drearier, it seemed, than at Neuchâtel. Nor was he popular with them. They thought he had become a courtier and had forgotten old friends; they were shocked by his behaviour to the Spaniards; and his strictures on Charles Edward, whom he accused of every vice under the sun, including cowardice, were badly received. The provincial Scotch were not aware of the depths to which their Prince had sunk since the romantic days of Flora Macdonald. Meanwhile, Frederick was imploring the Milord to go and live at Sans Souci.

> I read Virgil's *Georgics* and in the morning I send my gardener to the devil, for he says that neither Virgil nor I know anything about gardening. My parsley is up, my elder tree sprouting and the wild geese are back. Your strawberry seeds have come. I go into my garden to see at my leisure all the progress of springtime, the bursting and the flowering and, to use Fontenelle's expression, I take nature *in flagrante*. I thought, I presumed, dear Milord, that you knew you would be welcome here but as you want me to repeat it let me assure you that winter and summer and night and day, in all the seasons, at all times and every hour you will be received with open arms by your faithful friend.

Keith secretly sold the estates he had so recently recovered and turned his back on the Bonny Land for ever.

Milord Maréchal, one of those people who know everybody, had a very unexpected friend. In 1762 Jean-Jacques Rousseau wrote both to him and to Frederick asking for asylum at Neuchâtel. He told Keith that he was a persecuted author and begged for fire and water refused him elsewhere. To the King:

> I have said bad things about you and shall probably say more; driven away from France, from Geneva, and from the canton of Berne I seek an asylum in your dominions . . . I have deserved no favours from you and seek none but would inform His Majesty that I am in his power and that he can do as he likes with me.

It so happened that Milord Maréchal admired Rousseau's writings and he longed to meet him. Frederick, on the other hand, greatly disliked his books but immediately said that they must shelter the poor creature, whose only sin was to have a singular outlook on life. However, it might be a good idea to stop him writing while in Neuchâtel, where the inhabitants were ticklish enough and the clergy fanatical enough already. Rousseau sarcastically engaged not to read or write or do anything but think. He was lent a house in Môtiers and settled there with Thérèse Levasseur; he told Keith that he would spend his time making lace with the village women and conversing with him. The two men took to each other in a perfectly exaggerated way—'my son', 'my father'—they decided never to part again. 'The main point in life I consider to be perfect reliance on people with whom one lives—I should have had that with Jean-Jacques and Ermetulla.' When Milord went to Scotland Jean-Jacques was to join him there and live for evermore at Keith Hall, 'our castle in the air', while Frederick thought of building a hermitage for him at Sans Souci. Both these schemes fell through, or Frederick would certainly have had another resounding affair with another philosopher. Jean-Jacques soon made Neuchâtel too hot to hold him; people were beginning to notice that he was a little mad and, as Voltaire said, not one of those jolly madmen who do nobody any harm, but a particularly spiteful one. Milord continued to protect him, saying that he had been made unjust by misfortune and must be treated as an invalid; Frederick took the same view. But after some years, during which Milord had given himself much trouble over Jean-Jacques, he saw that his touchiness and devious ways made him

A detail from the top of a chest of drawers of tortoiseshell inlaid with mother-of-pearl by Spindler and J. M. Kambly, about 1765.

impossible as a friend. He settled some money on him and begged him to spare him any more letters, as he longed for peace and quiet in his old age.

Lord Keith's decision to go and live at Potsdam was never regretted either by him or by the King. Frederick built him a little house facing up the slope on which Sans Souci stands and backing on the town. It had a garden of its own with a door into the King's. Milord had to buy an extra plot, as the King, having designed the house himself, had forgotten sheds for the wood, the dung and for smoking the meat. He lived surrounded by pets as well as by his Tartars; a dog—Herr Schnell—and many monkeys who escaped so often that the path between his house and Sans Souci is called the Monkey Walk to this day. A place was always laid for the old man at Frederick's table which he could occupy or not, as he pleased, and they never seemed to tire of each other's company.

By degrees Frederick and Voltaire made up their quarrel. Voltaire's attitude to him was very much that of Prince Henry—he could not resist him yet there was a stinking little residue of hatred. They never risked another meeting but their correspondence was full of love and affection. Voltaire said his years at Sans Souci had been the happiest of his whole life: 'I shall never console myself for having to end my days far from you', while Frederick said, 'Whatever happens, I shall have been of your generation.' Voltaire began to wash the King's dirty linen (in other words, correct his verses) again, while he helped Voltaire with money and moral support for the victims of the French religious laws whose defence took up so much of the old poet's time and energy. Frederick, however, pointed out that a difference should be made between the appalling death of the innocent Calas and the fates of those who had knowingly and openly broken a law. In their case it was the law that should be changed. He added that no death sentence ought ever to be implemented without the considered assent of the ruler. As they grew old the two men hated organized religion more than ever for the cruelty it engendered. Frederick said that the knowledge of human nature which he had acquired in his profession made him doubt whether another two centuries would be enough to do away with the 'Superstition Christicol'. It was he who first used the word *l'infâme* (referring to clerical superstition), a term which Voltaire made famous in his phrase *écrasez l'infâme*.

When the widowed Queen Ulrica of Sweden visited Frederick, whom she had not seen since her marriage in 1746, she said that Berlin seemed dull without Voltaire. Frederick replied that he had been noticing that for sixteen years.

Air, a statue by L. S. Adam given to Frederick by Louis XV, now in the garden at Sans Souci.

CHAPTER TWENTY-ONE

The Potato War

The Emperor Francis died in 1765 and Archduke Joseph then became Emperor, and co-Regent, with his mother Maria Theresa, of her lands. Frederick was anxious to meet him but the *pédagogues*, Kaunitz and *elle*, forbade Joseph to have anything to do with the monster. In 1769, however, the international system received a jolt: the Turks attacked the Russians. They had managed their campaign so stupidly that there was no element of surprise and the Russians had a year in which to prepare. They did so with their usual inefficiency; when hostilities began the leadership and commissariat were equally bad on both sides; but the Russians were soon winning so easily that their neighbours became alarmed. It seemed sensible to draw together, so Kaunitz and *elle* allowed Joseph to meet Frederick at Neisse. He fell at once under the King's charm: 'a genius and a wonderful talker but one senses the rogue in every word he says . . . we talk sixteen hours a day. He is quite unlike any of his portraits.' Joseph, ever since the days when he had been lively as a squirrel in his mother's arms, had been taught to consider the Prussian King as a rogue. He was still lively and Frederick was attracted to him: 'His lovable nature was gay to the point of vivacity; but though he had a desire to learn he lacked the patience to study.' Frederick behaved with an almost ironical politeness to his Emperor; he quite embarrassed him by springing to his stirrup whenever he mounted or dismounted, like a knight of olden times with his liege lord. The Prussians wore white uniforms like the Austrians, not wishing to meet them in the field blue of their erstwhile foes. Unfortunately, Frederick's uniform was soon splattered with food and snuff and dogs' hairs. 'I am not clean enough for you,' he said, 'not fit to wear your colours.' After this meeting the world was told that the two rulers had signed a treaty of neutrality in case of war between France and England and that Frederick had given the Emperor a copy of Maurice de Saxe's *Mes Rêveries*. (It always lay by Joseph's bed but, at his death, the pages were found to be uncut.) But rumour had it that they had been seen, not once but many times, bending over the map of Poland. When Frederick got home he hung a portrait of Joseph in his bedroom. 'Better keep an eye on that young fellow', he said; he thought him devouringly ambitious.

Next year they met again in Moravia and this time Joseph was accompanied by Kaunitz, who had long political conversations with the King, preaching at him as he preached at

The Emperor Joseph II; terracotta bust by F. X. Messerschmied.

Maria Theresa. The burden of his song was supposed to be the danger to Europe of the quarrel between Russia and Turkey, but once more the map of Poland was laid upon the table. He urged Frederick to use his influence with Catherine to make good feeling between the two Empresses. Frederick honestly did what he could, without much result. Also in the Emperor's suite was the Prince de Ligne, one of the charmers of all time. His property near Brussels was in the Empire but he was more French than German—an enthusiastic soldier, man of letters and brilliant talker, he might have been made for Frederick. The two rulers found it easier to get on with each other when Ligne was there and they hardly let him out of their sight—a situation which was to be repeated when, eventually, Joseph met Catherine the Great. Ligne had fought in the Seven Years' War and he and Frederick had many a gossip about the battles seen from different sides. He speaks in his memoirs of the magic of the King's conversation. 'People think he was jealous of Keith and Schwerin and delighted to have got them killed. This is how mediocrities love to belittle great men.' Before they parted, the Prince was cordially bidden to Sans Souci.

A few months later, in the winter of 1770, Prince Henry paid a visit to Catherine the Great, whom he had known as a child. She was beginning to enlarge her empire towards the west; she had already seized the Danubian principalities and was cocking an eye on Sweden and Poland. At the death of Augustus III she had, with Frederick's approval and in defiance of Maria Theresa, placed her former lover, Poniatowski, on the throne and she now virtually controlled his anarchic country. The courtiers at St Petersburg thought Henry was a funny, stuffy little fellow with old-fashioned clothes and a most peculiar wig, but he got on with Catherine: they had the same taste for French literature and laughed at the same jokes. When he wrote home enthusiastic accounts of all he saw, Frederick replied, rather priggishly, that palaces and houses are of no interest compared with the establishment for educating girls which Henry had also been shown. The ostensible reason for his visit was to talk about the Russo-Turkish War; Frederick said that as, thank God, he was 900 miles from St Petersburg he left the discussions entirely to Henry. But presently a much more interesting subject came up. Somebody said the Austrians had seized two estates inside the Polish frontier on pretext of limiting the spread of the plague there. Catherine laughed: 'Why don't we all do that?' Soon the joke became a reality and in a few months the First Partition of Poland between the two Empresses and Frederick took place. It affected about a quarter of the country—Austria and Russia each took ten times more than Prussia did.

Frederick had long coveted the territory which lay between Brandenburg and East Prussia, so he made no difficulties and certainly felt no guilt at what others regarded as a robbery. Poland was as badly administered as Turkey and quite incapable of carrying out her historic mission of forming a barrier between Russia and the West; the people existed on the verge of starvation and lived more like animals than men; and Frederick knew that he could improve their lot. He made the common mistake of thinking that better living conditions make up to a people for loss of national identity. Maria Theresa did not see the matter

LEFT: *'The Polish Plum Cake', the partition of Poland; engraving by N. LeMire after J. M. Moreau le Jeune.*
RIGHT: *The Prince de Ligne; painting by the French school.*

with the same eye; she had always prided herself on never having broken the rules of international morality—furthermore she had not forgotten that it was the brave Poles under
John Sobieski who had saved Vienna from the Turks in 1683. She made strenuous objec-
tions to the partition but they were overridden by Joseph and Kaunitz, to the amusement of
Frederick who said, 'She weeps but she takes.' She took the province of Galicia, saying,
'*Placet*, since so many great and learned men will have it so, but long after I am dead it will be
known to what this violation of all that was hitherto held sacred will give rise.' It gave rise
to the total partitions of Poland in 1793 and 1795. Frederick would not have approved of
them: to do away with the Polish State had never been his aim.

When he went to inspect his new lands he told Prince Henry that West Prussia was a
considerable acquisition but that, as it wouldn't do to arouse jealousy, he was giving out
that all he found there was sand, pines, heather and Jews. Indeed it was in a fearful condition.
After a long visit in 1773 Frederick wrote to Voltaire:

> I have abolished serfdom, reformed the savage laws, opened a canal which joins up all the main
> rivers; I have rebuilt those villages razed to the ground after the plague in 1709; I have drained
> the marshes and established a police force where none existed . . . it is not reasonable that the country
> which produced Copernicus should be allowed to moulder in the barbarism that results from
> tyranny. Those hitherto in power have destroyed the schools, thinking that uneducated people
> are easily oppressed. These provinces cannot be compared with any European country—the
> only parallel would be Canada.

Frederick thought that education was of prime necessity for a state because all depended
on the next generation, but he had great difficulty in finding teachers. He was reduced to
using old or invalid soldiers in some schools. So now that the great educating Order of the
Jesuits was being turned out of every Catholic country, finally to be suppressed by a papal
bull in 1773, he was delighted to welcome the fathers into his kingdom.

273

One must never destroy things [he wrote to Voltaire]. It was a mistake to destroy the home of Jansenism at Port-Royal—how stupid the modern Jansenists have become! Why destroy those depositories of Greek and Roman civilization, those excellent professors of the humanities? Education will be the loser but as my brothers the very faithful, very Christian and apostolic Kings have thrown them out I am collecting as many as I can. I preserve the breed and presently I'll sell them back again. I tell them so—I will easily get 300 *thalers* for you, my Father, and 600 for the Father Provincial.

Voltaire remarked that Frederick, from having been a general in the army, was now the General of the Jesuits.

At this time Voltaire was obsessed by the idea that Greece ought to be freed from Turkish rule. Frederick complained that having been bitterly scolded for his wars and having been told by the *philosophes* that all warfare was immoral he now received no fewer than twenty letters from his friend urging him to get mixed up in the troubles of the East. 'Tell me,' he wrote, 'how can you stir up Europe to warfare when you and the *encyclopédistes* have expressed such sovereign contempt for warriors?' To be sure, Voltaire said that on no account must democracy be restored in Greece: '*Je n'aime pas le gouvernement de la canaille.*' Frederick had heard that the Greeks were quite as savage as the Turks, and he had no intention whatever of adding to his own problems by undertaking such a crusade. Catherine II played with the idea of putting her younger grandson on the throne of Constantine and gave him Greek nurses. When a third grandson was born Frederick said no doubt he was destined to become the Great Mogul.

It was lucky that Frederick had got Milord Maréchal for company; his few remaining friends were dying fast. Mitchell went in 1771—the King stood weeping on his balcony as the coffin passed by—and 'Maman' Camas had died, at an enormous age. Quantz died in 1773, Fouqué died in 1774 and Quintus Icilius, whose death specially worried Prince Henry for his brother's sake, followed in 1775, a horrible year for Frederick. He had lost too many teeth to be able to play his beloved flute any more (he allowed himself an extra hour in bed as compensation), was tormented by abscesses in his ear and on his knee and had a series of fearful attacks of gout. He kept his room for months and word went round that he was dying. The Austrian minister at Berlin duly informed Joseph, who sent a large army to Bohemia which, in the case of Frederick's demise, was to advance on Brandenburg and demand Silesia. Thereafter Frederick mistrusted him more than ever. It was becoming evident that the Emperor intended to bring the German princes to heel and would soon challenge Frederick's influence in the Empire.

'If the Elector of Bavaria dies before me,' Frederick wrote to Prince Henry, 'we shall have to get on our horses again.' Two years later, in 1777, this very thing happened: the senior branch of the Wittelsbachs became extinct and the Habsburgs decided to compensate themselves for the loss of Silesia by annexing Bavaria. Neither the distant and childless heir, nor his nephew the next heir, nor anybody else in the Empire, except Frederick, was in a position to do more than protest. Maria Theresa and Joseph had been told by their minister

Silberberg from the air.

in Berlin that the old King was far too ill to go to war. But, entirely opposed to such an enormous extension of Austrian territory, he began to mobilize.

Many people in Prussia were against this war, which seemed a great risk to take for an insufficient reason, and at their head were the King's brothers. Henry, now elderly and suffering from gout (though much less than Frederick was), no longer cared for soldiering and he was afraid that he would lose his high military reputation if things went wrong. However, when Frederick cracked the whip he reluctantly accepted to command an army. Ferdinand refused point-blank and got a sarcastic letter from the King urging him to take great care of his health and saying he was quite right to sacrifice his adored and favourite profession to it.

Frederick addressed his officers. He said that though he was obliged, now, to travel in a coach, they would see him on a horse when the day of battle dawned. He left Berlin in April 1778 with an army of 100,000 and waited with it at Silberberg, not far from Glatz, while Kaunitz tried to find out whether he was bluffing or not. This time Saxony came down on Frederick's side, so his communications were assured. The Austrian army was scattered and disorganized: had he wished to do so, he could easily have marched to Vienna and dictated his terms there. But he had lost his taste for warfare and would now do almost anything to avoid bloodshed. The disgust of his officers when this became apparent may be imagined but as usual he went his own way. Getting no further by negotiation, he and Henry took their troops into Bohemia in July. There was little fighting and most of what there was fell to Prince Henry, who distinguished himself in some minor actions brilliantly carried out. By this time the Austrians had assembled a large force; Frederick with his army sat on one bank of the Elbe, facing Joseph, Lacy and Loudon on the other. He never doubted that Joseph, in the prime of life, would be filled with an offensive spirit and he waited for this to manifest itself. Joseph was indeed longing to show the world what he could do with his fine army but he was held back by various considerations. Maria Theresa was against the war; the new accommodation between Russia and Turkey seemed to her an alarming factor in the balance of power; her French ally had refused to fight. In spite of an Austrian queen, France was returning to its old distrust of the Empire and the Foreign Minister, Vergennes, saw Frederick as the only brake on Austrian ambitions. Maria Theresa, saying that she and Frederick must not pull out each other's grey hairs, began writing to him behind Joseph's back.

The Austrian army never moved and in October the campaign came to an end. The chief business of this war lay in the feeding of vast static armies; the soldiers, who did more foraging than fighting, called it the 'Potato War'. By the Treaty of Teschen, May 1779, the

Key to colour plate overleaf:
1. *Frederick II*
2. *Prince Frederick William, later King Frederick William II*
3. *Prince Frederick William, later King Frederick William III*
4. *Prince Augustus Ferdinand*
5. *Ferdinand, Duke of Brunswick-Wolfenbüttel*
6. *General von Zieten*
7. *Frederick Louis Alexander, Prince of Württemberg*
8. *The Duke of York*
9. *General de Lafayette*

The front of Marshal Keith's house flanked by his outhouses. The back of it faced Frederick's windows at Sans Souci.

OVERLEAF: *Frederick returning from manœuvres; painting by E. F. Cunningham.*

Habsburgs gave up their claim to Bavaria, but took the small rich district of Burghausen. The Empress said, 'I am not partial to Frederick but I must do him the justice to confess that he has acted nobly and honourably; he promised me to make peace on reasonable terms, and he has kept his word.' So the Wittelsbachs were firmly established in Bavaria; they became kings in 1806 and produced the extraordinary Ludwig II. The influence of Prussia was now paramount in Germany.

As soon as Frederick got back to Potsdam he took up the case of the miller Arnold. One of his favourite nephews, Duke Leopold of Brunswick, had a Private Arnold in his regiment who told him a long story of legal injustice to his brother, a miller. As it seemed that the miller had indeed been treated badly, Leopold went to his uncle, who ordered an investigation. The facts were as follows: Arnold took his water-mill on lease from Count von Schmettau; further up, the river flowed through the estate of Landrat von Gersdorf who, in 1770, deflected some of the water by making a fish-pond. The miller said that there was not now enough pressure to turn his wheel and on this pretext he refused to pay his rent. Count von Schmettau said he must pay or be evicted—if Arnold was really short of water he must sue Gersdorf. He gave him four years' respite, then had him up in the local magistrate's court (where Schmettau was suspected of having undue influence). Arnold lost the case and was evicted; the technical reason for the verdict was that, by an old law, Gersdorf could do as he liked with the water in his own stream. Also there seems to have been some doubt as to whether the pressure at the mill-wheel was really too much reduced to work it. For years Arnold and his energetic wife took the case from court to court, but they always lost. It was the sort of story that infuriated Frederick, who saw it as an example of the nobility trampling on modest folk with the sanction of a too rigid judiciary. He ordered it to go to the highest court of all; but once more the verdict was against the Arnolds.

Frederick, suffering dreadfully from gout in his hands and his feet, and in a blinding rage, sent for Chancellor Fürst and the three judges who had tried the case. He was in his Berlin palace, his poor legs covered with rugs and his poor hands hidden in a muff. He told them that unjust judges were a greater danger to society than thieves. Fürst tried to speak. 'Quick march,' said the King, 'your successor is appointed.' As the Chancellor and the judges left the palace they were arrested and carried off to prison, where they found all the many magistrates who had had anything to do with Arnold. The next day the whole of the Berlin aristocracy and the high bourgeoisie called at Fürst's house to express sympathy; Frederick could see the queue of coaches from his window. But outside his palace there gathered a vast crowd of what Carlyle calls 'the dark peasant people', most of them bearing petitions to say they had been quite as badly treated as the miller, if not worse. The rights and wrongs of the Arnold case are still argued to this day; Frederick's interference angered the legal profession and complicated the administration of justice, especially in country places. Perhaps he felt that he had made a mistake; he never bothered his judges again.

Frederick, aged seventy; painting by Anton Graff.

CHAPTER TWENTY-TWO

Winter

So the King came to extreme old age. When he drove out in Berlin in his shabby carriage it went at a snail's pace in order not to tire the ancient soldiers who formed his guard. While he was away at the Potato War two key figures in his life had disappeared within five days of each other. On 24 May 1778 the Earl Marischal sent for Hugh Elliot, the English Minister at Berlin: 'Perhaps you have a message to give me for Lord Chatham [who had died on 11 May] whom I expect to see tomorrow. I will with pleasure take your dispatches.' He duly took them the next day. He was about ninety and had been too frail for some time to go to the King's suppers, but Frederick saw him every day and used to walk beside his bath chair in the gardens of Sans Souci. He was a grievous loss. Ermetulla went back to Neuchâtel where she lived to be a hundred, as boring as ever and in the end rather mad.

On 30 May Voltaire died in Paris. Society people there said he had done more harm to his fellow men than a war, a plague or a famine. His letters were Frederick's greatest joy, and latterly they had been so very affectionate, so filled with admiration, and so intimate that the quarrel seemed to be buried and forgotten at last. He used the same tone to other correspondents when writing about the King. Did he think he had destroyed that time bomb, the *Mémoires pour servir à la Vie de M. de Voltaire*, which is really a *mémoire* to serve for the destruction of the Great King? Had horrible Mme Denis hidden away a copy? It is only charitable to assume so, especially as in 1776 he wrote a second fragment of autobiography, *Commentaire historique sur les Œuvres de l'Auteur de la Henriade*, unfortunately much less well known than the *Mémoires pour servir*, in which his friendship with Frederick falls into its real perspective. Here he says that the King was unaware of Freytag's blunders at Frankfurt and that the adventure was very soon forgotten by both parties. It was a lovers' quarrel, and (says Voltaire), 'I must have been in the wrong'. It seems probable that Frederick never saw this work, which was not published under Voltaire's name. The first he knew of the *Mémoires pour servir* was when Beaumarchais offered to sell him the manuscript; he replied, in effect, 'Publish and be damned!' No doubt he was wounded in his soul, since the *Mémoires* showed that Voltaire had really hated him for over forty years, and that when he had been such a kindly mentor to a young man searching for light in particularly dark surroundings, Voltaire was laughing at him all the time and thereafter had used him to his own

Frederick's death mask.

Frederick reviewing his troops; engraving by Daniel Chodowiecki.

ends. Frederick's estimation of his fellow men was not improved by Voltaire's baseness and duplicity. 'You don't know this damned race', he said to a young schoolmaster who thought there was more good than evil in human beings. When a Berlin bookseller came to the palace and asked permission to sell the *Mémoires* Frederick said yes and hoped he would do well with it. He would merely ask him not to advertise it unduly. Autocratic though he had become, he never changed his attitude to free speech, especially where it concerned himself. Out riding one day he saw a crowd gazing at a vile caricature of him posted high above their heads. He told his A.D.C. to lower it. 'They can't see it properly up there', he said. The crowd cheered him to the echo as he rode away.

Frederick's popularity at the end of his life has always been a subject of controversy, though he is generally admitted to have been idolized by the poor, the disinherited and the old soldiers he had led to the wars. Frederick himself thought that he had lived too long and that his people were probably as tired of him as the French had become of Louis XIV and Louis XV. He viewed the future without optimism. The despised Frederick William grew even fatter and stupider and more taken up with his women and their children. The King hardly ever saw him and minded the idea of being succeeded by him. He told Prince Henry that he loved his country too much to say *après moi le déluge* and that he would do what he could until his dying day to ensure its future; but he knew that when things went wrong after his death he would be blamed.

According to the London papers Frederick was loathed in Berlin, but Hugh Elliot wrote to William Eden:

> You have no idea the joy the people express to see the King on horseback—all the Grub Street nonsense of a nation groaning under its burdens and governed with a rod of iron vanished before the sincere acclamations of all ranks who joined in testifying their enthusiasm for their monarch.

In Breslau, where he still went every year for the army manœuvres, he was warmly greeted by the people, who always turned out to see him riding home of an evening. Somebody remarked that he seemed much loved here. 'Put an old monkey on a horse', said Frederick, 'and they would cheer him the same.' These manœuvres were a magnet to officers from all over the world who came to see the great King at work with his army.

Sad to relate, he fell out with Catt after an association of twenty-four years. He suspected him of taking bribes—one feels that this could not have been true. Catt, in his usual measured and dignified way, merely says that he was innocent and that it was a great sadness to him to be deprived of the King's presence. There were no recriminations. He must have known that Frederick's illnesses had made him strange.

For company and jokes Frederick had a jolly young Italian, the Marchese Lucchesini, an excellent acquisition. Somebody said to the King that Lucchesini was clever enough to be used as an ambassador—Frederick agreed and said that was why he kept him in his household. After the death of the King he duly became an ambassador. He was not only very bright, well able to keep up with Frederick's conversation, but also easy and tactful. He made no enemies. The suppers at Potsdam generally consisted of a few silent generals and Frederick and Lucchesini chatting away in French. Sometimes Frederick invited members of his Academy, which had gone sadly downhill of late, and, several times a year, the widow of Maupertuis. He still liked to see foreign visitors, especially Frenchmen. Ten years after their first meeting, the Prince de Ligne wanted to present his son 'to the greatest man who ever lived'. He had to apply for permission to cross the Prussian frontier, which, since the Bavarian War, Frederick had closed to Imperial officers. Of course it was gladly given.

The account of Ligne's visit to Potsdam is the last portrait of Frederick written by a man of his own world, and it shows that in congenial company he could still be brilliant and gay—'an old wizard who knows what people are thinking'. Ligne observes the eyes, strange and expressive as ever, the beautiful voice, the fascinating movement of his lips when speaking, his encyclopedic conversation and his extraordinarily courteous manners. If he asked a personal question he always said, *Oserais-je vous demander?* (Dare I ask you?)

'I hadn't realized you had got a grown-up son.'

'He is even married, Sire, since a year ago.'

'Dare I ask to whom?'

'A Pole—a Massalska.'

Frederick recalled that this lady's grandmother had greatly distinguished herself by taking an active part in the siege of Danzig at the time of Stanislas Leczinski. They talked of all

LEFT: *Frederick William II of Prussia; painting by Anton Graff.*
RIGHT: *The Comte de Mirabeau; painting by A. P. Couderc.*

subjects under the sun; the King told stories of the wits he had known—Voltaire, Maupertuis and Algarotti (who had died in 1764), and then went back to the heroes of history: Francis I, Henri IV, Homer. Virgil was mentioned. 'A great poet, Sire, but what a bad gardener!' 'To whom do you say it! Have I not tried to plant, hoe, dig and sow with the *Georgics* in my hand? My man says to me, "Monsieur, you're a fool and so is your book—that's not the way to work." Oh my God, what a climate!' Whenever Frederick said 'Oh my God', he would bring his hands slowly together and clasp them, in a way which made him look very good.

He got the news that Charles of Lorraine had died and broke it to Ligne, who of course knew him well, having lived under his administration in the Austrian Netherlands. 'The poor Prince depended upon too many people—I only had myself to look to. He was badly served and not always obeyed—none of that ever happened to me.' Frederick went back to his pet theory, that one must cross the races of the Empire, and said that he had a liking for love-children. 'Look at Maurice de Saxe and Anhalt.' (A young Count von Anhalt, a bastard grandson of the Old Dessauer, was now one of Frederick's favourite officers.)

Ligne was more under the spell than ever. He went away and wrote what was, for a loyal subject of Maria Theresa's, an extraordinary defence of Frederick's policy, saying that the Empress had been wrong not to let him have Silesia in the first place and very wrong indeed to have instigated the Seven Years' War. (Even Thomas Carlyle hardly goes as far.) The only thing about Frederick that Ligne did not admire was his taste in buildings and interior decoration. Ligne went much to Versailles, where the severe, dry, classical *style Louis Seize* was now the fashion. Frederick's palaces seemed to him outmoded, provincial and overdone.

Like Voltaire (and like most old people), Frederick thought that taste was declining. Voltaire had been outraged, just before his death, by a sudden fashion for Shakespeare in Paris. He said he had been the first to introduce to France 'a few pearls I found in that vast manure heap'—now the manure heap was being swallowed whole. Frederick, who could only read Shakespeare in translation, had more excuse than Voltaire for seeing him as a barbarian. He had a horror of Romanticism in any form, and all savages—even noble ones, even if they were geniuses—filled him with despair. He found the new generation of writers unreadable and for his pleasure he went back to the great French classics of his youth. As for German literature, he doubted whether it would amount to much. He said two elements were missing: taste and language. The latter was too verbose: all civilized Germans spoke French so that their native tongue never became polished. Another draw-back was the dialects, which were practically incomprehensible from one district to the next and of which none served as a model. German writers fell into the error of telling everything —they were bad historians, pedantic and dull, and were at their best in legal documents. Then he had second thoughts. He said that all the same, a taste for letters was certainly spreading— nature must now do her part and give birth to a few prodigies. The country of Leibniz must be able to produce others of that sort. Frederick himself would not live to see these happy days—he was Moses on the edge of the Promised Land. Meanwhile, he read Goethe's *Goetz von Berlichingen* and said it was like a parody of the very worst efforts of Shakespeare.

When Maria Theresa died in 1780 Frederick said she had honoured her throne and her sex. He had fought her but had never been her enemy. To Prince Henry: 'Already half out of this world, I am obliged to redouble prudence and take steps and have my head full of all the odious projects to which that damned Joseph gives birth every day. I shall only be left in peace when my bones are covered with a little earth.' He countered Joseph's designs for the Empire with a Confederation of German Princes—that and signing a treaty of the most favoured nation with the future United States of America were his last political actions.

At the Silesian manœuvres of 1784 the King was displeased with his army—he said he would as soon take a lot of tailors into battle and that if his generals did not show some improvement they would find themselves in the lock-up. The next year he realized that an effort had been made to satisfy him. The weather, always uncertain in August, was particularly bad, and one day the King, who scorned to wear a topcoat, was on horseback from 4 a.m. to 10 a.m. in steadily pouring rain. When his boots were pulled off they were as full of water as two buckets. Then he gave a dinner for the generals and foreign visitors, among

The death of Frederick; painting by C. B. Rode.

others those two erstwhile enemies, Lord Cornwallis and the Marquis de Lafayette. He went to bed in a high fever and never really recovered, though he made a tour of inspection in Silesia and attended manœuvres near Berlin before going home to Potsdam, to fall desperately ill.

As well as all his usual miseries he now had appalling headaches and asthma, 'a pitiless torturer that smothers you without finishing you off'. For months he spent his wakeful nights in an armchair. 'If you are looking for a night-watchman,' he said to a visitor, 'you can employ me.' Doctors came—he received them with his usual courtesy, pretending to believe in their remedies; but he knew that there was no cure for him. Sans Souci, where there were no stoves, became too cold as the winter drew on and he decided to move into

288

the Potsdam town palace. But he always rode at Potsdam, keeping his carriage for Berlin, and he was too proud to break the rule; so he waited and waited, hoping in vain that one day he would feel able to get on his horse. In the end he had to be carried from Sans Souci to the palace in a sedan-chair at dead of night.

In January 1786 he received his last foreign visitor of note, Mirabeau. The meeting was not a success. Frederick, like many others, was put off him by his extraordinary clothes and wig, his bad manners and general clumsiness. Ill and suffering as Frederick was he failed to go below the surface and discover the political genius of the man. He told Prince Henry that Mirabeau was on his way to Russia where he would be safe to publish his sarcasms against his own country. Mirabeau, for his part, felt that he was not appreciated and Frederick did not charm him. His *Histoire secrète de la Cour de Berlin* is full of spiteful gossip about the King, who was not the only target; the book also aroused great fury in Dresden and Vienna. Prince Ferdinand, it said, was not the father of his children; Prince Henry, too, came in for some rough stuff: he was in Paris when the book appeared, and was asked what he thought about it. He replied with dignity that history would be his judge. Mirabeau's huge and serious *De la Monarchie prussienne sous Frédéric le Grand* was compiled by a Prussian, Mauvillon, and is full of information on the economics of the time, written from a free trade point of view.

Frederick on his deathbed, drawn from memory by Frederick William III of Prussia.

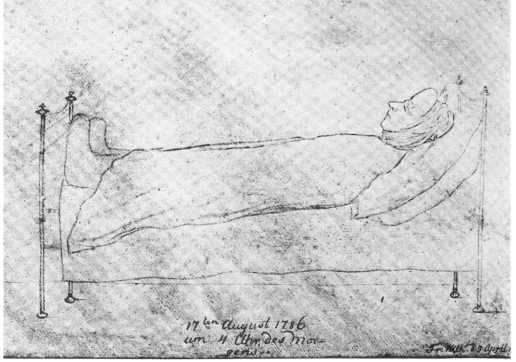

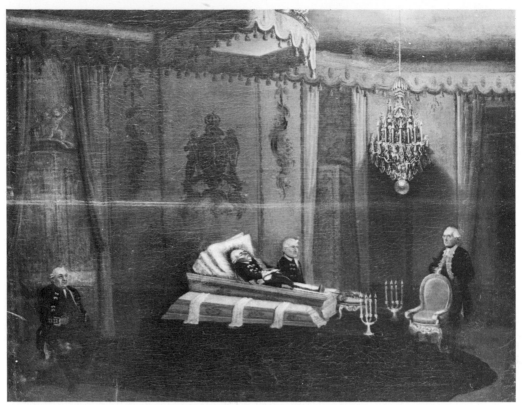

Frederick lying in state in the Potsdam town palace; painting by J. F. Bock.

To his own surprise Frederick lived through the winter, and was able to go back to Sans Souci, where he enjoyed a particularly mild spring, the season he loved so much; he was even able to go out riding once or twice on his white horse Condé. The rhythm of his day's work was never altered, and when it was over he supped with the generals and Lucchesini as usual. On 10 August he wrote to his sister the Duchess of Brunswick to say good-bye: 'The old must make way for the young.' The last bereavement of his life was the death of her young son Leopold some months before; he was drowned while gallantly trying to save a group of people trapped by the Oder in flood.

The Queen asked to be allowed to visit her husband. 'I am very much obliged for the wish you are so kind as to express but a high fever prevents me from answering.' He begged Prince Ferdinand not to come. On 15 August he started to work, as usual, at 5 a.m. The next day he did not wake until 11 a.m. and then tried in vain to give orders to a weeping general. All that day he was dying in his chair. He asked his reader for a chapter of Voltaire's *Précis du Siècle de Louis XV*, but he could not listen to it. Towards the evening he went to sleep again. He awoke at midnight and told the servants to throw a quilt over his dog who was shivering with cold. For two hours his orderly held him up in his chair so that he could breathe more easily. In the early morning, 17 August 1786, his sufferings were over.

He had prepared a grave for himself, with his dogs and his horse, on the terrace at Sans Souci. But after his lying in state, when thousands came from Berlin to see him for the last time, his nephew buried him in the Garrison Church next to Frederick William I. Twenty years later, Napoleon stood by his coffin. 'Hats off, gentlemen—if he were still alive we should not be here.'

Napoleon visiting Frederick's tomb,
25 October 1806;
engraving by J. F. Arnold after H. Dahling.

Sources

Most of the information in this book comes from the works of Frederick himself, that is to say his *Œuvres* (which include his private correspondence) published in Berlin in 1850, and the *Politische Correspondenz* (Berlin, 1879). Very valuable sources are also Voltaire's Correspondence, edited by M. Theodore Besterman, with its masterly index (107 vols., Geneva, 1953–65); *Mémoires de Frédérique Sophie Wilhelmine de Prusse, Margrave de Bareith* [*sic*] (2 vols., Paris, 1811); Henri de Catt, *Mes Entretiens avec Frédéric le Grand* (Paris, 1885). Thomas Carlyle's *History of Friedrich II of Prussia, called Frederick the Great* (centenary edition, London, 1899), is a gold-mine of information, both relevant and irrelevant: anybody who may have enjoyed this book should read it. Ernest Lavisse's *La Jeunesse du Grand Frédéric* (Paris, 1891), is full of brilliant flashes of light on Frederick's character. Sainte-Beuve, especially in his essay on Prince Henry in the *Causeries du Lundi*, sees things as they are; his understanding of human nature never fails. The *Encyclopedia Britannica* (11th edition) has a very good bibliography, including some first-class biographies. Albert Sorel's *Europe and the French Revolution*, translated and edited by Alfred Cobban and J. W. Hunt (London, 1968) would make an invaluable introduction.

Other books consulted are:

Barbier, Edmond J. F., *Chronique de la Régence et du Règne de Louis XV*, Paris, 1885

Barraclough, Geoffrey, *The Origins of Modern Germany*, Oxford, 1946

Besterman, Theodore, *Voltaire*, London, 1969

Bielfeld, Baron de, *Lettres familières et autres*, 2 vols., The Hague, 1763

Bisset, Andrew, *Memoirs and Papers of Sir Andrew Mitchell*, London, 1850

Börsch-Supan, Helmut, *Friedrich Rudolph, Comte de Rothenbourg*, in *L'Oeil*, Paris, December 1968

British Medical Journal, 'Porphyria—A Royal Malady', 13 April 1968, p. 105

Broglie, Duc de, *Frédéric II et Louis XV d'après des documents nouveaux*, 2 vols., Paris, 1885
Frédéric II et Marie Thérèse, d'après des documents nouveaux, 2 vols., Paris, 1883

Coxe, William, *History of the House of Austria*, 2 vols., London, 1807

Cuthell, Edith E., *The Scottish Friend of Frederick the Great, the last Earl Marischal*, London, 1915

Easum, Chester, *Prince Henry of Prussia*, University of Wisconsin, 1942

Gaxotte, Pierre, *Frédéric II*, Paris, 1938

Hervey, Lord, *Some materials towards memoirs of the reign of King George II*, London, 1848

Keith, Sir Robert Murray, *Memoirs*, 2 vols., London, 1849

Koser, Reinhold, *Geschichte Friedrichs des Grossen*, 4 vols., 1893–1905

Ligne, Prince de, *Mémoires et Mélanges historiques*, Paris, 1827

Macaulay, Lord, *Critical and Historical Essays*, London, 1891

Mirabeau, Comte de, *De la Monarchie prussienne sous Frédéric le Grand*, 4 vols., Paris, 1788

Oliver, Frederick Scott, *The Endless Adventure*, 3 vols., London, 1930–35

Pérey, Lucien, *Un Petit-Neveu de Mazarin (Duc de Nivernais, 1715–63)*, Paris, 1890

Reddaway, William F., *Frederick the Great and the Rise of Prussia* (in a French translation, Paris, 1932)

Ritter, Gerhard, *Frederick the Great, an historical Profile*, London, 1968

Rousset, Camille F. M., *Le Comte de Gisors*, Paris, 1868

Strangways, Giles (Earl of Ilchester) and Brooke (Mrs Henry Langford), *The Life of Sir Charles Hanbury Williams*, London, 1928

Thiébault, Dieudonné, *Mes Souvenirs de vingt ans de séjour à Berlin; ou Frédéric le Grand*, 5 vols., Paris, 1805

Valory, Marquis de, *Mémoires des Négotiations du Marquis de Valory*, Paris, 1820

William II, Emperor of Germany, *My Ancestors*, London, 1929

Wraxall, Sir Nathaniel William, *Memoirs of the courts of Berlin, Dresden, Warsaw, Vienna, 1777–9*, London, 1806

Monochrome Plates

198 An episode in the Seven Years' War by J. B. Le Paon (*c.* 1737–85). *Musée Condé, Chantilly. Photo: Giraudon.*

200 LEFT: Marshal von Browne by J. Glatz. *Bildarchiv der österreichischen Nationalbibliothek, Vienna.*
RIGHT: Maria Josepha of Habsburg, Electress of Saxony and Queen of Poland by Rosalba Carriera. *Gemäldegalerie, Dresden; Staatliche Kunstsammlungen, Dresden. Photo: Deutsche Fotothek, Dresden.*

201 The Battle of Lobositz, 1 October 1756, by P. P. Benazech (1730–83). *Photo: John Freeman Ltd.*

202 *La Notte* by Correggio (1494–1534). *Gemäldegalerie, Dresden; Staatliche Kunstsammlungen, Dresden. Photo: Deutsche Fotothek, Dresden.*

204 The bombardment of Prague, 29–30 May 1757, by P. P. Benazech. *Photo: John Freeman Ltd.*

206 LEFT: Augustus William, Prince of Prussia, by J. C. Sysang (1703–57). *Staatsbibliothek, Berlin (West).*
RIGHT: The Prince de Soubise by an unknown artist. *Musée de l'Histoire de France. Photo: Archives Nationales.*

207 Glatz; an eighteenth-century engraving. *Photo: John Freeman Ltd.*

214 The castle at Lissa by J. C. Richter. *Silesian Museum, Wrocław. Photo: Edmund Witecki.*

216 Wilhelmine; copy of a painting by Antoine Pesne. *Neues Palais; Staatliche Schlösser und Gärten, Potsdam-Sans Souci. Photo: Roland Handrick.*

220 Stone sphinxes erected by Prince Henry in the garden at Rheinsberg. They are reputed to be Mme de Pompadour (left) and the Empress Maria Theresa. *Photo: R. Law.*

222 The siege of Schweidnitz, 1758, after P. P. Benazech. *Staatsbibliothek, Berlin (West).*

223 The siege of Olmütz, 1758. *Staatsbibliothek, Berlin (West).*

224 General von Loudon by J. Steiner. *Staatsbibliothek, Berlin (West).*

225 Porcelain soldiers by J. J. Kändler (1706–75). *Galerie Jürg Stuker, Berne. Photo: H. Meier.*

226 A ribbon commemorating Frederick's victory at the Battle of Leuthen. *Photo: John Freeman Ltd.*

231 Sir Andrew Mitchell by an unknown artist. *National Portrait Gallery, London.*

234 The Kreuzkirche, Dresden, by Bernardo Bellotto. *Kupferstichkabinett, Dresden; Staatliche Kunstsammlungen, Dresden. Photo: Deutsche Fotothek, Dresden.*

236 Frederick writing dispatches in a church after the Battle of Torgau by C. B. Rode (1725–97). *Verwaltung der staatlichen Schlösser und Gärten, Berlin.*

239 LEFT: Hubertusburg. *Photo: Lichtbildarchiv Löhrich, Munich.*
RIGHT: The picture gallery at Sans Souci. *Staatliche Schlösser und Gärten, Potsdam-Sans Souci. Photo: Roland Handrick.*

241 The Empress Catherine II of Russia by Vigilius Erichsen (1722–82). *Bobrinskoy Collection. Photo: George Rainbird Ltd.*

243 An allegorical representation of the Peace of Hubertusburg by J. D. Schleuen. *Archiv für Kunst und Geschichte, Berlin.*

244 A porcelain teapot, 1762. *Schloss Charlottenburg; Verwaltung der staatlichen Schlösser und Gärten, Berlin.*

248 The Brandenburg Gate, Berlin, in 1764, by Daniel Chodowiecki. *Landesbildstelle, Berlin.*

249 Frederick inspecting the plans for mining galleries by J. C. Frisch (1738–1815). *Photo: Bildarchiv Foto Marburg.*

250 Claude Adrien Helvétius by A. de Saint-Aubin (1736–1807) after C. A. van Loo. *Bibliothèque Nationale, Paris. Photo: Roger-Viollet.*

251 Two porcelain plates from the Berlin factory. *Schloss Charlottenburg; Verwaltung der staatlichen Schlösser und Gärten, Berlin.*

253 Frederick with two of his greyhounds by Johann Gottfried Schadow (1764–1850). *Staatliche Schlösser und Garten, Potsdam-Sans Souci. Photo: Roland Handrick.*

254 The Empresses Maria Theresa and Catherine, and Mme de Pompadour on the top of the cupola at the Neues Palais. *Photo: Staatliche Schlösser und Gärten, Potsdam-Sans Souci (Archives).*

260 LEFT: Jean Le Rond d'Alembert by Maurice Quentin de La Tour. *Louvre, Paris. Photo: Giraudon.*
RIGHT: Maria Antonia of Bavaria, Electress of Saxony, by Anton Raphael Mengs (1728–79). *Gemäldegalerie, Dresden; Staatliche Kunstsammlungen, Dresden. Photo: Deutsche Fotothek, Dresden.*

262 The Unter den Linden, Berlin, by J. Rosenberg (1739–1808). *Landesbildstelle, Berlin.*

263 LEFT: Jean-Jacques Rousseau by Allan Ramsay. *National Gallery of Scotland. Photo: Annan.*
RIGHT: Prince Henry by Anna Dorothea Therbusch. *Staatliche Schlösser und Gärten, Potsdam-Sans Souci, Photo: Roland Handrick.*

264 The Empire, showing Austrian and Prussian territories, in 1786.

265 A view of Potsdam in 1772 by J. F. Meyer (1728–89). *Staatliche Schlösser und Gärten, Potsdam-Sans Souci. Photo: Roland Handrick.*

270 The Emperor Joseph II by F. X. Messerschmied (1737–83). *Staatliche Museen; Preussischer Kulturbesitz, Berlin. Photo: Walter Steinkopf.*

273 LEFT: 'The Polish Plum Cake' by N. LeMire (1724–1800) after J. M. Moreau le Jeune (1741–1814). *Staatsbibliothek, Berlin (West).*
RIGHT: The Prince de Ligne; French school. *Wallace Collection, London.*

275 Silberberg from the air. *Photo: J. G. Herder Institut, Marburg-Lahn.*

282 Frederick's death mask. *Potsdam-Sans Souci. Photo: Edwin Smith.*

284 Frederick reviewing his troops by Daniel Chodowiecki. *Staatsbibliothek, Berlin (West).*

286 LEFT: Frederick William II of Prussia by Anton Graff. *Neues Palais. Photo: Staatliche Schlösser und Gärten, Potsdam-Sans Souci.*
RIGHT: The Comte Mirabeau by Couderc (eighteenth century). *Château de Versailles. Photo: Mansell Collection.*

288 The death of Frederick by C. B. Rode. *Staatliche Schlösser und Gärten, Potsdam-Sans Souci. Photo: Roland Handrick.*

289 Frederick on his deathbed, drawn from memory by Frederick William III of Prussia (1770–1840). *Staatliche Schlösser und Gärten, Potsdam-Sans Souci (Archives).*

290 Frederick lying in state in the Potsdam town palace by J. F. Bock (eighteenth century). *Photo: Bildarchiv Foto Marburg.*

291 Napoleon visiting Frederick's tomb, 25 October 1806, by J. F. Arnold (1780–1809) after H. Dahling (1773–1850). *Bibliothèque Marmottan. Photo: Archives de France.*

Index

Figures in *italic* type with an asterisk indicate pages on which are to be found plates in colour; figures in *italic* type indicate pages containing illustrations in monochrome.